P9-CQQ-064

DISCARD

*f*P

MAKE THE BREAD, BUY THE BUTTER

What You Should and Shouldn't
Cook from Scratch—Over 120 Recipes
for the Best Homemade Foods

JENNIFER REESE

FREE PRESS

New York   London   Toronto   Sydney   New Delhi

FREE PRESS
A Division of Simon & Schuster, Inc.
1230 Avenue of the Americas
New York, NY 10020

Copyright © 2011 by Jennifer Reese

All rights reserved, including the right to reproduce this book or portions thereof
in any form whatsoever. For information address Free Press Subsidiary Rights Department,
1230 Avenue of the Americas, New York, NY 10020.

First Free Press hardcover edition October 2011

FREE PRESS and colophon are trademarks of Simon & Schuster, Inc.

For information about special discounts for bulk purchases,
please contact Simon & Schuster Special Sales at 1-866-506-1949
or business@simonandschuster.com.

The Simon & Schuster Speakers Bureau can bring authors to your live event.
For more information or to book an event contact the Simon & Schuster Speakers Bureau
at 1-866-248-3049 or visit our website at www.simonspeakers.com.

DESIGNED BY ERICH HOBBING

Manufactured in the United States of America

1   3   5   7   9   10   8   6   4   2

Library of Congress Cataloging-in-Publication Data

Reese, Jennifer.
Make the bread, buy the butter / Jennifer Reese.—1st ed.
p. cm.
1. Natural foods—Processing. 2. Processed foods—Costs. 3. Agricultural processing.
4. Cookbooks. I. Title.
TX551.R35 2011
641.3—dc22
2011009088

ISBN 978-1-4516-0587-7
ISBN 978-1-4516-0589-1 (ebook)

To Mom, coauthor

CONTENTS

INTRODUCTION

Boil peanuts until tender; remove hulls in cold water; mash. Season with buttr [*sic*] and salt; When cold spread between slices of bread. Good for school lunch.

—*Los Angeles Times Cookbook, No. 2,* 1905

Until recently, I never considered making my own peanut butter. Skippy was good enough for me.

Until recently, I never considered buying a frozen peanut butter and jelly sandwich. I hadn't even known such a thing existed. I first read about Smucker's popular frozen peanut butter sandwich—the Uncrustable—in a *New York Times Magazine* article by (of course) Michael Pollan. He wrote, "People think nothing of buying frozen peanut butter and jelly sandwiches for their children's lunch boxes." I thought: *They don't? What people? What frozen peanut butter and jelly sandwiches? What's next, frozen buttered toast?*

I felt briefly smug in the certainty that I was not so lazy or compromised that I would ever buy mass-produced peanut butter and jelly sandwiches. Then I thought, *People probably once said that about peanut butter. And bread. And jelly.* They almost certainly said it about waffles, and pie crust, and pudding. Not so long ago, people must have wondered who couldn't fry her own donuts, grind her own sausage, cure her own bacon. Kill her own bacon! The more I thought about it, the more arbitrary it seemed to draw a line in the sand at the frozen PB&J.

Yet drawing and redrawing just such arbitrary lines had become one of my primary preoccupations in recent years. The most irksome decisions I faced as an adult and working mother seemed to be made at the supermarket. Fundamentally trivial, they were nonetheless maddeningly fraught, involving questions of time, quality, money, First World guilt, maternal guilt, gender, meaning, and health. I had only to step through those automatic Safeway doors for the nattering mental calculations to begin: *Owen needs cupcakes for school and look, here they are, ready to go, packed in clamshells. Nutritionally irredeemable—but made. Sixteen dollars for twenty-four supermarket trans-fat packed cupcakes? Good grief. I'll bake. That means I need eggs and the eggs here sure are cheap. But I can't buy them here because these eggs are laid by debeaked chickens living in cages the size of Tic Tac boxes. If only I'd gone to the farmers' market on Sunday and bought eggs there . . . But how do I know that guy treats his chickens well just because the eggs are blue? And honestly, do I even really care about chickens? I can't believe I'm spending three dollars per pound for these crunchy tomatoes. I should grow them, just like Barbara Kingsolver. How does she find the time to make her own cheese and breed her own heritage turkeys and write books? I need to work harder, sleep less, never watch TV again. Wait, there's high-fructose corn syrup in Campbell's vegetable soup? Isn't that supposed to be a deal breaker?*

Every choice I made was loaded, and every choice I made was wrong. The mental conversation was circular and chronically irritating and I couldn't seem to shut it down.

Then I lost my job.

Instantly, I was stabbed with the predictable financial anxiety, which I attended to by taking an overdue video back to the video store and calling my husband to make sure that he still had his job. It was 2008 and a lot of people were losing their jobs. I made myself a cup of tea and walked out the back door of our house and sat on the steps leading down to our unkempt suburban yard, strewn with deflated soccer balls and broken deck chairs and gravel. The sky had fallen, yet there it was, vast and blue above me. A few end-of-the-season red apples weighted down the branches of our tree. I thought, *I should really pick those, before the squirrels get them. I can make applesauce. I can make apple butter. I can make chutney. Who needs a job when you have an apple tree? They didn't have jobs in* Little House in the Big Woods.

Even as I thought this, sitting on my steps, I knew it to be completely ridiculous. A job is more valuable than an apple tree. People can't live on applesauce and no one even likes chutney. Plus, I hate canning.

And yet a question lodged in the forefront of my mind. Where is that sweet spot between buying and making? What does the market do cheaper and better? And where are we being deceived, our tastes and habits and standards corrupted? Could I answer this question once and for all? I didn't want an answer rooted in ideology, or politics, or tradition, or received wisdom. I wanted to see the question answered empirically, taking into account the competing demands—time and meaning, quality and conscience, budget and health—of everyday American family life.

And so, over the next months and years, I got some chickens, which I loved; and some ducks, which I loathed; and some turkeys, which we slaughtered. I learned to make cheese and keep bees and worried that the neighbors were going to call Animal Control. I cured bacon and salmon, canned ketchup, baked croissants, and made vanilla extract and graham crackers. I planted tomatillos and potatoes and melons and squash. My son, Owen, joined 4-H and practically moved into the yard, while my teenage daughter, Isabel, refused to step outside the back door at all, especially after the goats turned up. My husband, Mark, rolled his eyes at all of it except the homemade yogurt. That, he ate by the quart. At the height—or maybe it was the depths—of my homemaking experiment, I had pickles lacto-fermenting on the counter and seven varieties of jam, ranging from banana-chocolate to plum, arrayed in the pantry, and absinthe and Taleggio cheese mellowing in the crawl space behind my closet. I was overwhelmed and a bit of a mess, but I had my answers.

PEANUT BUTTER AND JELLY SANDWICH

Let's get back to the PB&J. One day, I bought some Uncrustables, the Smucker's frozen sandwiches, which come in a carton decorated with a quaint gingham check. Then I made a peanut butter and jelly sandwich the usual way, which took less time than finding the car keys to drive to buy the Uncrustables. Unwrapped, Uncrustables do not look like sandwiches, but like dainty white turnovers with sealed, crimped edges. They look wonderful, the bread downy and soft and white as a stack of Kleenex.

I took a bite. The jelly was gelatinous and supersweet, as in a jelly donut, one of my favorite foods. I loved it. The second bite was less delightful—a bit cloying and yet oddly desiccated. By the third bite, I was done. This was a stupid little sandwich.

"It's like the peanut butter is a solid mass," said Isabel, then twelve years old, plucking out a flat shard of tan paste and holding it up for inspection. "Look, it's a thing."

The homemade peanut butter and jelly sandwich, on the other hand, was luscious and sloppy and extravagant and fresh, and it easily carried the day. *If this is the best Smucker's can do*, I thought, *civilization is safe.*

I assumed that the Uncrustables would turn out to be a bargain. Isn't the whole point of industrial food that it is cheap? Well, cheap to make, maybe, but not all that cheap to buy. This fact has repeatedly taken me by surprise, though it probably shouldn't have. Inferior mass-produced food often costs more—and sometimes quite a bit more—than homemade food. The homemade sandwich cost fifty-one cents and was roughly twice the size of the wee Uncrustable, which priced out at sixty-three cents.

There is market research that answers the question of who buys these expensive sandwiches when it is so easy and inexpensive to make one at home. Just to show how loaded this subject of food can be, how much socioeconomic and gender baggage we attach to the shopping and production of what we eat, I'll describe the "research" that I performed in my own brain while standing in my kitchen. Who buys Uncrustables? I saw a woman in a peach velour tracksuit with a Kate Gosselin haircut loading up her cart at a big-box supermarket. She appeared pouty and spoiled and indolent, someone who would recline on the sofa watching *Real Housewives* and eating fat-free bonbons rather than make her kids' sandwiches. A mother who buys Uncrustables: bad mother.

Then I tried to picture a man buying a box of Uncrustables. He came to me just as instantly and fully formed. A widower, he pushed a cart through the IGA after a long day of honest toil, perhaps in the construction trade. He wore a rumpled flannel shirt and looked a lot like Aidan Quinn. He was noble and long-suffering, a devoted dad, out there shopping for his kids' food when he deserved to put his feet up and crack open a cold one. He needed to meet a really nice woman, someone just like me, except single.

I thought this. I was appalled at myself.

PEANUT BUTTER

Until I actually did it, I thought you had to be compulsive and controlling to grind your own peanut butter. But it turns out to be almost as worthwhile as making your own PB&Js. (Though not quite.) Home-ground peanut butter is nubbly, rich, intensely peanutty. Mass-market brands like Jif and Skippy have been sweetened and homogenized to the point where they resemble peanut-flavored Crisco. I still love Jif and will almost surely buy it again, but homemade is better next time you have seven minutes to spare.

Make it or buy it? Make it.

Hassle: Scant

Cost comparison: Per cup, homemade peanut butter is 80 percent the price of Jif.

1 pound unsalted roasted peanuts, shelled and skinned
2 tablespoons oil (preferably peanut)
Salt

1. Put the peanuts and oil in a food processor or blender and grind until you have a creamy paste. Add more oil if necessary to thin. Make this peanut butter a little thinner than you think it should be, as it will firm up a lot in the refrigerator.
2. Salt to taste. Store in a jar in the refrigerator for several months.

Makes 2 cups

Now what about the bread? What about the jelly? What about all of it?

A few caveats before we get started. First, although, like most people, I think about money, I've always been able to clothe my children and pay the mortgage and if I couldn't, whether I bought or made crème fraîche—or bread, to use a less absurd example—would make no difference. It is frivolous and deluded to think it would. I just wanted to address and answer some middle-class home economics questions that nagged my Michael Pollan–reading, price-checking, overthinking self. This is *not* a book about how to scrape by on a budget and it is not a book about how to go off the grid.

Second, prices of food vary from day to day, shop to shop, region to region. I did my best to price ingredients consistently and accurately as of late 2010 and early 2011, but the prices you see here might not always reflect what you pay, where you live, today.

When I started this project I had a lot of time on my hands—more than I'd ever had before as an adult. A lot of these projects are very ambitious, and I've tried to make clear which are particularly time consuming. But when you're exhausted and overworked, even the simplest kitchen job—even mixing a jar of salad dressing—can seem like too much. When I say "make it," I mean that when you have the time and the inclination, the recipe in question is something you can do better, and/or more cheaply, than the supermarket. By no means do I think everyone should make all (or even any) of these foods, all of the time. I sure don't.

Moreover, if you don't enjoy messing around in the kitchen, you probably aren't going to end up making your own Camembert and pancetta, despite the fact that they're better and cheaper than what you can buy. Nor should you. As my son, Owen, said one day—a little spitefully—while he was reluctantly doing his homework and I was happily stuffing pot stickers, "Mom, I think if you didn't like to cook we'd eat canned soup every night."

He is right.

CHAPTER 1

BREADS AND SPREADS

Laurel was just setting out four long, fat strips of dough to rise for French bread. A light dusting of flour was especially visible on her black cat, but it covered everything in the room. Framing the whole scene was the most luxuriant sweet potato plant I had ever come across. It shot up from one corner, curled up across the ceiling, meandered along the far wall, and darted out a window. Laurel herself was right out of Vermeer.

—*Laurel's Kitchen*

When I was growing up in the 1970s, my mother had a battered copy of *Laurel's Kitchen* that I used to pore over when I was bored on a Saturday afternoon. *Laurel's Kitchen* painted a vivid, highly romantic portrait of a vaguely counterculture vegetarian home, lush with houseplants, infused with the aromas of baking bread and bubbling soups, and I was captivated. It was one of those books that were always lying around in homes of that era, like *I'm OK—You're OK* and *Fear of Flying*, from which I gleaned many seductive, misleading ideas about the way the world operates.

I opened *Laurel's Kitchen* recently, for the first time in twenty-five years. The frontispiece features a black-and-white photograph of the three authors, all of them wearing prairie skirts, smiling beatifically at one another, not one of them looking at the camera. They are drinking mugs of tea—or perhaps it is their beloved Gandhi's coffee, a "good warming drink" made from toasted wheat—and their long hair has been pulled back in old-fashioned buns that make them look like Manson sisters, or Amish wives, or Ma Ingalls.

I started reading. Was I hallucinating? Had I really once loved this book? And were these truly the views of groovy Berkeley, California, women in the 1970s? Interspersed between paeans to the glory of homemade bread and recipes for cashew gravy were meditations on the nature of women that struck me as so essentialist and retrograde that they might have come from a fundamentalist religious sect. "I would never go on record as saying 'a woman's place is in the home,'" wrote one of the authors. "But to my mind the most effective front for social change, the critical point where our efforts will count the most, is not in business or profession . . . but in the home and community, where the problems start." In the home, kneading a big batch of cracked wheat bread, was where women—the "nurturant" sex—belonged: "No paycheck comes at the end of the month," the authors wrote, "and no promotion: the incentive here is much less obvious, and much more worthy of you as a human being."

If I saw my teenage daughter reading this today, I would gently remove it from her hands and suggest that she go to the library and find herself something energizing and appropriate for a girl her age, like *Wifey* or *Scruples*.

This is not to say I don't think that making bread is a worthwhile pastime. I emphatically do. I've made almost all of my family's bread for the last fifteen years but I don't equate bread baking with a higher morality or the eternal feminine. And I will attest that you don't need to look like a Vermeer to make bread. You can look like an R. Crumb and smoke Parliaments while drinking Sanka spiked with Jim Beam, and still bake amazing bread. It's one of the easiest ways to upgrade (and sabotage) your diet while saving a little money. Moreover, it takes less time to mix bread dough than drive to the supermarket, and you won't run into anyone you don't want to see. I have often baked bread for this very reason.

EVERYDAY BREAD

I make this straightforward bread once a week, sometimes twice. It has a hard, chewy crust and the texture of a peasant loaf, but you bake it in a pan, which makes it more tidily sliced for sandwiches. Though I've changed it significantly, the recipe is originally from the British cookbook *Moro*.

For a while I felt I should bake all our bread—that it was spendthrift and lazy not to. I didn't want my husband to buy bread, even when we ran out, and I got snippy when he did. But I also got snippy when he'd remind me that we were running out of bread—I felt like I was being nagged to put on my apron. I think everyone in my family is glad I've stopped wearing that particular hair shirt. Homemade bread is better but still: it's just bread.

Make it or buy it? Make it.

Hassle: Can you stir? You can make this bread.

Cost comparison: Homemade: Less than one dollar a loaf, including fuel to heat the oven. A 1-pound loaf of levain bread made by Acme, a local artisanal bakery, costs $5.50. A loaf of Sara Lee classic 100% whole wheat: $4.39.

Neutral vegetable oil, for greasing
1 teaspoon instant yeast
3½ cups whey from making yogurt (page 47) or water, at room temperature
5½ cups all-purpose flour
1¾ cups whole-wheat flour
⅓ cup flaxseeds (optional)
4 teaspoons kosher salt

1. Oil the inside of two 9 by 5-inch metal loaf pans.
2. In a large bowl, mix the yeast, liquid, flours, seeds (if using), and salt. Scrape the dough into the pans. Drape with a clean, damp dish towel and let rise for about 2 hours until level with the tops of the pans. Many recipes specify plastic wrap

YEAST

These recipes all call for instant yeast. If you bake bread even just a few times a month, you should absolutely order your yeast in bulk from King Arthur Flour (see Appendix). Supermarket yeast costs as much as $4.50 per ounce. A one-pound sack of instant yeast from King Arthur costs $0.75 an ounce, including shipping. A pound is a lot of yeast, but you're far more likely to bake if you have abundant cheap yeast in the refrigerator. I decant my yeast into a clean quart jar and it has so far never gone bad on me.

to cover rising bread; I don't use it because a) it's plastic and b) it never stays in place. Occasionally this dough rises extra high and sticks to the towel; just pull it off the best you can. If the prospect of this bothers you, cover with lightly oiled plastic wrap instead.

3. Preheat the oven to 450 degrees F.
4. Bake loaves for 30 minutes.
5. Remove the bread from the pans, return to the oven, and bake directly on the rack for 15 minutes more. The bread is done when it is richly colored and sounds hollow when tapped.
6. Ordinarily, you should cool bread before slicing, but a hot, crispy heel of this bread is too delicious to forgo, especially with butter. Store in a paper bag for up to a week. For longer storage, wrap tightly and freeze.

Makes 2 loaves

BUTTER

I was very proud of my first homemade butter. Then, for comparison, I tasted a bit of unsalted butter from the supermarket and it was also smashing. I made cultured butter, which entails ripening the cream with yogurt, and it was delicious as well. Homemade butter is good, but because it costs so much more to make it, unless you have a cow, I don't see the point.

Make it or buy it? Buy it.
Hassle: With a mixer, little
Cost comparison: A $3.39 pint of cream yields a half pound or so of butter, which you can buy for $1.75.

1 pint heavy cream

Pour the cream into a large bowl and beat hard with a mixer. Over the course of 10 minutes it will go from liquid to softly whipped to stiffly whipped to overwhipped, then grainy and curdled, then shrunken, and suddenly you will hear liquid sloshing around the bowl, which will contain two distinct entities: clumps of butter clinging to the whisk, and thin, cloudy buttermilk. Pour off the buttermilk (it's sweet and drinkable if that's the kind of thing you like), whisk some more, and drain off any additional buttermilk that accumulates. Take the butter in your hands and rinse it under ice-cold running water. Pat it dry. Use immediately if possible—it's at its most exquisite right now—or pack in a bowl, cover tightly with plastic wrap, and store in the refrigerator for a week.

Makes ½ pound

BREAD CRUMBS

You can make bread crumbs that are the size of Grape-Nuts to add crunch to pasta or the crust of a casserole, and you can make bread crumbs with the consistency of sand to plump up a hamburger patty or line a cake pan. At the store you can usually find only sandy bread crumbs and panko—the wispy, flaky Japanese bread crumbs used for coating foods before deep-frying. Panko you should buy, but all other bread crumbs you should make.

Make it or buy it? Make it.
Hassle: None
Cost comparison: Homemade bread crumbs cost nothing if you make them from bread you would otherwise throw away. Store-bought crumbs range from $2.50 to $6.00 per pound, which is more than ground beef and completely insane.

Every time you find yourself with some bread—baguette, whole-wheat, bagel— that's starting to get stale, break it into smallish pieces and put them in a bag in the freezer. Keep filling the bag as bread accumulates. One day when you're heating the oven for some other purpose, spread your stale bread collection on a cookie sheet and pop it into the oven for 10 to 15 minutes. When the pieces of bread are golden and toasted all the way through, take them out of the oven and grind in the food processor. (If you don't have a food processor, place in a plastic bag and crush with a rolling pin.) Store in the freezer indefinitely.

RYE BREAD

Unless you use a high-gluten flour (see Appendix), this seedy rye bread will be very tender, not quite as sturdy as supermarket rye. If you're making a burly sandwich like a Reuben (see page 180), you might want to go with store-bought.

Make it or buy it? Your call. Better flavor or stronger crumb?
Hassle: Easy
Cost comparison: Homemade: $0.13 per slice. Oroweat: $0.19 per slice.

2¼ cups all-purpose flour, plus more for shaping
1⅓ cups rye flour
1 tablespoon caraway seeds
2 teaspoons kosher salt
1 tablespoon sugar
2 teaspoons instant yeast
¼ cup neutral vegetable oil, plus more for the bowl and pan
1¼ cups warm water or whey from making yogurt (page 47)
1 egg, for brushing

1. Whisk together the flours, seeds, salt, sugar, and yeast in a large bowl. Add the oil and liquid and stir until you have a shaggy dough. Knead the dough for 10 minutes, until it is smooth and firm. Form into a ball, remove it from the bowl, lightly oil the bowl, and put the dough back in. Cover with a clean, damp dish towel. Let rise until doubled in bulk, about 2 hours.
2. Oil a 9 by 5-inch metal loaf pan. On a lightly floured surface, shape the dough into an 8-inch log and place in the pan. Cover with the same damp towel and let rise until it reaches the top of the pan, about 1 hour.
3. Preheat the oven to 350 degrees F.
4. Beat the egg with 1 tablespoon water and brush over the top of the loaf. Bake for 35 minutes.
5. Remove from the oven, slide the bread out of the pan, and cool on a rack. Cool completely before slicing. Store in a paper bag at room temperature for up to a week.

Makes 1 loaf

BAGUETTES

In the San Francisco Bay Area, the Acme baguette—a long, crenellated wand of bread with a shiny, crackly crust—is the best you can get. I've never baked a baguette that came close. After producing countless indifferent baguettes, I found Acme's own recipe in Maggie Glezer's *Artisan Baking Across America*. Glezer agrees with me about the Acme baguette: "Their Rustic Baguette has a soft, creamy yellow crumb almost frothy with huge gas cells, and a lightly flavored crust that is brittle eggshell thin. Its flavor is pure sweet wheat." The recipe covered four oversize pages and I got very amped up about the whole endeavor. I started the night before by making both a poolish and "scrap dough." In the morning I mixed the poolish with flour and yeast, put it down for a rest, got it up again to mix in the scrap dough, kneaded, let it rise, rotated it, let it rise, and rotated it, for what sometimes felt like ad infinitum. There were many steps, staggered at intervals until I baked the baguettes. They emerged from the oven like very thick bread sticks. They were not beautiful; the flavor was not pure sweet wheat. Baguettes are tricky and they're for the serious bread hobbyist, which, after years of experimenting, I have figured out that I am not. Unless you want to devote yourself to the worthy and venerable craft, buy your baguettes.

APRICOT-GINGER BREAD

I first tasted the apricot-ginger bread from the Noe Valley Bakery in San Francisco, while chaperoning a third-grade field trip. I bought a loaf, took it home, and ate the whole thing. If I lived closer I would buy a loaf every other day and they'd have to bury me in a piano case. To come up with this recipe, I adapted the no-knead technique developed by Jim Lahey, owner of New York City's Sullivan Street Bakery, and popularized by *New York Times* columnist Mark Bittman. This bread is chewy, tangy, and studded with apricots that make it look like a stained-glass window. For this you want plump, bright orange dried apricots, not the shriveled, dark, unsulfured ones.

Eat this bread with almond butter (page 16) or Camembert (page 204), or plain.

Make it or buy it? Make it, though if I lived next door to the Noe Valley Bakery I'd give them my business.

Hassle: Easy

Cost comparison: It costs $2.60 to bake this bread at home, including fuel to heat the oven. It costs $5.30 to buy a slightly smaller loaf from the Noe Valley Bakery.

2½ cups all-purpose flour, plus more for dusting
¼ teaspoon instant yeast
1 cup plus 2 tablespoons cold water or whey from making yogurt (page 47)
1 tablespoon ground ginger
1 tablespoon kosher salt
¾ cup dried apricots, cut into quarters

1. In a big bowl, mix all the ingredients. Stir briefly; do not knead. The mixture will seem very wet and clumpy, which is as it should be.
2. Cover with a clean, damp dish towel and let the dough rest for 18 hours in a draft-free spot. No need to dampen the towel again and don't worry too much about the time; a little more or less makes no difference.
3. Dust a clean, dry dish towel with flour. Scrape the dough into a round onto the flour. Gently nudge into a ball, and then swaddle in the towel. Let the dough rise for 1 or 2 hours.

4. Preheat the oven to 475 degrees F with a covered cast-iron Dutch oven inside. I use an oblong 2-quart Le Creuset, though you can use a bigger pan if you like. (The pan does not serve to give the bread shape but to trap heat and steam as the inside of a brick oven does, yielding bread with a crunchy, hard crust.)

5. When the oven reaches 475 degrees F, open the Dutch oven and carefully slip the dough inside. Cover and bake for 30 minutes.

6. Take the lid off the pot and bake for 15 to 30 minutes more, until, as Lahey writes, the bread "is a deep chestnut color but not burnt." Cool completely before slicing. Store in a paper bag at room temperature for up to a week.

Makes one 20-ounce loaf

MILK CHOCOLATE–CHERRY BREAD

Omit the ginger and apricots and replace with ⅓ cup dried tart cherries and ½ cup milk chocolate, chopped in nuggets the size of the cherries. The bread should rise to cover most of the fruit and chocolate, but if chunks are sticking out aggressively after the first rise, try to poke them back into the dough. Cut a piece of parchment paper to neatly fit the bottom of the Dutch oven, because the sugars in the chocolate and cherries can leak during baking. You won't enjoy scrubbing the pot. You will, however, enjoy eating this bread.

ALMOND BUTTER

Almond butter might have been invented to go with apricot-ginger bread.

You can make almond butter with toasted almonds, which I love, or raw almonds, which I don't love as much. Toasted almonds won't require any additional oil, but raw almonds might need a few tablespoons of neutral vegetable oil to form a spreadable butter.

Make it or buy it? Make it.

Hassle: Easy

Cost comparison: Per cup, homemade almond butter costs about $3.75. Supermarket almond butter such as MaraNatha (which contains both sugar and palm oil): $6.40.

2 cups almonds, skin on, about 10 ounces
Neutral vegetable oil (optional)
Pinch of salt (optional)

1. If you want toasted almond butter, preheat the oven to 375 degrees F. If you're making raw almond butter, skip to step 3.
2. Spread the almonds on a baking sheet. Toast for 10 minutes, until just fragrant. Cool to room temperature.
3. Put the almonds in a food processor and grind for about 5 minutes, until the nuts release their oils and become almost runny. If you're using raw almonds, you might need to add a spoonful of oil. Add a pinch of salt, if you like. Store in a jar in the refrigerator.

Makes 1 cup

BAGELS

It's untraditional to bake bagels at home. Dating back to at least the sixteenth-century in Poland, when village bakers sold them strung from ropes and piled in baskets on market days, bagels have always been a commercial product. Jewish immigrants in the nineteenth century brought the bagel to New York City, where, according to bagel historian Maria Balinska, they were produced in fetid and vermin-infested basements (often using spoiled ingredients) and sold by street vendors. There's no sense romanticizing the New York sweatshop bagels of yore, but when you bite into a hygienic and vacuous supermarket bagel today you might wonder why anyone bothered carrying the tradition across the Atlantic.

To understand, you might just have to bake your own. I've baked just about every bagel recipe I've come across, from honey-sweetened Montreal bagels and puffy egg bagels to the two-day bagel recipe from Peter Reinhart's epic *The Bread Baker's Apprentice,* and they've all been good, but the quickest and easiest recipe I found turned out to be the best. It comes from *The New Complete Book of Breads* by Bernard Clayton, who in turn took it from Jo Goldenberg's, a legendary Jewish restaurant in Paris that closed in 2006. These bagels are delicious when baked with ingredients you probably have in the cupboard right now, but if you want to raise your game, order high-gluten flour (see Appendix), save the whey from making yogurt (page 47), and track down a jar of barley malt, which you can find in specialty groceries, health food shops, and some Whole Foods stores. The high-gluten flour makes for a superdense, chewy body, the whey provides tang, and the malt syrup gives both the bagels and your kitchen a toasty fragrance.

The crust on these bagels is hard and shiny, as if the bagel has been shrink-wrapped then shellacked, and the interior is dense and yeasty. Even without cream cheese, a homemade bagel is a meal. My sister, Justine, a former New Yorker, says, "Homemade bagels are better than 99 percent of the bagels I've ever eaten, including H&H and Murray's, but not as good as Columbia Bagels on 110th Street in Manhattan." Last time she went back to New York and made a pilgrimage to Columbia Bagels, she discovered it had closed. I think this means that these bagels are now officially the best.

These take about two hours start to finish, so if you start at eight in the morning the bagels will be ready to serve hot from the oven at ten o'clock brunch, with plenty of downtime in between for frantically cleaning the house and setting the table.

Make it or buy it? Make it.

Hassle: Moderate

Cost comparison: If you bake your bagels with all-purpose flour, these cost about $0.16 apiece. By contrast, one of Sara Lee's presliced so-called bagels costs $0.85, a bagel from the chain Noah's costs $0.99, and a bagel from New York City's hallowed H&H, $1.40. However, if you make your bagels with high-gluten flour, the price goes up to more like $0.48 per bagel. Not the cheapest bagel you will find (that would be Thomas' at $0.42 per bagel), only the best.

> *3½ cups high-gluten flour, such as King Arthur Flour's Sir Lancelot,*
> *or all-purpose flour, plus a bit more if necessary*
> *4½ teaspoons instant yeast*
> *3 tablespoons granulated sugar*
> *1 tablespoon kosher salt*
> *1½ cups warm whey from making yogurt (page 47) or water*
> *Neutral vegetable oil, for greasing*
> *2 tablespoons barley malt syrup or dark brown sugar*
> *Coarse cornmeal, for sprinkling*
> *Optional toppings: sesame seeds, poppy seeds, caraway seeds, coarse salt, etc.*

1. In the bowl of a mixer, combine the full 3½ cups flour, the yeast, sugar, and salt. Add the whey or water and beat hard with the paddle for a few minutes, switching to the dough hook when the mixture comes together. (You can do this mixing by hand, but prepare for a workout.) If the mixture seems overly wet, add some additional flour, a tiny bit at a time. Stop adding flour as soon as you have a stiff dough. Knead for 5 minutes.

2. Place the dough in a greased bowl, cover with a clean, damp dish towel, and let rise until doubled in bulk, about 1 hour.

3. Preheat the oven to 400 degrees F. Bring a large pot of water to a boil. While the water is heating, sprinkle a baking sheet generously with cornmeal and lightly grease another.

4. Deflate dough and divide into 10 pieces. Roll each piece into the neatest, round-

est ball you can and then, with your thumb, poke a hole into the middle and coax the dough into a bagel shape. Leave the bagels on the lightly greased sheet to rest for 10 minutes.

5. When the water comes to a rolling boil, add the malt syrup. Drop the bagels into the water three at a time. Let them simmer for a minute, then flip them over and simmer for another minute. Remove with a slotted spoon, return to the oiled sheet to dry just a bit, and proceed with the remaining bagels.

6. Move all the bagels to the cornmeal-sprinkled baking sheet. If you want to add toppings, now is the time to sprinkle them on top of the damp bagels.

7. Bake for 25 to 35 minutes, until golden brown. Store in a paper bag at room temperature for up to a week, or freeze, tightly wrapped, for longer storage.

Makes 10 bagels

CINNAMON RAISIN BAGELS

Add 1 tablespoon ground cinnamon along with the flour and increase the granulated sugar to 5 tablespoons. Toward the end of the kneading, add 1 cup raisins.

BAGEL CHIPS

If your bagels are getting stale, this extends their life. Bagel chips are great with hummus, or plain, for mindless snacking.

Make it or buy it? Make it.
Hassle: Trivial
Cost comparison: A 6-ounce bag of New York Style bagel chips (they contain both palm oil and sugar) costs $4.39. To make 6 ounces of chips from bagels you'd otherwise throw away: less than a dollar.

For every bagel, you need 2 tablespoons of olive oil and 1 garlic clove
Pinch of sea salt

1. Preheat the oven to 300 degrees F. Heat the olive oil in a small pan. Add the garlic and cook until the garlic softens and just begins to color. Let cool.
2. Set a bagel on a cutting board, press down with the flat of your hand, and slice horizontally as thinly as you can. You'll get 8 to 10 slices from a bagel—don't worry if some of them are raggedy. Spread the slices on a baking sheet.
3. Brush each side of each bagel slice with the oil. Bake for 20 minutes, until crispy and tan, then salt to taste. Cool and store in a sealed plastic bag or a cookie tin.

One bagel yields about 3 ounces of chips

The classic partners to a good bagel: some cream cheese and a few slices of cured salmon.

CREAM CHEESE

To make cream cheese, you need to order a tiny and inexpensive packet of something called mesophilic culture from a cheesemaking supply company (see Appendix). This packet will produce many pounds of cheese, and not just cream cheese, but Camembert, cheddar, and Taleggio, should you get ambitious. (See pages 196-207.) It lasts indefinitely in the freezer. You also need a small bottle of liquid rennet, equally cheap, useful, and long-lived.

I love homemade cream cheese, which is fluffy, snowy, and tart; by comparison, store-bought seems gummy and inert. But there are mixed feelings in our household. Once I watched Mark reach past a bowl of homemade cream cheese to pull out a silver-wrapped brick of Philadelphia to spread on Owen's bagel. "Why did you buy that?" I asked. I would have described my tone of voice as "sharp." Mark probably would have said "shrill."

"Owen says the homemade cream cheese is too sour," Mark replied.

It's not sour, but it *is* tangy.

Make it or buy it? Try it once and decide for yourself.

Hassle: You will be amazed by how simple this is.

Cost comparison: Less than half the price per ounce of Kraft Philadelphia. Even made with premium organic milk from a local dairy, homemade cream cheese costs less than Kraft, which is neither organic nor local. Nor, in my view, as delicious.

1 quart whole milk
1 quart half-and-half
¼ teaspoon mesophilic culture
2 drops liquid rennet
1 teaspoon kosher salt

1. Cooking equipment should always be clean, but cleanliness is especially vital when you're making cheese. In a very clean stainless-steel pot, over very low heat, combine the milk and half-and-half. Heat it to about 80 degrees F, barely lukewarm. You don't want the milk hot; you're just trying to take the refrigerator chill off. Remove from the heat.
2. Sprinkle the culture over the milk. To mix, gently lift a slotted spoon up and down beneath the surface of the milk to draw the cultures down and help them permeate the entire pot of milk.
3. Add the rennet and again stir with the up-and-down motion. Cover the pot, find a quiet corner where no one will disturb the mixture, and let it sit at room temperature for 24 hours.
4. Place a colander over a large bowl and line the colander with cheesecloth. Gently ladle in the curd. Cover with a clean towel and let it drain for 8 hours or so at room temperature, until the cheese is thick and has ceased to drip. (Store the whey in a jar in the refrigerator for up to 10 days to use in bagels or bread.)
5. Stir the salt into the creamy cheese. Scoop the cheese into a container and store, tightly covered, in the refrigerator. Cream cheese does not improve with age, so try to eat it within a week.

Makes 1½ pounds

WHY IS KOSHER SALT CALLED KOSHER?

Kosher salt has large, flaky crystals that are particularly effective at drawing blood from meat to render it kosher under Jewish dietary law. A more accurate name would have been "koshering salt." Other salts, such as sea salt, may be kosher—but they're not "kosher salt."

CURED SALMON

There are two types of smoked salmon: Hot-smoked salmon, opaque and rust-colored, has been cooked, as the name suggests, by gusts of warm smoke. Cold-smoked salmon (or lox) is supple, bright, and nearly translucent, flavored—but not cooked—by cool smoke. Lox is what you eat on bagels with cream cheese and capers on Sunday mornings. In his book *Essentials of Cooking*, James Peterson shows how to rig up a cold smoker by attaching some piping to a hot smoker, but this is unhelpful if you don't have a hot smoker. Lacking either a hot smoker or a cold smoker, the closest most of us can come to replicating lox at home by using gravlax, the ambrosial Swedish cured fish. It is easy and the variations are endless. I've cured gravlax in oil (it was not, in fact, oily), with Pernod (reminiscent of a black jelly bean), with fresh dill, with ground coriander and brown sugar, and with mountains of lemon zest. The one universal is salt.

I had made and served much gravlax when I first read about anisakis, a parasitic nematode routinely found in wild salmon. When a larva makes its way into a human body, the human body may end up in the hospital. I had just eaten a slice of gravlax when I learned about anisakis and all afternoon my throat felt oddly scratchy, as if . . .

I did not in the end have anisakis, but just thinking I might was bad enough.

Preventing it is easy. If you use farmed salmon for your gravlax, you are in luck: anisakis is rarely found in farmed salmon. Unfortunately, farmed salmon is often full of fungicides, pesticides, PCBs, and antibiotics. Moreover, salmon farms can pollute the surrounding waters and endanger wild fish populations. I prefer to buy wild salmon, and wild salmon is frequently host to anisakis. To destroy the parasite, you simply need to freeze the fish and keep it below −4 degrees F for 7 days. I worried that freezing would also destroy the flavor and texture of the salmon, but it doesn't.

This is a simplified version of a citrus-cured salmon recipe from Boston chef Barbara Lynch. It's dazzling, this fish, salty and sweet with a fleshiness you seldom find in lox.

Make it or buy it? Make it.

Hassle: Truly easy

Cost comparison: Salmon prices vary depending on the time of year, the type of salmon, and whether the fish is farmed or wild. If you buy wild salmon in season at $14.99 per pound, you can just about match the price of most smoked salmon, which ranges between $15.00 and $24.00 per pound. I would skip the gravlax when salmon costs $26.00 per pound.

1 pound skin-on salmon fillet
½ cup coriander seeds
¼ cup black peppercorns
1 cup kosher salt
1 cup sugar
Finely grated zest of 3 lemons (optional)
Finely grated zest of 3 oranges (optional)

1. If you're using wild salmon, begin by wrapping it tightly and freezing it for 7 days. Thaw completely in the refrigerator.
2. In a spice grinder, grind the coriander and peppercorns. Toss with the salt, sugar, and citrus zests, if using, and spread half the cure mixture in a container just slightly larger than the salmon, such as a small glass pie plate.
3. Place the salmon on the bed of cure mixture and cover with the rest. You want the salmon immured in cure. Cover with plastic wrap and refrigerate for 48 hours.
4. Remove from the cure, rinse well, dry, and slice thinly as needed. Store it unsliced, tightly wrapped, in the refrigerator. I wouldn't keep it more than a week.

Makes 1 pound

HOT DOG BUNS

One day we had a package of hot dogs to use up, but no buns. I've served naked hot dogs rolling around on a plate before, but no one in my household is very happy when I do. Likewise, I'm never very happy to go to the supermarket. I decided to try out the bun recipe in *The King Arthur Flour Baker's Companion,* a cookbook that has seldom steered me wrong. Mixing and kneading the dough took five minutes. I left it to rise for three hours and went about my day.

Shortly before dinner, I shaped the dough into logs, let them rise briefly, and put them in the oven. They were lopsided and lumpish when they emerged, and didn't offer a perfectly tidy cradle for the hot dogs. "People rely on hot dog buns to hold their hot dogs," said Mark, frowning. But once he started eating, even he had to concede that these were superlative hot dog buns, slightly sweet and yeasty, soft and rich.

I found myself reflecting on how bad most hot dog buns are. How we take for granted their badness, how inured we are to their badness. How I always throw away what's left after the last bite of hot dog because the bread has the texture of foam rubber. But hot dog buns don't need to be bad! We were eating these hot dog buns as if they were warm sourdough rolls. Moreover, they were cheaper than buns from the supermarket.

Make it or buy it? If you have time, make it. You can buy delicious bread and adequate bagels but you cannot buy a good hot dog bun.

Hassle: Slight, though you have to plan ahead

Cost comparison: Homemade: $0.17 a bun. Ball Park buns: $0.37. Sara Lee: $0.55.

1 cup milk
2 tablespoons unsalted butter, softened
1 large egg
2¾ cups all-purpose flour
½ cup whole-wheat flour
¼ cup sugar

1 teaspoon kosher salt
1 tablespoon instant yeast
Neutral vegetable oil, for greasing

1. In the bowl of a stand mixer, combine the milk, butter, egg, flours, sugar, salt, and yeast and knead with the dough hook until you have a smooth dough.
2. Scoop up the dough, grease the bowl, and return the dough to the bowl. Cover with a clean, damp dish towel and let the dough rise. It will be puffed and ready in about 1 hour, but you can leave it longer.
3. Gently deflate the dough and divide into 10 pieces. Shape each lump of dough into a petite bun-sized log. Make them as neat as you can, because every flaw in the design will be exaggerated in the finished product.
4. Place on a greased or parchment-lined cookie sheet, 1½ inches apart. Drape with the same damp towel. Let rise for 30 minutes. This is dough with Frankenstein inclinations, so don't let the buns rise much longer than 30 minutes.
5. Preheat the oven to 375 degrees F.
6. Bake the buns for 12 to 15 minutes, until golden. The original recipe says to cool the buns, but I would eat them soon. Like, immediately. If you don't eat them immediately, store in a plastic bag at room temperature for up to 5 days. Freeze for longer storage.

Makes 10 buns

HAMBURGER BUNS

Because hot dog buns were such a revelation, I assumed the same would be true of hamburger buns. This didn't turn out to be so. In my experience homemade hamburger buns are always too stiff and substantial, not fluffy enough. Here's the issue: Unlike hot dogs, hamburgers are sloppy and effusive and you need a bun to work as both a sponge to soak up juices and a mitt to hold the burger itself. While I can bake a really outstanding mitt, it never quite doubles as a sponge. I have to hand it to Big Food: it has mastered the spongy bread.

Make it or buy it? Buy it. (I recommend the Crustini sandwich rolls from Francisco. Since giving up on trying to bake my own, I've become very brand loyal.)

OIL SPRAYS

For all recorded history until 1959, when adman and entrepreneur Arthur Meyerhoff, Sr., and a partner began marketing the first nonstick cooking spray, people got by without spritzing oil out of a can. Meyerhoff named his product PAM (it stands for Product of Arthur Meyerhoff) and cooking sprays are now ubiquitous. My mother never bought PAM and I hardly ever use it, as I never got into the habit. But my husband cannot live without. According to him, we go through two cans of PAM a year at $3.00 per can. According to the label, a can provides "529 ¼-second sprays." Or: six ounces of canola oil, soy lecithin, dimethyl silicone, rosemary extract, and propellant.

The oil in that can is by my estimate worth about $0.36 and what you're paying for is the functionality of the disposable can. Is there a cheap, reliable, reusable alternative? Ten dollars will buy an aluminum canister that you can fill and refill with the oil of your choice. I bought one, loaded it up, started spraying, and noticed immediately that the spray wasn't quite as powerful as PAM's. If we use twelve ounces of oil spray in the first year, as our track record suggests we will, we'll spend $10.72 on spray oil for the year versus $6.00 for PAM. The first year we're in the red, but in the second year we go into the black, and every year after that we go deeper into the black.

Unless, of course, the canister breaks. I have quietly noted that whenever it's sitting on the counter or the table, my ten-year-old son, Owen, must play with it. It is, after all, a shiny gadget. And we know what happens to those. If our canister lasts two years, I will declare it a success. Meanwhile, it's an open question.

PITA BREAD

The trick to getting pita to form a pocket is to put a baking stone on the lowest rack of the oven and heat it to 550 degrees F at least 30 minutes before you bake. (You really need a bakery store for this recipe.) A baking stone absorbs and holds heat, and when you put the flat bread on top, it immediately starts cooking the crust. But even on a hot baking stone, sometimes pita just won't bubble. Nevertheless, warm homemade pita, with a pocket or without, is more supple and flavorful than the pita you buy at the supermarket—and you can just fold the pita around the filling. Or you can cut the pita in triangles and eat it with hummus, which requires no pocket.

Make it or buy it? How much do you need that pocket? Make it.

Hassle: Moderate

Cost comparison: The ingredients are humble, and homemade pita is cheap. Ounce for ounce, store-bought pita, such as Sara Lee, costs 5 to 10 times as much.

1¼ cups warm water
1 teaspoon instant yeast
1 tablespoon sugar
1 tablespoon olive oil
1½ teaspoons kosher salt
1½ cups whole-wheat flour
1½ cups all-purpose flour, plus more as needed
Neutral vegetable oil, for greasing

1. In the bowl of a stand mixer, beat together the water, yeast, sugar, oil, salt, and whole-wheat flour until creamy. Add the all-purpose flour ½ cup at a time, until you have a smooth dough (you might need a little extra if the dough seems sticky).
2. Switch to the dough hook, or knead by hand, until the dough is velvety and springy.
3. Lift the dough out of the bowl, oil the bowl, and cover with a clean, damp dish towel. Let rise at room temperature until doubled in bulk, about 1½ hours.
4. At least 30 minutes before you bake, preheat the oven to 550 degrees F with a baking stone set on the bottom rack.

5. Gently deflate the dough and divide it into two portions. Cover half with the damp towel to keep it from drying out. Divide the dough you're holding into 8 chunks of roughly equal size and form each into a ball. Let rest 10 minutes while dividing the rest of the dough into 8 portions.
6. Dust a work surface with flour and, using a rolling pin, roll each ball into a 6-inch circle, about ¼ inch thick. Loosely cover the circles with a few clean, dry dish towels.
7. Transfer the breads to the blazing hot stone, as many as can fit without crowding, about three at a time. Do not open the oven door for 8 minutes, then check the pitas. They should be puffed and light brown. Remove to a rack and repeat with the remaining pitas. Eat immediately, or cool and store in a bag at room temperature for up to a week. Freeze, tightly wrapped, for longer storage.

Makes 16 pitas

HUMMUS

Rich, nutritious, filling, and inexpensive, hummus is one of those foods that make vegetarianism seem doable.

Make it or buy it? Make it.
Hassle: Once you have the chickpeas, there's little more to making hummus than turning on the blender.
Cost comparison: Homemade hummus: $0.85 per cup. Sabra: $3.10 per cup. Athenos brand: $4.45 per cup.

4 garlic cloves, peeled
4 cups drained cooked chickpeas (recipe follows) or canned
Liquid from the chickpeas
2 teaspoons ground cumin
Pinch of ground coriander
5 tablespoons tahini (page 30)
Juice of 3 large lemons

3 tablespoons olive oil, plus more as needed
Salt

In a blender or food processor, puree all the ingredients until smooth. Thin with chickpea cooking liquid and some additional olive oil, if necessary. Salt to taste. Add another squeeze of lemon if you think the hummus needs more acid. Store in the refrigerator, where it will keep for about a week.

Makes 4 cups

CHICKPEAS

Dried or canned chickpeas? Some people don't mind canned, but for me there's a sliminess to them that comes through even in hummus. Plus: expensive.

Dried or canned chickpeas? Dried.
Hassle: Slight
Cost comparison: A cup of chickpeas starting with dried: $0.24. A cup of S&W canned chickpeas: $1.08.

1 pound dried chickpeas
Salt

1. Cover the chickpeas in water to soak overnight. Or, if you're in a hurry, boil the chickpeas for 2 minutes, turn off the heat, and let sit at room temperature for 2 hours. (This is what cookbooks call a "quick soak.")
2. Drain off the soaking water. Put the chickpeas in a medium pot, add fresh water to generously cover again, bring to a boil, and simmer gently until tender. This will take as little as 40 minutes or up to a few hours, depending on the age of the beans. Salt to taste only after the chickpeas have softened. Store in the refrigerator for 5 days, or freeze for longer storage.

Makes 7 cups

TAHINI

Store-bought tahini is plush and sand-colored, with a pronounced sesame flavor. Home-ground tahini is coarse, the flavor more muted.

Make it or buy it? Buy it.

Hassle: Easy

Cost comparison: Homemade: $0.15 per tablespoon. Indo-European brand imported from Lebanon: $0.15 per tablespoon.

½ cup sesame seeds
4 teaspoons olive oil

1. Preheat the oven to 375 degrees F.
2. Spread the sesame seeds on a baking sheet and toast for 10 minutes.
3. Cool. Grind with the oil to form a smooth, runny paste. Store in a jar in the refrigerator.

Makes ⅓ cup

CORNBREAD

Jiffy mix makes a fair cornbread. It's not quite as lofty as homemade, you can't tailor the sweetness, and it does contain partially hydrogenated lard. But the bread tastes fine and it's marginally cheaper and quicker than homemade. That said, I've been baking my husband's grandmother's cornbread recipe for fifteen years, and I think of her every time I do it. She was lovely with a cloud of white hair and the gift of making everyone feel appreciated, from the smallest child to the most shy and awkward adult. She called recipes "rules" and she wrote out this rule for "Aunt Sally's cornbread" for me in her own hand. Whoever Aunt Sally was, she was definitely a Yankee. This cornbread is *sweet*.

Make it or buy it? Make it.

Hassle: Not as jiffy as Jiffy but quite easy

Cost comparison: Jiffy costs about two cents per ounce less than homemade. A piece of Jiffy cornbread: $0.18. A piece of homemade: $0.22.

6 tablespoons (¾ stick) unsalted butter
1 cup all-purpose flour
1 cup white or yellow cornmeal, whatever grind you like
½ cup sugar
4 teaspoons baking powder
1 teaspoon kosher salt
2 large eggs
1 cup milk

1. Preheat the oven to 375 degrees F. Put the butter in a 10-inch pie plate and place it in the oven to melt.
2. Mix the flour, cornmeal, sugar, baking powder, and salt in a large bowl. In a smaller bowl, whisk together the eggs and milk. When the butter has melted, take the pie plate out of the oven and swirl the butter around to coat the pan. Let it cool for 1 or 2 minutes, then pour the butter into the milk-egg mixture. Whisk to combine.
3. Whisk the liquid into the dry mixture—not too strenuously. A few lumps are okay.
4. Pour into the pie plate and bake for 25 minutes. When it is done, the bread will be slightly puffed and a toothpick inserted in the middle will come out clean. Serve immediately. Leftovers keep for a few days, covered, at room temperature.

Serves 8

NUTELLA

Delicious on toasted English muffins and by the spoonful, straight from the jar, homemade Nutella is nubblier than the Ferrero product, but also more hazelnutty and intense. I thought the recipe from the archives of the *Los Angeles Times* was so perfect I decided to teach the sixth-grade girls in my cooking class how to make it. They were very stoked—until they tasted it. They frowned. They were not pleased. So we added sugar and cocoa powder until we got the Nutella closer to the supersweet, fudgy, slightly waxy spread they know and love. I began to wonder if they would care if hazelnuts were eliminated entirely. Perhaps not. This recipe reflects the happy medium between my ideal Nutella and theirs.

Make it or buy it? Give it a try.
Hassle: Skinning hazelnuts is maddening.
Cost comparison: Homemade: $0.22 per tablespoon. Store-bought: $0.20 per tablespoon.

2 cups hazelnuts (about 9 ounces)
¾ cup cocoa powder
1¼ cups confectioners' sugar
½ teaspoon vanilla extract (page 260)
⅛ teaspoon kosher salt
¼ cup neutral vegetable oil, plus more as needed

BUYING NUTS

The plastic sacks of nuts from the baking section of a big-box supermarket cost more—often a few dollars per pound more—than nuts you scoop from the bins at a health food store, a co-op, or even the very same big-box supermarket. Moreover, if you buy your nuts chopped, you may pay half again as much for the same variety of nut. Diamond chopped walnuts: $0.71 per ounce. Diamond walnut pieces: $0.50 per ounce. Whole Foods bulk walnuts: $0.37 per ounce. So learn to chop nuts and buy them from the bulk bin—but don't buy too many. If you store nuts in a tightly sealed container in the freezer they should keep for many months, but even there they eventually become rancid. You can taste it immediately when nuts have turned. Throw them out, because baking them or turning them into butter isn't going to bring them back to life. It's tempting to hoard nuts, like a chipmunk, but it's also a mistake.

1. Preheat the oven to 400 degrees F.
2. Spread the hazelnuts on a cookie sheet and toast for 10 minutes until they begin to darken. Transfer to a clean, damp dish towel and rub until the skins loosen. Don't worry about getting all the skins off; you never will.
3. In a blender or food processor, grind the hazelnuts into a butter. This takes about 5 minutes—don't stop when the hazelnuts are merely ground up; you want them shiny and pourable.
4. When the hazelnuts are liquefied, add the remaining ingredients and grind until you have a mixture with the consistency of peanut butter, pausing once or twice to scrape down the sides of the bowl. If it seems too dry, add a bit more oil.
5. Refrigerate in a covered container until needed. It lasts indefinitely, though you need to bring it to room temperature before you can spread it, which is actually the only drawback to this recipe. When people want Nutella, they want it *now*.

Makes 2 cups

CHAPTER 2

EGGS

It was spring break and the children and I were home and bored. One sunny morning, we drove up to a feed store in rural Sonoma County just to check out the day-old chicks. This was a little like dropping by See's just to see if the chocolates look good. The only real surprise was that we didn't also come home with ducklings, which were even cuter than the chicks. But I was not ready to install a pond. Yet.

My mother called just as we were walking in the door with our box of cheeping chicks.

"Do you hear that?" I asked.

"No!" she said. "You didn't!"

"We did!"

"So you got Mark to agree?"

"No," I said. "I didn't."

"Oh, dear," she said. "Well, you're an original."

Actually, I was a cliché. In 2009, it seemed that everyone was getting chickens, citing sustainability and the economy. In the lower part of our hilly yard we had a derelict playhouse, creaking of floor and leaking of roof, that could easily be converted into a poultry shelter. This seemed like a clever way to stick it to the economy that didn't need me anymore. Take that, Big Egg. The six (supposedly) female chicks we brought home that day were Buff Orpingtons, a British bird that begins life resembling a marshmallow Peep and matures into a voluptuous hen with a raspberry-red comb and apricot-colored feathers. We bought a sack of pine shavings for bedding, a plastic feeder, and some chick feed that looked exactly like kitty litter, and set the babies up in a cage on the floor with a lightbulb for heat. They huddled under the lightbulb, every few minutes falling asleep en masse and toppling over.

My brother-in-law, Michael, broke the news to Mark. As reported to me later, their conversation went something like this:

Michael: "Hey, dude, congratulations."
Mark: "For what?"
Michael: "The chickens!"
Mark: "What?"
Michael: "I heard you got these awesome chickens."
Mark: "Are you effing kidding? Goddamn it."

My mother came over that very afternoon and we sat around the cage, observing and admiring the little birds in much the same way we had sat around observing and admiring my children when they were newborns lying on a receiving blanket. We were sitting there when Mark came home and stood, arms folded across his chest, looking down at the cage.

"Oh, dear," said my mother. "I think I'll let you handle this in privacy."

"Don't we have enough going on without adding complications?" Mark asked.

"Probably," I said. I thought: *What exactly do we have going on?*

He was silent for a minute. "Well, they are cute."

They were cute. Almost immediately, I wanted more chickens. Having an all–Buff Orpington flock is a little like having a closet that contains nothing but khaki. There's no prettier or friendlier fowl, but reading about poultry, as I found myself idly then avidly doing, I coveted variety. Chickens come in scores of colors and sizes and breeds, and they seized my imagination in a way probably familiar to collectors of orchids or antique watches. I wanted a gold-laced Wyandotte, whose plumage resembles a tortoiseshell comb; and a shiny black Australorp, the breed that holds the world record for egg production; and a blue-egg-laying Ameraucana, beloved by Martha Stewart; and a Cuckoo Marans, which produces the chocolate-colored eggs favored by James Bond. Our town's laws allow us to keep up to twelve hens, so we got nineteen. I found another feed store with a wider selection and bought a Polish chick with a white topknot, and a Silkie bantam whose downy feathers lined her legs like tiny black pajamas, and a footloose white Leghorn, and an ill-tempered Frizzle with feathers that resembled a black shearling coat. The chicks were adorable and noisy and inquisitive and did not seem nearly as stupid as everyone said.

When they were six weeks old, the birds moved outside. In the mornings, released from their coop, they raced around the yard flapping their wings and squawking joyfully. We fed them everything we didn't eat. (Everything, that is, except chicken.) They ate Total dregs from the bottom of Owen's cereal bowl, cold spaghetti scraped from a plate, the core from a head of lettuce, a damp sandwich crust rescued from a dank lunch box, failed cakes, steak bones. Whenever I emerged onto the deck above the yard I sang out, "Hey, girls!" and they came racing from all directions to see what I was going to toss them. I was very proud of our smart chickens and their evident affection for me. One day I noticed Isabel watching me as I carried food out for the chickens.

"What is it?" I asked.

"Nothing," she said.

"There's something wrong."

"Okay," she said, "I really hate it when you say, 'Hey, girls.'"

I said, "You do?"

"You sound dorky."

"I do?"

"Kind of," she said. She did not meet my gaze.

It's a testament to the withering power of the adolescent female that I never called "Hey, girls" again. I took to saying, in a flat, almost contemptuous tone, "Okay, chickens, here you go." As time passed, I stopped flinging platters of food off the deck, which seemed a little too Ma Kettle. I began to carry the food down and set it discreetly under a tree.

Pastoral literature suggests there's a glorious synergy between chickens and gardens, that the birds eat up all the bugs and convert them into fertilizer, which they deposit directly in the beds, like little fairies spreading fairy dust. And they were indeed very picturesque, in those early weeks, roaming around the garden like moving flowers, bobbing and fluttering amid the greenery.

One morning, I stepped outside and noticed the hens were eating the squash starts. A few days later, every last leaf had been plucked from the melons. Then with their increasingly enormous, scaly claws, the birds trampled the pole beans and overnight, it looked as if the entire patch had been stomped by the yeti. After this, we shut them out of the "productive" area of the garden, restricting them to the lower part of the yard. But they repeatedly and cleverly breached the little fence we built and even as I mourned the plants they devoured, I was perversely proud of my girls' ingenuity.

The first egg was a miracle. So was the second. So, really, was the five-hundredth. By the end of summer, the eggs were coming on like zucchini in August, at least zucchini in a garden without chickens. Every day, a half dozen more eggs waited in the henhouse and though I cooked eggs every way I knew how, and gave them to my sister and my friends and our neighbors, there were always forty or fifty eggs in a bowl in the refrigerator.

It was very simple and joyful, until it wasn't. I've come to believe that having chickens is like having foxy teenage daughters. Trouble will find you.

In the fall, we discovered a hen lying dead in the bushes with a mysterious puncture wound to her throat. A month or so later, I walked outside to find a bobcat crouched over the corpse of another hen. We don't live in the country. I had never seen a live bobcat before, let alone in my backyard, fifteen feet away. In October, a husky broke through the fence and killed four hens in five minutes. A few days before Christmas, a raccoon got her claws on Sally, one of my favorite chickens, and gnawed all the feathers and skin from her back before she ran shrieking out of the bushes. You know what her back looked like? It looked like skinless chicken from the supermarket, pink and tender and raw. Epic amounts of bacitracin and hydrogen peroxide saved her life and she was outside again in a month, laying again in two.

We decided we couldn't let our chickens range around the yard anymore. Although the yard was secured by a tall wire fence, the sight of all those chickens drove the local predator population mad with bloodlust. I disapprove of factory farms, but I understand why people who depend on chickens for their livelihood might decide to keep them in a big, window-less room. I paid a carpenter $350 to build a fifteen-by-fifteen coop adjoining the hen-house, complete with a chicken wire roof to deter hawks. Now there were two wire fences between our chickens and dogs and bobcats. Three hundred and fifty dollars was more than twice what I used to spend on eggs in an entire year, but it was no longer about the money.

The chickens resented the coop. They paced the perimeter, yelling, looking out through the chicken wire. I liked them less almost immediately. I found them irritating with all their complaints and demands, and somewhat contemptible. I had an inkling of how becoming a prison guard might corrode the soul.

But I thought we were all set, that our chickens were now safe.

And so they were, for a couple of months. And then, three days after my mother died, two terriers broke through the outer fence one day, and then dug their way into the chicken coop. It was the same afternoon my sister and I met the pastor to plan our mother's funeral. I drove home from the meeting in a heavy March drizzle and found an animal control van and a police car blocking the road. A dozen or so neighbors stood on the street outside our yard and a cop walked down the street, holding two bulging garbage bags that, it took me about three seconds to understand, were stuffed with dead chickens. *Ten* dead chickens.

I stood there in the middle of the street in my makeup and meet-the-priest dress, tears and mascara streaming down my cheeks. We've become a sideshow, I thought. The silly suburban people with their chickens that are always getting eaten. I looked at our yard, scratched and grassless and now strewn with feathers, as if a giant duvet had exploded. All we needed were a junked car and sprung sofas to complete the look. I was devastated, furious, and embarassed

After that, I did what I should have done the day we got the chickens: I went down to the lumber company and found someone to build us a wooden fence so the dogs and bobcats couldn't see the birds and the neighbors couldn't see our mess. I paid him $3,500 to take down the wire fence and replace it with redwood planks, and into the pocket of that carpenter's holey jeans disappeared forever the illusion of cheap backyard eggs. The fence went up in a week, and once again, we set the surviving chickens free in the yard. Within hours of their release from the coop, they charmed and fascinated me with their habits and their foibles, their dust baths, their rogue nests. Owen and I promptly ordered more chicks.

Given that you can buy a live chick for $3.00 and chicken feed is synonymous with cheap, raising hens might seem like a brilliant way to provide affordable eggs to your household. Is it? If you've read this far, you are smirking, and rightly so. But I'll break it down just for the record.

We collected approximately 450 eggs in the first nine months of keeping chickens. We spent $954.86 on chicks, feed, lightbulbs, wire, carpentry, medicine, lice powder, bedding, and hiring neighbor kids to tend the birds when we went on vacation. This works out to $2.12 per egg. Safeway eggs: $0.18 apiece. Even if you buy pastured eggs from the farmer's market, you probably won't pay more than $0.50 per egg.

Granted, for most of this time, most of our chickens were not yet laying. Moreover, there were onetime start-up expenses, like carpentry, that inflated the cost. I expected the equation to improve during the second nine months. It only got worse, because in addition to replacing ten dead chickens, we shelled out $3,500 for that fence. At some point

I stopped counting eggs and keeping receipts. It's hard to earn back $3,500 in eggs. At Safeway prices, that's almost 2,000 dozen.

Of course, you can't get fresher eggs. When you crack a homegrown egg next to a supermarket egg, the yolk is brighter and rounder. Does this matter? I can't taste a difference, though others insist that they can. Moreover, apart from the lower risk of contracting salmonella from a backyard egg, I'm not even sure you can make a health argument. According to some studies, eggs from chickens that are raised on "pasture" (i.e., the backyard) are significantly more nutritious than supermarket eggs, with less cholesterol and more healthy omega-3 fatty acids. According to other studies, however, they also contain higher levels of carcinogenic dioxins and PCBs, which they pick up from pecking around in our (apparently) almost universally polluted soils.

There is an ethical component to chickens that I find compelling. However expensive—and keeping chickens can be expensive—I do believe that it is one of the most ecologically and morally important changes you can make in your eating habits. The eggs require no packaging or trucking, and our chickens compost many pounds of lettuce cores, eggshells, carrot peels, and sandwich crusts every week.

That said, you can buy humanely raised, local, organic eggs in most parts of the country and it will very likely cost you less than keeping them. The truth is, my family and I keep chickens now because we think they're beautiful and funny and we like to watch them scratching around. They make me smile, they make me think, and they come when I call. They are my chickens and I am their person. I have become the kind of dope who buys a tea towel because there's a picture of a hen on it. I am a chicken fancier, and although it wasn't at all what I'd intended or expected when we bought those first chicks, enthusiasm is its own reward.

MAYONNAISE

Like whipped cream, homemade mayonnaise is a magical food that manages to be simultaneously rich and ethereal, almost evaporating on the tongue. Sadly, homemade mayonnaise lasts only a couple of days and it would be both exhausting and expensive to emulsify mayonnaise every time you wanted to make a tuna salad sandwich. There's little more sumptuous than homemade mayo—on a BLT, for dipping french fries—but Hellmann's has its place.

Make it or buy it? Both
Hassle: Slight
Cost comparison: It costs $1.51 to make a batch of mayo. Best Foods: $1.75.

> *1 large egg yolk*
> *1½ teaspoons Dijon mustard*
> *Kosher salt to taste*
> *Juice of half a lemon*
> *1¼ cups neutral vegetable oil*

1. Place the egg yolk, mustard, salt, and lemon juice in a bowl or blender. (A hand-held blender works best, but a standing blender does the job.)
2. While the blender is running, add the vegetable oil in a *very* slow and steady drizzle. Whip until thick. Store in the refrigerator for up to 3 days.

Makes 1½ cups

Like factory-raised birds, backyard chickens can become infected with salmonella, the bacteria that sickened 1,600 Americans and led to the recall of a half billion eggs in 2010. But salmonella is relatively rare among hens raised in clean conditions with room to range. I'm not going to say you'd want to eat off the floor of our henhouse, or even in its vicinity, but you will find no eight-foot piles of manure crawling with mice and maggots such as inspectors found in the offending factory farms. You can feel considerably more confident serving dishes made with raw eggs, such as mayonnaise, when those eggs come from your backyard.

MILK MAYONNAISE

If you don't want to consume raw eggs, try this dreamy sauce from David Leite's *The New Portuguese Table*.

> *⅓ cup cold whole milk*
> *¾ teaspoon fresh lemon juice*

1 small garlic clove, minced
⅛ teaspoon freshly ground white pepper
½ cup neutral vegetable oil
¼ cup olive oil
Kosher salt

1. Combine the milk, lemon juice, garlic, and pepper in a small bowl (if you're using an immersion blender or a whisk), or in a standing blender. Blend until frothy.
2. With the blender running or whisking constantly, in a very slow, steady drizzle add the oils and beat until, as Leite puts it, "the mixture thickens lusciously." Salt to taste. Keeps tightly covered in the refrigerator for up to a week.

Makes about 1 cup

EGGNOG

With backyard eggs, you can serve homemade eggnog at a holiday party with *almost* complete confidence that you won't make anyone sick—from salmonella, anyway. Because drink enough homemade eggnog, and the race is on between heart failure and liver disease, unless a stroke fells you first. But life is short. Especially if you drink eggnog. When we throw a Christmas party, which we do once every decade, I pull out my grandmother's purple cut-glass punch bowl and fill it with this alcoholic eggnog. Then I open a square box of store-bought vanilla ice cream—trying to preserve the boxy shape—and drop it into the middle of the bowl of nog, where it both looks and functions like a giant ice cube. (Homemade ice cream is better, but it doesn't come shaped like an ice cube.) The next morning, use the leftovers to make eggnog French toast.

Make it or buy it? Make it.
Hassle: A production, but festive
Cost comparison: Tricky to price, but basically a draw. If you subtract liquor from the equation, homemade costs about $1.50 per quart—except a lot of that is

air. If you try to squeeze the air out of the equation as well, homemade costs just over $3.00 per quart. Our local market last holiday season sold eggnog for $3.00 per quart. But it wasn't nearly as good.

6 large eggs, separated
1 cup sugar
1 to 1½ cups bourbon (start with the smaller quantity, taste, and see
*   what you think)*
1 to 1½ cups rum (see bourbon)
2 cups whole milk
2 cups heavy cream
Lots of freshly grated nutmeg
A box of vanilla ice cream (optional)

1. In a large bowl, beat the egg yolks until bright yellow. Add the sugar and beat until smooth. Stir in the bourbon, rum, and milk, scraping the sides of the bowl.
2. In another bowl, beat the cream until it forms soft peaks. Fold this into the eggnog.
3. Beat the egg whites until stiff and fold this into the eggnog.
4. Pour the eggnog into a punch bowl—it should be able to hold about 2 gallons. Sprinkle generously with nutmeg. If you want, float a brick of vanilla ice cream in the eggnog.

Makes about 1½ gallons

EGGNOG FRENCH TOAST

To make eggnog French toast, pour leftover eggnog into a shallow pan and soak a few slices of bread for 5 minutes. Fry in hot butter until browned on both sides.

CHAPTER 3

BREAKFAST

Sometimes it seems that food fads have never been wackier than they are today (wheat-grass juice? Atkins?), but a few minutes spent reading about the diet gurus of 150 years ago suggest we've always been crazy on the subject of food. Nineteenth-century health food nuts were particularly fixated on breakfast. Back then, many Americans began the day with foods we now eat for dinner—meat, potatoes, biscuits, pie. But John Harvey Kellogg, the eccentric vegetarian director of a Michigan sanatorium, strongly disapproved. As obsessed with discouraging sexual activity ("We have not the slightest hesitation in pronouncing flirtation as pernicious in the extreme") as he was with administering yogurt enemas, Kellogg began touting the virtues of high-fiber cereals, including the precursor to the cornflake. His younger brother, Will, eventually took John Harvey's ideas to market and built the company we now love and revile. Meanwhile, one of Kellogg's patients, Charles Post, launched a cereal company of his own, marketing Grape-Nuts and a caffeine-free grain beverage called Postum. They had the best of intentions, those Victorian dieticians, and it's a sad irony that they are the reason so many of us wake up today to Cocoa Pebbles and Frosted Flakes.

OATMEAL

The difference between the now-ubiquitous presweetened instant oatmeal from a brown paper envelope and old-fashioned rolled oats cooked on the stove (or in a microwave) is like the difference between Taster's Choice and freshly ground Ethiopian Yirgacheffe brewed in a French press pot. Why have we raised the bar for coffee in the last thirty years and lowered it for oatmeal? Cooked oats are a noble food, firm and starchy and ribsticking. A bowl of Quaker instant oatmeal—bits of oat product swimming in a thin, sickly sweet brown fluid—is not.

Do I allow instant oatmeal in the house? Sure. And I'm not too happy about it. But my children like to make it for themselves for breakfast and I can't quite muster the indignation to cut them off. Sugar Pops for breakfast are one thing; instant oatmeal is something else.

Make it or buy it? Unless you're camping, or unless you are a kid, make oatmeal from real rolled oats.

Hassle: It takes about 5 minutes longer to make old-fashioned oats than to hydrate a pouch.

Cost comparison: Old-fashioned homemade oats cost about $0.23 per ⅔ cup serving when you factor in a tablespoon of brown sugar. Quaker Instant: $0.68.

GRANOLA

How funny that granola acquired a reputation as a health food. True, granola is full of nuts and seeds and oats and fiber, and Honey Smacks are full of corn syrup. But if America's number one health problem is obesity, based on the calorie counts, aren't we better off with a bowl of Honey Smacks? Of course, we are probably better off with a spoonful of granola than a bowl of Honey Smacks, but no one ever eats a spoonful of granola. Not when it's as good as this granola.

The beauty of homemade granola is that you can customize. I personally don't like fruit in granola, but you can add raisins or dried papaya—or chocolate chips. If you don't like maple syrup (or think it's too expensive—it's the single costliest ingredient in this recipe), you can substitute honey. Don't care for walnuts? Use peanuts, hazelnuts, or cashews. Add cinnamon. Add orange zest. Omit coconut. Et cetera. Fun.

Make it or buy it? Make it.
Hassle: One bowl, one pan, mix, bake

Cost comparison: This granola costs about $1.10 per cup to make. Quaker 100% Natural: $0.60 per cup. Bear Naked: $2.21 per cup. Fiber Power Triple Berry: $2.56 per cup.

3 cups rolled oats
1 cup almonds, slivered or roughly chopped
½ cup chopped pecans
¼ cup wheat germ
⅓ cup maple syrup
¾ cup sweetened flaked or shredded coconut
⅓ cup light brown sugar, packed
¼ cup melted butter
¾ teaspoon kosher salt

1. Preheat the oven to 250 degrees F.
2. Mix all the ingredients and spread on a cookie sheet.
3. Bake for 1 hour and 15 minutes. No need to stir while it's baking. You'll know the granola is done because it will be crunchy and golden.
4. Remove from the oven, break apart any large clumps, and cool. Store in a resealable plastic bag or 2-quart jar.

Makes 7 cups

GRAPE-NUTS

Since childhood I have been a Grape-Nuts devotee. I love that they're not sweet, that they're filling, and that they're nutty without being unctuous and oily in the way of nuts. Grape-Nuts is my cereal.

And so, when I saw a recipe for Grape-Nuts in Kim Boyce's multiple-prize-winning (and deserving) book, *Good to the Grain* (in which she calls them graham nuts), I had to try it.

Here's how it went: First, I mixed a simple dough of whole-wheat flour, buttermilk, and brown sugar, and spread it on a cookie sheet. Then I baked this big flat cracker in a slow oven. It smelled lovely.

When the biscuit was baked, I broke it up into shards. Boyce directs you to put the pieces of biscuit through the grating attachment of a food processor, but since my grating attachment was broken, I tried other methods of pulverizing the biscuit: rubbing it on a box grater, chopping it with the metal blade in the food processor, hitting it with a rolling pin. Nothing broke the biscuit down into sufficiently small and evenly sized "nuts." Finally, I carried the sack of roughly broken biscuit to my sister's house and we ran it through the grating attachment of her food processor.

This was unpleasant. The roaring and crashing sounded like a wood chipper, and it woke my sister's baby from his nap. That noise alone was enough to discourage me from making Grape-Nuts again. Moreover, the nubbly bits were not as uniform as what you get in the box—some emerged powdered, and some were overly chunky. And the cereal was sweeter and more fragrant than the Post product. That sounds like an improvement, but it's not. If you truly embrace the Grape-Nut, you want a severe little pebble. One day Post might do something unforgivable, like oversweetening Grape-Nuts, and then I will be glad to have this recipe. Meanwhile, Grape-Nuts stays on the grocery list.

YOGURT

When I was growing up, my mother cultured yogurt in a Salton machine, but she really didn't need one. Yogurt dates back millennia and was eaten throughout the Mediterranean and Indian subcontinent long before electricity, not to mention the Salton Corporation. You can make yogurt from a packaged starter; thicken it with gelatin and powdered milk; boil it and reduce it and augment with cream and swaddle the ripening container in towels or heating pads and generally make the process a lot more complicated and esoteric than it needs to be. Although the simple way is not always the best way, with yogurt it is. Homemade yogurt is richer and thicker and denser and (of course) fresher than anything on the shelf at the supermarket. No commercial yogurt can touch it, including the much-loved Fage.

Make it or buy it? Make it.
Hassle: Minor
Cost comparison: A quart of homemade yogurt costs $1.75. The cheapest factory-made yogurt at Safeway: $3.15. Mountain High: $3.89. Fage: $8.00.

½ gallon milk (whole is best, but you can use 2%, 1%, or fat-free)
¼ cup yogurt (store-bought yogurt that contains live cultures, or homemade yogurt
from a previous batch)

1. In a large saucepan over moderate heat, warm the milk until it is on the verge of a boil. You can either stir constantly to prevent the milk from sticking to the bottom of the pan, or spend five minutes scrubbing when you're through. Your call.
2. Remove from the heat, pour the milk into a bowl, and let cool to lukewarm. If you're in a hurry, you can put the bowl in a larger bowl filled with ice cubes; just don't let the milk cool completely. It should be between 110 and 115 degrees F to activate the cultures. If you don't have a thermometer, you should be able to put your clean finger in the milk and hold it there comfortably for 10 seconds, but still feel heat.
3. Stir the starter yogurt into the lukewarm milk. Cover with a clean, damp dish towel and leave the mixture undisturbed in a warm place overnight. Don't get hung up on the temperature of the warm place. You can just turn the oven on for a few minutes, turn it off, and put the yogurt inside.
4. The next day, you will have about a half gallon of yogurt. If you like runny yogurt, you're done, but if you prefer thick Greek-style yogurt, you'll need to drain it. Put a piece of cheesecloth or white cotton, such as a clean old pillowcase, in a sieve set up over a bowl. Scoop the yogurt into the sieve and drain for a few hours at room temperature until the yogurt is as thick as you like it. Depending on the fat content of the milk and how long you let it drain, you'll have between a quart and a quart and a half of yogurt. (Don't discard the whey, which you can store in a jar in the refrigerator for up to 10 days and use instead of water in bread and bagels.) Scoop the yogurt into a jar, cover tightly, and refrigerate. It will keep a week or so.

Makes 1 to 2 quarts

SOY YOGURT

Homemade soy yogurt is quavery and faintly sweet—like a delicate pudding. It is more temperamental than dairy yogurt, so you'll want to experiment with brands of soy milk and cultures. I've had the best luck using Silk and yogurt cultures from New England Cheesemaking Supply (see Appendix).

Make it or buy it? Make it.
Hassle: Minimal
Cost comparison: Homemade: $4.00. Store-bought: $6.50.

To culture soy yogurt, follow the directions above for dairy yogurt, but instead of cow's or goat's milk, use a half gallon of supermarket soy milk. Replace the starter yogurt with a packet of powdered yogurt cultures. You can find these at some supermarkets and co-ops, or order them from a cheesemaking supply company (see Appendix).

The only hitch with my yogurt making is that my children eat only what Greg Malouf and Lucy Malouf in their cookbook *Artichoke to Za'atar* dismiss as "a gloppy, gelatinous substance, usually sweetened beyond belief." In other words, Yoplait. A lot of people don't approve of flavored yogurt, and I can see their point, but it is nonetheless a staple in many American households, including mine. It contains sugar but also protein and calcium, and as a portable snack for children, it could be much worse.

That said, after I started making yogurt I got carried away with yogurt mystique, and wanted my children to partake in its ancient, probiotic, homemade goodness. I was making this amazing stuff and they were taking plastic containers of key lime pie yogurt to school. How to replicate the sweetness and portability of Yoplait? The portability was the biggest problem. Perhaps now as I look back on it, the only problem. One day I sent Owen to school with a small canning jar that contained an inch of strawberry jam topped by homemade yogurt, an attempt to replicate "fruit at the bottom." I explained to him that the jar was reusable and we were therefore making a proper ecological choice. He is ordinarily a patsy for any green argument, but he came home after school, the yogurt barely touched. "It's not flavory enough," he said.

I sent him the next day with more jam in the yogurt, and the jar came back full again. "I wasn't that hungry," he said.

I tried lemon the next day, using lemon curd, since lemon is his favorite yogurt flavor.

Again, the jar returned untouched. I thought about this. I thought that perhaps it is embarrassing for a fourth-grade boy to extract a canning jar from a Transformers lunch box at the picnic tables of a public elementary school. Perhaps this is the twenty-first-century equivalent of sending a child off to the one-room schoolhouse in a flour-sack dress with a lard sandwich in her lunch pail. I retired the canning jar.

However, if you're eating at home or don't mind the canning jar, homemade lemon yogurt is terrific—much better than Yoplait.

LEMON YOGURT

Make it or buy it? Make it.
Hassle: None, once you have the lemon curd
Cost comparison: Homemade: $0.49 per ¾-cup serving. Yoplait "lemon burst": $0.90.

> *1 tablespoon lemon curd (recipe follows)*
> *Squeeze of lemon juice or ½ teaspoon water*
> *¾ cup plain yogurt*

Thin the curd with the lemon juice or water. Stir into the yogurt.

LEMON CURD

A company called Dickinson's makes a lemon curd you can find in the jam section of some supermarkets. The label on the jar features a pastoral vintage design much like what I imagine is the chintz upholstery pattern in a Cotswold cottage. It looks vaguely British and I assumed the curd was imported, but it is actually made in Oxnard, California, by a division of Smucker's. When I learned this I instantly liked it less, for no admirable reason. It's fine, but not in the same category with homemade lemon curd.

Make it or buy it? Make it.
Hassle: Squeezing and grating lemons. A double boiler. Constant whisking. Sieving. *Hassle.*
Cost comparison: Homemade: $0.16 per tablespoon. Dickinson's: $0.34 per tablespoon.

> *½ cup fresh lemon juice (about 5 lemons)*
> *Finely grated zest of 1 lemon*
> *½ cup sugar*
> *3 large eggs*

1. In the top of a double boiler set over simmering water, whisk together all the ingredients. Continue whisking until the curd is thick and shiny, about 10 minutes.
2. Pour the curd through a fine-mesh sieve into a bowl to strain out any bits of zest and egg.
3. Keeps about a week, tightly covered, in the refrigerator.

Makes 1 cup

COFFEE YOGURT

Homemade is creamier than Dannon, with a robust mocha flavor.

Make it or buy it? Make it.
Hassle: None
Cost comparison: Homemade: $0.35 per serving. Dannon: $0.89.

> *1 tablespoon sugar*
> *1½ tablespoons warm brewed coffee*
> *¾ cup homemade yogurt*

Dissolve the sugar in the coffee. Cool. Stir into yogurt.

(If you don't have brewed coffee on hand, dissolve ¾ teaspoon instant coffee and 1 tablespoon sugar in 1 teaspoon of hot water to form a thin paste. Stir into ¾ cup yogurt and adjust for sweetness.)

HASH BROWNS

I assumed diner hash browns were homemade until I made hash browns at home, at which point it became clear that most diner hash browns come out of a freezer bag. Mine are even better than french fries and will spoil you forever for truck stop breakfasts. The outer layer of potato forms a salty, crunchy, toast-colored crust while the inner shreds soften and melt.

Make it or buy it? Make it.

Hassle: It takes less time to make hash browns from scratch than to wait for grub-like Ore-Ida shreds to cook.

Cost comparison: Homemade: $0.11 an ounce. Ore-Ida prepared according to the package instructions: $0.18 per ounce.

3 tablespoons unsalted butter
1 pound russet potatoes (2 or 3 medium)
⅓ cup heavy cream
Salt and freshly ground black pepper

1. Start heating the butter in a wide skillet right before you begin peeling and shredding.
2. Peel the potatoes and shred on the coarse blade of a grater, either a box grater or a food processor.
3. When the butter is hot, add the potatoes and spread across the surface of the pan in a single layer. Let them sizzle and cook until you have a good, brown bottom crust, about 10 minutes or so. Don't rush this; patience is the key to crispy hash browns.
4. When the crust is golden brown, pour the cream over the potatoes and sprinkle with salt and pepper. Flip. Don't worry about keeping it all in one piece. Hash browns are plural. Cook until golden on this side. Serve immediately, ideally, with ketchup, hot sauce, and fried eggs.

Serves 4

BUTTERMILK PANCAKES

Homemade pancakes are lopsided, mottled, creamy, and soft. Eggo frozen pancakes are stiff, yellow, and perfectly round, like miniature Frisbees. "They're kind of crunchy," said Owen. "Like a cross between a pancake and a Ritz cracker."

Make it or buy it? Make it.

Hassle: Homemade require four minutes to mix, 5 minutes to cook. Versus: 90 seconds to unwrap and microwave frozen pancakes.

Cost comparison: Homemade pancakes: $0.10 per ounce. Eggo frozen pancakes: $0.27 per ounce.

1¼ cups all-purpose flour
½ teaspoon baking soda
2 teaspoons baking powder
½ teaspoon kosher salt
2 tablespoons sugar
1 large egg, beaten
2 cups buttermilk, homemade (recipe follows) or store-bought
2 tablespoons unsalted butter, melted
Butter, for the skillet
Maple syrup, for serving

1. In a large bowl, whisk together the flour, baking soda, baking powder, salt, and sugar.
2. Beat in the egg, buttermilk, and melted butter. Stir until smooth.
3. In a large skillet, melt a chunk of butter over medium heat. Ladle ½-cupfuls of batter into the skillet and cook, watching closely and waiting until the bubbles burst on each pancake before flipping it. Add more butter to the skillet and proceed until all the pancakes are cooked. Or store the excess batter in the refrigerator for up to 5 days.
4. Serve with maple syrup.

Makes about 10 pancakes

BUTTERMILK

If you enjoy a big, creamy glass of buttermilk sprinkled with salt, as my grandmother does, you're very strange and you should definitely buy fresh buttermilk in a carton. You should also buy fresh buttermilk if you're making buttermilk soup or a Southern buttermilk pie—or anything that relies heavily on buttermilk's unique satiny-rich-sour personality. But for biscuits or pancakes, you can improvise buttermilk by souring ordinary milk: mix a tablespoon of vinegar (distilled white or cider) in a cup of milk, and let it sit for a minute to sour. Another alternative is to buy powdered buttermilk: dilute about 2 tablespoons of the powder in a cup of water and mix well. The beauty of powdered buttermilk is that it doesn't go bad. Although if you make the mistake of tasting it freshly mixed, you might argue that it already is. Don't drink it; just bake with it.

Make it or buy it? Make it.
Hassle: Easy
Cost comparison: A quart of store-bought buttermilk costs about $2.50. A quart made with powder: $0.94. A quart of soured milk: $0.90.

WAFFLES

A staple of the motel complimentary breakfast buffet, Eggos—or more likely a cheap knockoff—are about as special as the nondairy creamer tublets sweating in the bowl of melted ice. This recipe makes a thin, crispy, and tangy waffle. It's a variation on the raised waffles from *The Breakfast Book* by Marion Cunningham.

Make it or buy it? Make it.
Hassle: This is a bowl, a beater, and 3 minutes more time than some people, like my husband, are up for. Plus, you have to remember to mix the batter 12 hours ahead.
Cost comparison: These cost about $0.18 per ounce to make. Eggo: $0.31 per ounce.

1 cup all-purpose flour
½ cup whole-wheat flour
2 tablespoons sugar
1 teaspoon instant yeast
1 teaspoon kosher salt
8 tablespoons (1 stick) unsalted butter, melted
2 cups warm milk
1 teaspoon vanilla extract (page 260)
2 large eggs, separated
½ teaspoon baking soda
Neutral vegetable oil, for greasing the waffle iron

1. The night before you plan to eat the waffles, in a large bowl beat together all the ingredients except the eggs and baking soda. Cover and let sit at room temperature overnight.
2. In the morning, whisk the egg yolks and soda into the batter, which will look puffy, crusty, and tired, but quickly revives. In another bowl, beat the egg whites until stiff. Fold them into the batter.
3. Cook the waffles on a lightly greased iron. Re-grease between batches. Leftover batter keeps for 3 days in the refrigerator.

Makes 8 to 10 waffles

EGGS BENEDICT

Eggs Benedict are fairly easy to make at home, and if you've read Anthony Bourdain's *Kitchen Confidential,* home is the only place you'll ever want to eat them. Bourdain writes: "Nobody I know has *ever* made hollandaise to order. Most likely, the stuff on your eggs was made hours ago and held on station. Equally disturbing is the likelihood that the butter used in the hollandaise is melted table butter, heated, clarified, and strained to get out all the bread crumbs and cigarette butts."

Make it or buy it? Make it.

Hassle: These take less time to pull together than waiting in line for brunch, but they're definitely a hassle.

Cost comparison: Hard to calculate. Restaurants typically throw in extras, like wedges of orange or a parsley sprig. Plus they wash the dishes for you. Then again, you have to tip the waiter. Today, urban brunch factories charge about $12.00 for a serving of eggs Benedict. To make one serving of eggs Benedict costs between $1.50 and $3.00, depending on how you acquire the components.

4 English muffins, homemade (recipe follows) or store-bought, split and toasted
8 slices Canadian bacon, homemade (page 170) or store-bought
2 tablespoons distilled white vinegar
8 eggs
1 recipe hollandaise sauce (page 58), warm
Cayenne pepper

1. Arrange the muffin halves, two to a plate, on four plates.
2. Fry the bacon until it acquires some dark brown spots and the edges are starting to curl up. Top each muffin half with a disk of bacon.
3. Bring a pan of water to a simmer—it should be bubbling, but not actually boiling. Add the vinegar. Crack an egg into a small measuring cup, lower the cup into the water, and let the egg slip out. Repeat with three eggs and cook until firm, about 3 minutes. When the eggs are cooked—the whites set, but the yolks still glowing and molten—remove from the water with a slotted spoon and slip onto

a piece of paper towel to dry for a minute. Repeat with the remaining eggs. Trim the ragged edges of the white, if desired. Place each egg on a circle of bacon.

4. Pour warm hollandaise over each egg, sprinkle with cayenne, and serve immediately.

Serves 4

Now to that interesting question of how you acquire the components. As is usually the case, the more of them you make from scratch, the cheaper and more delicious the dish will be. But is it really worth the effort? Starting from the bottom:

ENGLISH MUFFINS

English muffins are fun to make—they rise straight up in the skillet like the flat-topped towers of storybook castles. I've never been able to match the nooks and crannies of a Thomas' muffin, but homemade muffins easily trump lesser brands like Oroweat.

Make it or buy it? If you have the time and inclination, make them, though to be honest their loveliness is lost under the hollandaise of eggs Benedict.

Hassle: A lot more hassle than going to the store

Cost comparison: To make English muffins from scratch costs about $0.10 per muffin. Thomas': $0.42. Sara Lee: $0.55.

¼ cup warm water
1 tablespoon instant yeast
2 tablespoons sugar
4 cups all-purpose flour, plus more as needed
2 teaspoons kosher salt
1 large egg
1¼ cups warm milk
2 tablespoons unsalted butter, melted
Neutral vegetable oil, for greasing the bowl
Cornmeal, for sprinkling

1. In the bowl of a mixer, combine the water, yeast, sugar, 2 cups of the flour, and the salt and beat to combine. Add the egg, milk, and butter and continue beating until creamy. Add the remaining flour and knead until smooth and bouncy, adding additional flour by the tablespoon only as necessary. You want the dough to be manageable, but soft and moist.
2. Remove the dough from the bowl, oil the bowl, and return the dough to the bowl. Cover with a clean, damp dish towel and let rise until doubled, about 2 hours.
3. Sprinkle a work surface with cornmeal. Place the dough on the cornmeal, and sprinkle the top with additional cornmeal. Roll the dough into a 9 by 15-inch rectangle, about ½ inch thick. Don't stretch the dough. Using a 3-inch biscuit cutter, cut out muffins. Reroll the scraps and cut out the rest of the muffins.
4. Heat a cast-iron skillet until very hot.
5. Place as many muffins in the hot pan as will fit without crowding. Immediately turn down the heat to medium so the muffins cook through without burning—10 to 15 minutes per side. They should be a light hazelnut brown.
6. Remove muffins to a cooling rack. Split with a fork before toasting. Store in a bag at room temperature for up to a week. Freeze for longer storage.

Makes about 16 muffins

ENGLISH MUFFINS

Before there were muffins as we know them in the United States today—shaped like cupcakes and often just as sweet—there were English muffins. These were the unsweetened flattish breads peddled by the Muffin Man of childhood song and Drury Lane. According to Elizabeth David, the earliest published recipes for such muffins appear in eighteenth-century cookbooks and typically include flour, yeast, salt, and water, which you mix and let "lie" in your "Trough." Here's Hannah Glasse in the 1754 edition of *The Art of Cookery Made Plain and Easy:* "When you eat them, toast them crisp on both sides then with your hand pull them open, and they will be like a honeycomb; lay in as much butter as you intend to use, then clap them together again, and set it by the fire." Good advice, now as then.

CANADIAN BACON

You can and should try making your own Canadian bacon, which is meatier and sweeter than anything you can buy. See page 170 in the chapter about meats.

POACHED EGGS

The geniuses at Nestlé and Kellogg haven't yet figured out how to vacuum-pack eggs, so for now we must poach our own.

Regrettably, it is possible to buy powdered hollandaise.

HOLLANDAISE SAUCE

Everything about homemade hollandaise is golden: it's sunny yellow with the richness of butter and the clean, precise bite of lemon. Knorr's powdered hollandaise, when prepared, tastes like a beef bouillon cube and is slimy and semicongealed, like room-temperature gravy. It is without question one of the most repulsive things I have ever eaten. You make hollandaise, to quote Julia Child, by "forcing egg yolks to absorb butter and hold it in creamy suspension." Its reputation for difficulty is undeserved.

Make it or buy it? Make it.
Hassle: Hollandaise from scratch: 7 minutes. Mixing powdered hollandaise from the Knorr packet: 4 minutes.
Cost comparison: Homemade: less than $2.00. Prepared using the Knorr packet: $3.50.

3 large egg yolks
1 tablespoon fresh lemon juice
8 tablespoons (1 stick) unsalted butter, melted
Kosher salt
Dash of hot sauce (page 81)
Freshly ground white pepper

1. In a bowl that can serve as the top of a double boiler, whisk the egg yolks and lemon until very thick and opaque.
2. Put the bowl over (not in) simmering water and, whisking constantly, drizzle in

the melted butter. Whisk until light and billowy. Add salt to taste, a generous dash of hot sauce, and a grinding of white pepper. Remove from the heat. The hollandaise will keep for 45 minutes or so if you leave the bowl over a pan of warm water, but you should serve it as soon as possible. Thin if necessary with a little warm water.

Makes about 1 cup

COCOA

Very economical and tasty.

Make it or buy it? Make it.
Hassle: None at all
Cost comparison: Swiss Miss charges about $0.38 per 1-ounce packet of cocoa. One ounce of homemade costs about $0.18.

1½ cups dark brown sugar
1 cup cocoa powder
2 teaspoons kosher salt

1. Sift the ingredients into a bowl. If any salt or sugar gets left in the sifter, just pour it into the cocoa mix and whisk to blend. Keeps indefinitely in a lidded jar.
2. To make hot chocolate, use 2 tablespoons per cup of hot milk. Stir in ¼ teaspoon vanilla (page 260).

Makes 2½ cups mix, enough for about 20 cups of cocoa

CROISSANTS

Most commercial croissants are spongy, pale, scorpion-shaped pastries that deposit flakes all over your clothes but no delicious butter flavor on your tongue. Today, croissants are often made with shortening instead of butter—even in France! Here in Northern California, where you can't throw a Birkenstock without hitting an artisanal bakery, it's still hard to find finicky butter-based pastries like the croissant, let alone the long-lost petit four and nearly extinct Napoleon. Every crumb of this homemade croissant is saturated with butter, from the crispy crust to the tender interior.

Because the butter flavor is so important, you should use the freshest butter you can find.

Make it or buy it? Make it, unless you live near a French bakery that bakes all-butter croissants. In which case, you're very lucky and should buy your croissants.

Hassle: Unbelievable hassle, requiring not just time but concentration

Cost comparison: From the in-store bakery of Safeway, croissants made with margarine and high-fructose corn syrup cost $0.80 each. The all-butter croissant from Whole Foods costs $2.29. A homemade croissant of equivalent size and much greater deliciousness: $0.29.

¾ pound (3 sticks) unsalted butter
1 tablespoon instant yeast
¼ cup light brown sugar, packed
1¼ cups warm milk
2¾ cups all-purpose flour, plus more for rolling
½ cup whole-wheat flour
1½ teaspoons kosher salt

1. Cut each stick of butter lengthwise into 4 slices. Place on a plate and refrigerate.
2. In the bowl of a stand mixer, mix the yeast, sugar, and milk. Add the flours and the salt and mix just until smooth, about 30 seconds.
3. Place the dough on a floured countertop and roll it out to form a rectangle about 18 inches long and 8 inches wide. If one of the short edges of the rectangle is not directly in front of you, turn the pastry so that it is. Arrange the butter atop the pastry, leaving about a ½-inch margin around the edge, start-

ing at the short end nearest you and extending two-thirds up the length of the pastry.

4. You now have a long rectangle of dough, two-thirds of it covered with butter slices, one-third of it still bare. Lift up that flap of unbuttered dough and fold it over the nearest segment of butter-covered dough. Now fold that thick double layer of dough over the third of the dough nearest to you. You should be looking at a smallish rectangle of dough separated by layers of the butter, which is completely covered now. Press the edges so the pastry layers seal.

5. Turn the dough so a short side is facing you. Roll it out to a rectangle 18 inches long and 9 inches wide. Fold the 2 short ends so they meet in the middle, and then fold them together. Your dough now has 4 layers.

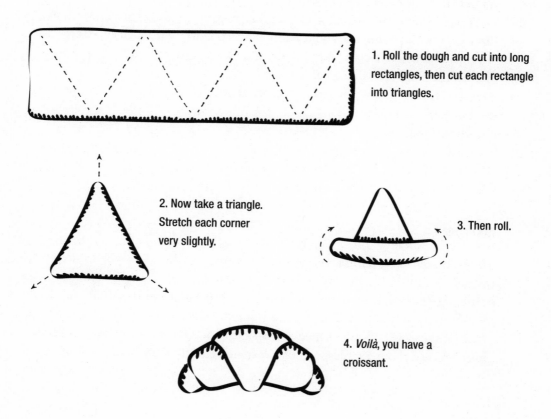

1. Roll the dough and cut into long rectangles, then cut each rectangle into triangles.

2. Now take a triangle. Stretch each corner very slightly.

3. Then roll.

4. *Voilà*, you have a croissant.

6. Wrap and refrigerate for about 45 minutes.

7. Return the dough to the counter with a short side facing you. Repeat steps 5 and 6.

8. Repeat step 7.

9. Now you can put the dough in the refrigerator overnight. It will rise a lot, so if it's in a resealable plastic bag you might have to cut it away in the morning.

10. In the morning, line two cookie sheets with parchment paper. Lightly flour the work surface and roll the dough into a 20-inch square. It will be thin. Trim the raggedy edges so you have a nice, neat square.

11. If you have a rolling pizza cutter, now is the time to pull it out. You want to cut the dough into three long, narrow rectangles. (You cut it into four rectangles if you want miniature croissants.) Cut each of these rectangles into triangles. You'll get between five and eight per strip of dough.

12. Working from the wide end, roll each croissant up very tightly. (See illustrations.) Place on the cookie sheets, about an inch apart. Cover with a clean, damp dish towel and let rise in a cool place for about 2 hours, until puffed.

13. Preheat the oven to 400 degrees F.

14. Bake the croissants for 15 minutes, or until golden. When you pick one up it should feel firm and light.

15. Eat immediately.

Makes 2 pounds, 15 to 20 croissants

VARIATIONS

To make chocolate croissants—*pains au chocolat*—when you get to step 11, instead of cutting the dough into triangles, cut it into rectangles and spread a small amount of shaved dark chocolate along the length of the short end. Roll up the pastry jelly-roll fashion. Bake as for croissants.

Chestnut croissants are formed exactly like chocolate croissants, but instead of chocolate, use about a tablespoon of sweetened chestnut cream per pastry.

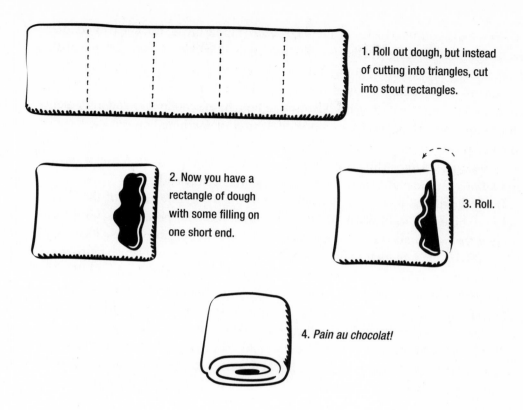

1. Roll out dough, but instead of cutting into triangles, cut into stout rectangles.

2. Now you have a rectangle of dough with some filling on one short end.

3. Roll.

4. *Pain au chocolat!*

DANISHES

In the house where I grew up in San Francisco, my mother sewed quilts and Halloween costumes, and knit sweaters, and stripped all the paint off of the banisters with turpentine-soaked rags, and installed skylights and bookshelves and linoleum tile bathroom floors. She was manually dexterous, bossy, and industrious. When I was ten, she tried to teach me to sew a cotton jumper and ended up making all the seams herself—it was just so much more efficient—while I looked on and felt like an oaf.

In the kitchen, she relished the industrial-scale engineering challenge, like canning 100 pounds of organic apricots or juicing five lugs of tomatoes and grinding wheat to bake fourteen loaves of *Laurel's Kitchen* hippie bread. But she had no interest in everyday cooking whatsoever. No interest at all in pots de crème or meatballs, or cookies or Welsh rabbit or anything you might find in *Ladies' Home Journal*.

Starting very young, I staked out the kitchen as my territory, a place where I could develop my own expertise. My mother bought me cookbooks and ingredients and complimented me profusely. She thought almost anything home-cooked tasted "divine," provided she did not have to cook it herself and could therefore spend more time rewiring a lamp while drinking black coffee, reading the *Wall Street Journal*, and talking on the phone to one of her several hundred friends.

In the living room, she kept a display set of the *Time-Life* Foods of the World, right up there next to Edward Steichen's *Family of Man*. Display, that is, until I discovered them. (Ubiquitous at garage sales, these books belong in every cook's library.) In *The Cooking of Scandinavia*, on page 174, next to the recipe for Danish pastries, is a comment in my twelve-year-old's print: "Difficult but worth the effort—SUPERB!"

"Superb"—along with "divine"—was one of my mother's adjectives. I hadn't yet discovered my own. I wince to imagine what the kitchen looked like after an unsupervised twelve-year-old got through making superb Danish pastries, especially because I know who that twelve-year-old was. My mother couldn't teach me to sew, but she opened the door to the kitchen and let me make a mess and discover on my own one of the great joys of my life, which is pretty much the nicest thing a parent can do.

Recently, I tried that Danish recipe again and it was as "superb" and "worth the effort" as I remembered—like a cross between a croissant and a butter cake. But it was also very, very "difficult," requiring the rolling and chilling and rerolling and chilling of the dough over several hours and then the shaping of that dough into strange, ornate forms. In hopes of shaving some time off the process, I turned to a recipe that Beatrice Ojakangas contributed to *Baking with Julia* by Dorie Greenspan, in which you throw the ingredients into a food processor: "Don't think you're cheating by taking the fast track—this is the way it's done these days all over Denmark, where they know great Danish when they taste it."

Obviously, all that social welfare has been making those Danes soft. Though I'm not Danish, I think the old-fashioned Danishes are better. Harder—and better. If you're going to the trouble to make something as fattening as a Danish, you may as well go whole hog. So to speak. You can make the dough the night before, and

4. Liberally sprinkle the counter with flour and roll the chilled dough into an 11 by 18-inch rectangle, about ⅛ inch thick. Mentally divide the dough into thirds. Place half the butter slices in the middle third of the dough in a single layer, crowding if necessary. Fold over the top third of dough and on top of that place the remainder of the butter. Fold the bottom third of the dough up over that. Seal the edges. Sprinkle with flour again, wrap, and refrigerate for 20 minutes.

5. Turn out the dough so the narrow side faces you. If you've already wiped down your work surface, flour again. Roll out the dough to an 8 by 18-inch strip. Fold both narrow ends in to meet in the center, then fold in half, making four layers. Wrap again and chill another 20 minutes.

6. Repeat step 5.

7. Repeat step 5 again, but this time chill for 2 to 3 hours or overnight, until you are ready to shape, bake, and eat your pastries.

8. Cut the dough into quarters. Line a baking sheet with parchment paper. Flour a surface and roll out the dough into a rectangle that's less than ¼ inch thick.

9. There are dozens of shapes for Danish pastries. Here are two easy ones.

    a. Envelopes: Cut dough into 3-inch squares. Now roll out just a bit more—you want the dough quite thin. Fold each corner of the square in toward the middle so they all meet. Press to seal. Place on the baking sheet. Cover with a cool, damp dish towel.

    b. Snails: Cut the dough into 1-inch-wide strips, each about 10 inches long. Gently twist each strip of dough so it coils. You'll end up with a long, twisted strip. Now form each strip into a round nest. Place on the baking sheet and cover with a cool, damp dish towel.

10. Let the dough rise for about an hour and a half in a cool place.

11. About half an hour before you bake, preheat the oven to 400 degrees F.

12. About 10 minutes before baking, put the pastries in the freezer. Take them out when you're ready to bake and, using your thumbs, make a deep indentation in the center of each nest or snail. Put about 2 teaspoons of jam in the indentation. Slide the sheets into the oven.

13. Bake for 15 to 20 minutes, until golden.

14. Pour yourself a shot of aquavit. *Skoal!* You've earned it.

Makes about twenty-one 3-ounce pastries

SCONES

Even though they were supersized, doughy, and coated with artificial-tasting maple frosting, I could not get enough of the 500-calorie scones in the display case at my local Starbucks, circa 1995. Then I started making scones at home and I loved them more. Homemade scones are delicate and moist, tender and buttery, and you can make them very petite, which is better for your BMI.

MAPLE NUT SCONES

Make it or buy it?: Make it.
Hassle: These aren't effortless. Scones are a weekend treat.
Cost comparison: Homemade scones: $0.18 per ounce. A Starbucks scone: $0.39 per ounce. The frosting on these tastes artificial—in the Starbucks tradition.

⅓ cup walnuts
2½ cups all-purpose flour
½ cup rolled oats, whirled briefly in the food processor to break down
⅓ cup light brown sugar, packed
1 tablespoon baking powder
½ teaspoon kosher salt
8 tablespoons (1 stick) cold unsalted butter, cut into tablespoons
2 teaspoons maple flavoring
1½ cups heavy cream

ICING
2 cups confectioners' sugar
7 tablespoons heavy cream
½ teaspoon maple flavoring

1. Preheat the oven to 400 degrees F. Put the walnuts in a small pan and toast while the oven heats. Cool and chop into pieces the size of chocolate chips.

2. Combine the flour, oats, sugar, baking powder, and salt in a wide, shallow bowl.
3. Add the cold butter to the dry ingredients. Mix with a pastry cutter or your fingertips until the dough has the appearance of cornmeal.
4. Stir in the toasted walnuts. Stir the maple flavoring into the cream and stir this into the dough.
5. Divide the dough in half and form each portion into a 7-inch circle, roughly ⅓ inch thick. Cut each circle into eight wedges, like a pie.
6. Place the wedges on an ungreased cookie sheet. Bake for 20 minutes, until golden. Cool for 10 minutes.
7. Meanwhile, in the bowl of a stand mixer, combine the ingredients for the icing. Beat until you have a thick, but pourable, mixture. When the scones have cooled, pour the icing over them. You should eat these as soon as possible, though leftovers can be stored for a few days in a cookie tin.

Makes 16 dainty but craggy scones

CLOTTED CREAM

Clotted cream, the traditional British accompaniment to scones, is like the love child of butter and whipped cream, and it's almost worth traveling to England just to eat it. In theory and unreliable recipes, you make clotted cream by ripening milk at room temperature for a day, heating it to just below a simmer, and letting it hover there, quivering on the brink of a boil, for an hour. Then, in theory, you chill the milk and eventually lift off a raft of bewitching cream. I have ripened, heated, and chilled gallons of milk—testing different brands and grades—and never lifted off a raft of cream. Just slimy skin. I had given up when I got my hands on a copy of *The One-Block Feast* by Margo True and the staff of *Sunset Magazine*. This superb recipe is just one reason I recommend buying that book.

Make it or buy it?: Make it.
Hassle: None

Cost comparison: Imported Somerdale brand clotted cream costs about $8.60 for a 6-ounce jar of waxy, off-tasting spread. Ounce for ounce, homemade clotted cream is a third of the price.

5 cups heavy cream (not ultrapasteurized)

1. Preheat the oven to 175 degrees F. Pour the cream into a wide heatproof bowl and place in the oven. No need to cover. Let it "cook" for 12 hours.
2. Remove the bowl from the oven, cover, and refrigerate overnight. In the morning you will have a bowl that contains 2 layers of cream—one very thick, one very thin. With a slotted spoon, scoop the thick cream into another bowl or a jar. You can eat it immediately, slathered over warm scones, or cover and chill for up to 5 days.

Makes 1¼ cups

PUMPKIN–CHOCOLATE CHIP MUFFINS

It is a truth not sufficiently acknowledged that chocolate chips and pumpkin are made for each other. Muffins, like scones, have been perverted by Starbucks. Starbucks muffins are almost always bloated yet dry. And honestly, I think even good bakery muffins are overpriced, given how easy they are to make. Save your bakery money and calories for pastries that are hard to make—like all-butter croissants.

You can grease the muffin pans or use paper cupcake liners, which cost about four cents apiece. To me, they're worth it.

Make it or buy it? Make it.
Hassle: Some stirring is all.
Cost comparison: Starbucks muffin: $1.85. Homemade muffin of equivalent size: $0.60.

> 1½ cups all-purpose flour
> 1 teaspoon ground cinnamon
> ½ teaspoon freshly grated nutmeg
> ¼ teaspoon ground cloves
> ½ teaspoon ground ginger
> ¼ teaspoon ground allspice
> 1 teaspoon baking soda
> 1 teaspoon kosher salt
> 1 cup pumpkin puree (page 224)
> ½ cup neutral vegetable oil
> 1 cup granulated sugar
> ⅓ cup light brown sugar, packed
> 2 large eggs
> 1 teaspoon vanilla extract (page 260)
> ⅔ cup semisweet chocolate chips
> Neutral vegetable oil, for greasing (if not using paper liners)

1. Preheat the oven to 350 degrees F.
2. In a large bowl, whisk together the flour, cinnamon, nutmeg, cloves, ginger, allspice, baking soda, and salt.

3. In another bowl, beat the pumpkin with the oil and sugars. Add the eggs, one at a time. Beat in the vanilla.
4. Stir in the dry ingredients, then the chocolate chips.
5. Line 12 muffin cups with paper liners, or lightly grease. Scoop in the batter.
6. Bake for 22 to 25 minutes. A toothpick inserted in the center of a muffin should come out clean. Serve warm, or cool and store at room temperature in an airtight container for up to 5 days.

Makes twelve 2½-ounce muffins

SPICES

Because the supermarket spice business is a racket, one of the best investments you can make in your kitchen is to buy a small electric spice grinder. Then you need to find an ethnic market—Indian, Chinese, Middle Eastern, Mexican—and buy your spices whole. To begin with, whole spices will last a year or more, while ground spices lose their potency after six months. (Do people really throw them away after six months? I know I'm supposed to, but don't.) A container of McCormick's ground allspice at Safeway costs $6.59. An equivalent amount of allspice berries from Haig's, a great Middle Eastern market in San Francisco: $0.56. Almost all spices, from black pepper to nutmeg to cumin, are significantly cheaper bought whole from ethnic markets. This is not to say that ethnic markets are across-the-board cheaper. Just as you might expect, they offer deals on the foods that sell quickly with their clientele. At the Chinese supermarket where I can buy red pepper flakes for a seventh of what I pay at Safeway, butter costs $7.00 per pound.

BISCUITS

One chilly fall morning I found myself in an apron, before dawn, making biscuits for breakfast. The hard drive on the computer had just crashed and I couldn't find a clean mug, so I was drinking coffee out of a quart canning jar. I stood there patting out the clammy dough on the kitchen counter, listening to rain pelt the windows as I glumly contemplated the chores ahead, like scraping bits of wet dough off the counter and slogging off to the Apple Store. I had bought a tube of Pillsbury buttermilk bake-and-serve biscuits to compare with the homemade. I peeled back the label on the canister, which sprang open with a cheerful pop. *Good morning!* cried the flabby biscuits, practically leaping from the tube onto the cookie sheet. I was momentarily enchanted.

Biscuits were once a morning (and noontime and evening) staple in America. Having made my share of biscuits over the years, I can see why women of a previous generation turned to refrigerated dough with such alacrity. If I were *expected* to produce biscuits once, twice, or three times a day, I might become very resentful and very grateful for the tube.

Today, though, biscuits are not a staple. I am not *expected* to make biscuits, and when I do, I am applauded. It is my choice to make them. Or not. They are also a treat, and treats are worth taking pains over. The Pillsbury biscuits were satisfactory, but as Owen put it, they tasted "kind of dull." Also, they contain both trans fat and sugar, neither of which makes a nutritionally empty biscuit any more defensible.

These biscuits—from a recipe by the chef Scott Peacock—are cream of tartar biscuits, the kind Jeff Bridges uses to woo Maggie Gyllenhaal in the movie *Crazy Heart,* at least when he's not falling down drunk.

Assemble all your ingredients and cooking implements before you begin—buttermilk, cutter, baking pan. Once you get your hands covered with biscuit dough, you don't want to be fishing around in the fridge for the buttermilk or in the drawer for the biscuit cutter.

Make it or buy it? Make it.
Hassle: Surprisingly messy

Cost comparison: Homemade: $1.75 per pound of baked biscuits. Pillsbury: $2.00.

> 1 tablespoon cream of tartar
> 1½ teaspoons baking soda
> 5 cups sifted all-purpose flour, plus more for kneading
> 1 tablespoon kosher salt
> ½ cup plus 2 tablespoons cold lard (page 155) or 10 tablespoons (1¼ sticks)
>   cold unsalted butter, cut into pieces
> 2 cups cold buttermilk (page 53)
> 3 tablespoons unsalted butter, melted

1. Preheat the oven to 450 degrees F.
2. Sift the cream of tartar and soda together into a large bowl. Whisk in the flour and salt, then add the fat. Working quickly, rub the mixture between your finger-

BAKING POWDER

If biscuits are wonderful made with cream of tartar and baking soda—the building blocks of baking powder—why do we need store-bought baking powder at all? To find out, I made my own baking powder by sifting together 1 part baking soda with 2 parts cream of tartar. I baked two batches of sugar cookies, one using this homemade baking powder and the second using Clabber Girl Double Acting baking powder. Some people think there's a tinny taste to double acting baking powder, but to me, the cookies tasted identical. However, they didn't look identical. The commercial powder produced a tidier, cakier cookie while the cookies made with homemade powder spread and sprawled and were generally ungainly. That said, my baking powder experiments—and the testimony of people with fine palates—have made me reconsider Clabber Girl. Henceforth, I intend to buy aluminum-free baking powder, such as Rumford or the Whole Foods house brand.

tips or use a pastry cutter until half is coarsely blended and the remaining pieces are clumpy.

3. Add the buttermilk and stir until a sticky dough forms. If it seems dry, add a bit more buttermilk.

4. Turn the dough onto a floured surface. Knead until it forms a ball. Flatten the dough and roll it out until it is ½ to ¾ inch thick.

5. Cut the dough into 2½-inch rounds. Roll out the scraps and cut until all the dough is gone. Place on an ungreased cookie sheet, about an inch apart.

6. Bake until golden, about 15 minutes. While the biscuits are still hot, brush with the melted butter. These are best eaten soon, ideally within the hour. Once they're cool, though, you can zap them for 5 seconds in the microwave. They keep 3 days in an airtight container.

Makes about nineteen 2-ounce biscuits

PARCHMENT PAPER

Kitchen parchment is shiny brown paper that has been coated with silicone, rendering it nonstick and ideal for baking. It looks a lot like waxed paper, but don't confuse the two. If you try to bake cookies or biscuits on waxed paper, smoke will start seeping out of your oven. For baking, it's parchment you want. Parchment costs about $3.99 for a 30-foot roll, or $0.13 per foot. Since most cookie sheets are about 17 inches long, that means for each batch of cookies it costs $0.18 to line the sheet with parchment. Is this a good deal? To grease a cookie sheet with butter costs about $0.09. On the other hand, you can often reuse parchment paper once or twice, depending on how dirty it gets. (After the second or third use it becomes brittle, and it's time to toss it.) On the *other* hand, I often grease pans with scrag ends of butter that no one is eager to spread on toast. And while you would think you wouldn't have to wash the cookie sheet after it's been lined with parchment, often the fat from the biscuits or cookies soaks right through. It's a draw: If you like using parchment, use parchment. If you don't, use butter. Or PAM (see page 26).

LEFTOVER BISCUITS: BISCUIT PUDDING

There's bread pudding, so why not biscuit pudding? Why not indeed. After even just a few hours, once rich and tender biscuits become about as appetizing as a child's board book. The idea for this pudding came from a *Salon* story by a writer reminiscing about his Southern grandmother's biscuit pudding. I took some liberties with the recipe as written and ended up with a dessert that I love more than any bread pudding I've ever eaten. However, if you're one of those people who think pecan pie is too sweet, this isn't the right recipe for you.

> *4 tablespoons (½ stick) unsalted butter, plus more for the pan*
> *4 large egg whites*
> *1 cup sugar*
> *2 large eggs*
> *2 cups whole milk*
> *2 teaspoons vanilla extract (page 260)*
> *Big pinch of salt*
> *Six 2½-inch biscuits (or thereabouts)*

1. Generously butter a 1½-quart casserole or baking pan. Preheat the oven to 325 degrees F.
2. Put the 4 tablespoons butter in a small heatproof dish in the oven to melt.
3. With a mixer, beat the egg whites until stiff. Add ¼ cup of the sugar and whisk until combined.
4. In a big bowl, beat the eggs with the remaining ¾ cup sugar, the milk, vanilla, and salt. Break the biscuits into the bowl in large chunks. Let them soak for 5 to 10 minutes.
5. When the oven is hot, pour the biscuit mixture into the casserole. Heap the meringue on top. Bake for 40 to 60 minutes, until the meringue is well browned and when you give the casserole a shake, the pudding beneath doesn't quiver too much. Remove from the oven and serve just slightly warm. It's also good cold and keeps for several days, tightly covered, in the refrigerator.

Serves 8

CHAPTER 4

VEGETABLES

Michelle Obama is beautiful and smart and I loved it when she planted the vegetable garden on the White House South Lawn in the spring of 2009. One sunny morning over breakfast, I was reading a story about this garden when I came to a quote from Alice Waters, the owner of Chez Panisse restaurant in Berkeley, California. "To have this sort of 'victory' garden, this message goes out that everyone can grow a garden and have free food," burbled Waters. My brow furrowed.

It must be fun to be a true believer, to know that earthly paradise is within reach if we would all just quit buying Fritos, pull out our hoes, and sign on with the Delicious Revolution. But on that sunny morning, I had recently paid a guy with a Bobcat steam shovel to clear the gravel patch from our yard and shore up the collapsing retaining wall. You can't plant a garden in 4 inches of gravel that are sliding down a Northern California hill. My husband has a job, but no steam shovel, and neither of us was capable of tackling a project like this one. It was either pay or not plant a garden. I paid. That's how much I love gardens.

I wrote a sarcastic essay about Alice Waters and her twitty quote that got published in *Slate* and for a year afterward, when I would go to gardening blogs, which I did all the time, I stumbled over stinging allusions to my article, which gardeners, to a one, hated. One woman called me "granite-toppy," the kind of person who owned a Viking range but couldn't fry an egg. Boy, did she get that wrong. I have a Wolf range and I'm really good at frying eggs.

Around the time that Mrs. Obama put in that garden, I sat down with the Baker Creek Heirloom Seed Company catalog and ordered $163 in seeds. I knew it was excessive at the time, but I was carried away and it can be healthy, not to mention joyful, to get carried away, at least when what you're talking about is as harmless, wholesome, and comparatively cheap as seeds. A few days later, the seeds arrived and I planted them in flats and little yogurt containers that I put in a bright corner of the living room. The water stains they left behind on the hardwood floor always take me right back to that hopeful spring.

I planted thyme, asparagus, onions, black basil, red basil, cinnamon and Thai basil; cardoons and artichokes; seven varieties of tomato and one variety of tomatillo. I planted four varieties of pole beans; chard; Charentais melons and scalloped summer squash, blue Hubbard squash, and pumpkins. I planted cilantro and epazote, a Mexican herb that improved every pot of black beans I cooked; and parsley, sage, and lemon verbena. I planted exactly six Victoria rhubarb seeds.

It sounds like I have an enormous yard. It was actually just really crowded.

I had planted gardens in years past, but this was the garden to end all gardens. The spring warmed into summer, the seedlings burgeoned into a jungle, and we harvested enormous thin-skinned tomatoes and a few tiny white eggplants and a lot of purple amaranth that was amazing sautéed with olive oil and garlic. I got chard, more chard than I wanted, and I have never seen more tomatillos. The tomatillo plants were spidery and unstoppable. Unlike tomatoes, which collapse in a hysterical puddle if you do not stake them, these grew wild and rangy and when they reached the brink of collapse, simply collapsed and kept on going, crawling over the yard like monsters—but generous, benevolent monsters. I picked the tomatillo bushes clean and a day or two later they would be loaded with pale green fruits bursting through their papery husks. I used them in salsas and the best guacamole I've ever eaten.

I had every intention of planting another fabulous garden the following year, but that next spring my mother died. A few weeks after her funeral, Owen and I took some seed potatoes and planted them. I'd read that two pounds of seed potatoes will yield up to forty pounds of potatoes at harvest. *We'll just see about that*, I thought sourly.

"Pretty soon everything is going to have high-fructose corn syrup in it," Owen said, helping me dig in a few carrot seeds. "Except the trusty vegetable."

I planted several white onions and a single yellow squash seedling. I had thought it would be peaceful and restorative to work in the garden, but contemplation amid the bees and the tender shoots of April just made me want to go lie on my bed and stare at the ceiling. I didn't lift a trowel again for the rest of the year.

And the garden went feral on me. The epazote I'd planted the year before metastasized into a forest of chest-high shrubs with serrated foliage, brutish and everywhere. Where last year had flourished tomatoes and pole beans and cilantro and eggplant, now grew epazote, and, where they could fight their way through, some purple-flowered thistles and blackberry vines. I'd grown a bramble, not a garden.

Yet a tomatillo came back, struggling through the epazote, laden with fruit. I was touched. *That* is the kind of vegetable you need in your platoon. And the six rhubarbs were not just holding their own, they were thriving. By summer, I had thigh-high plants with green stalks almost as wide around as my wrist, leaves the size of doormats. Given that I'd paid $2 for the seeds and rhubarb sells for about $3 a pound, planting rhubarb had turned out, in the end, to be a very sound decision: I harvested fifteen pounds.

The biggest surprise, though, were the potatoes, buried with so little expectation of success. Idly one day that summer I went out and scrabbled around with my hand in the earth and hit a small, solid orb. I reached around some more and found scores, some of them the size of jelly beans and some the size of golf balls and some as big and lumpish and dusty brown as spuds from the supermarket. I carried them in and boiled the babies for dinner and ate them with a salad. They were hands down the best potatoes that I have ever tasted—milky and sweet. I knew right then that I was never going to harvest forty pounds of potatoes in the fall because I was going to eat them all before the end of summer. Far too much has been written about the glories of the vine-ripened tomato and far too little about the pleasure of eating steamed just-dug potatoes on a balmy summer evening. I almost had the heart to garden again, but by then the days were already starting to get short.

GUACAMOLE

Everything lovely about avocado perishes when it is mashed, packed in a pouch, and shipped to a supermarket. Avocados don't keep. I started making this fantastic guacamole, inspired by a Rick Bayless recipe, because it uses up tomatillos, but if you don't have tomatillos, forget the tomatillos. For that matter, forget the cilantro, garlic, onion, and chiles. You can just mash avocado with lemon juice and salt and spread it on toast and it will surpass any guacamole you'll find at the supermarket.

Make it or buy it? Make it.

Hassle: Not bad, though this isn't the easiest of all guacamoles.

Cost comparison: It costs about one and a half times as much to buy your guacamole as to make it, depending on the price of fresh avocados.

8 ounces tomatillos (about 8 crab apple–size tomatillos), husked
2 fresh serrano chiles
2 garlic cloves, unpeeled
½ onion, finely chopped
¼ cup chopped cilantro
4 ripe avocados
Kosher salt

1. Preheat the broiler on high.
2. Put the tomatillos, chiles, and garlic on a baking sheet under the broiler. When they've blistered and blackened on one side, after about 3 minutes, turn them over and broil on the other side. Cool.
3. Pull the stems from the chiles and peel the garlic.
4. Combine the chiles, tomatillos, and garlic in a food processor or blender. Process until coarsely pureed. Transfer to a bowl and add the onion and cilantro.
5. Scoop the avocado from the shells and mash. Add to the tomatillo mixture and stir. Season with salt. Eat promptly, as this doesn't keep for more than a few hours.

Makes 4 cups—enough for a crowd

HOT SAUCE

I first made this salsa with habaneros, which produced a tangerine-colored salsa so hot that I worried I'd seared my tongue when I tasted it. For the next batch, I moved down the Scoville heat scale to serranos, which were still too fiery for me. You can use any chile, but I like Fresnos, which make a cherry-red sauce with the perfect bite. This sauce is vibrant and fruity, and to me, Tabasco now tastes thin and musty.

Make it or buy it? Make it.

Hassle: Approximately 4 minutes of labor, then you put the sauce in the cupboard and blender jar in the dishwasher.

Cost comparison: Homemade: $0.02 per teaspoon. Crystal brand: $0.05 per teaspoon. Tabasco: $0.18 per teaspoon.

1 pound Fresno chiles
1½ cups cider vinegar
4 garlic cloves, peeled
2 teaspoons kosher salt

1. Cut the stems off the chiles but leave the seeds. Combine the chiles with all the other ingredients in a blender or food processor. Puree until liquefied. Pour the contents into a jar with a lid and cap tightly. Store in a dark place for 6 weeks.
2. Refrigerate. The sauce will keep indefinitely.

Makes 3 cups

SALSA

Unlike store-bought guacamole, store-bought salsa can be quite tasty, but in summer, when local tomatoes are in season, homemade can't be beat.

Make it or buy it? Make it.

Hassle: Lots of wet chopping

Cost comparison: In high summer, this costs between $0.50 and $1.00 per cup. Year-round, barring a sale, Tostitos medium chunky salsa costs $2.00 per cup.

3 tablespoons chopped onion

2 cups chopped tomatoes

2 chiles, such as jalapeños or serranos, minced

3 tablespoons finely chopped cilantro

2 teaspoons sugar

2 teaspoons kosher salt

Juice of 1 lemon or lime

1 unpeeled peach, chopped (optional, but great)

Combine all ingredients and mix well. If you have time, let the salsa sit for an hour at room temperature so the flavors can mingle. Use immediately. This doesn't keep well overnight.

Makes 2 cups

CHAPTER 5

RESTAURANT FOOD

Here are words I like to see on a menu when I go to a restaurant: Soft-shell crabs. Wood-burning oven. Lobster rolls. Peking duck. Marrow bones. *Sous vide.* Sweetbreads. I don't necessarily love to eat sweetbreads, but their presence on a menu suggests that the cook is doing something I can't, don't, or won't do at home.

Here's what I don't like to see on a menu: Meat loaf. Meatballs. Roasted chicken. Pot roast. Macaroni and cheese. I see those words a lot.

"We're in uncertain times, and this is the time when we crave comfort food," said a commentator on NPR not long ago. I disagree. In the Depression, which pretty much defined "uncertain times," people who could afford to splurge splurged on mock turtle soup and saddle of venison. They didn't dress up and go out for meat loaf. I think we go out for meat loaf because a lot of us have stopped cooking meat loaf.

A short alphabetical survey of dishes to order in a restaurant and dishes to make:

BANH MI

Unless you live next door to a Vietnamese gorcery, just assembling the components for this classic sandwich is drudgery. For a single banh mi you want meat—sweet barbecued pork, spiced liver pâté, Vietnamese cold cuts, maybe even all three. You need some freshly pickled daikon; freshly pickled carrots; a crusty French roll, preferably made by a Vietnamese bakery; cilantro; sliced chiles. It is, probably, easier to find a Vietnamese deli and buy a $3 banh mi, and the deli will appreciate your business.

Make it or buy it? Buy it.

RESTAURANT FOOD   83

BARBECUE

In the first draft of this manuscript I wrote that the only place to eat proper Southern barbecue is in the American South. That you can drop your "g's" and play with your Big Green Egg and debate the merits of ketchup-based sauce versus mustard-based sauce till the cows come home, but no barbecue you produce in your suburban backyard north of the Mason-Dixon Line will ever match what you might find in, say, Holly Hill, South Carolina. Even if the meat is succulent and perfectly spiced, it will lack mystique.

And yet it weighed on my mind. I hadn't ever actually tried to make barbecue.

So I did. I spent a day poking coals, mixing sauce, worrying over my first attempt at Carolina-style pulled pork. It was the middle of the week and I took a child to the oral surgeon and ran to the bank and to the supermarket and all the while, there was pig smoking in my yard. We had people over for that pork. A crowd. There was coleslaw, and there were drinks, and there was onion dip (page 114) and there were kids running around and I realized that no matter where you are, barbecue becomes an occasion. The meat was succulent and perfectly spiced and it also had mystique.

So I take it all back. Make your barbecue. It's cheaper than flying to South Carolina, though you should do that too. Go to Sweatman's and be sure to try the hash.

To make this pulled pork, you'll need wood chunks, which are like wood chips, but bigger, each chunk about the size of a lemon. You can find them at a well-stocked hardware store. I've done a few pulled porks and I recommend using "natural" charcoal briquettes. Barbecue is supposed to be smoky, but I think standard commercial briquettes make it a little too smoky.

Two 4- to 6-pound pork butts

FOR THE SPICE RUB

2 tablespoons paprika

2 teaspoons cayenne pepper

2 tablespoons garlic powder

2 tablespoons brown sugar

1 tablespoon ground cumin

1 tablespoon ground coriander

1 tablespoon dried mustard

1 tablespoon dried oregano

3 tablespoons freshly ground black pepper

⅓ cup kosher salt

FOR THE VINEGAR SAUCE

1½ cups cider vinegar

1 tablespoon kosher salt

1 tablespoon sugar

2 teaspoons freshly ground pepper

1 teaspoon crushed red pepper flakes

Barbecue sauce, on the side

1. The night before you plan to serve the barbecue, mix the ingredients for the spice rub in a small bowl. Unwrap the pork, pat it dry, and then coat with the spices, working them into every crevice. Place the pork in a large bowl, cover with foil, and refrigerate.

2. It's a good idea to prepare for smoking the night before, as you will have to start at 5 or 6 in the morning to have barbecue in time for dinner. If you're going to use a smoker, follow the instructions that came with your equipment. I use an ordinary charcoal kettle grill, and here's how it works: Put the wood chunks in a large bowl of water to soak overnight. If you're using a chimney to start the fire, prepare it now so you'll have less to do in the morning. Fill the chimney with your charcoal and stuff balled-up newspaper underneath to help it light. Make a drip pan out of two layers of aluminum foil and place on the lower rack of your grill. Locate your matches or lighter.

3. Early next morning, about 12 hours before you want to eat, light the chimney and take the pork out of the refrigerator. When the coals have all ignited and are smoking and gray, put them on the lower rack of the grill across from the drip pan. Now put about 4 wet hardwood chunks on top of the charcoal and replace the top grill.

4. Place the pork on the grill over the drip pan. Now put the lid on the grill with the vent directly over the meat. Place a long-stemmed thermometer through one of the holes in the vent. Your goal now is to keep the temperature between

200 and 250 degrees F for the rest of the day. You do this by adjusting the vents. Open them wider if the temperature falls, and close them a bit if it gets too hot. Keep checking every 30 minutes or so, and add fresh charcoal and wood chunks as necessary. (If the heat gets really fierce, put a small pan of water on the grill.)

5. About 6 hours after you started cooking, prod the meat with a fork to see how it's coming along. It will probably look cooked, but will not feel very tender. It is not done. In my experience it takes between 8 and 10 hours before the meat is ready. You'll be able to tell because it will almost fall apart when you push at it with a fork.

6. Toward the end of the cooking time, mix the ingredients for the vinegar sauce in a medium bowl.

7. Lift the pork onto a platter, wrap in foil, and let it rest for 10 minutes.

8. Transfer the pork to a wide bowl, unwrap, and shred the meat. If it's too hot, use rubber gloves or a wooden spoon to separate the pieces and break them down into shreds and chunks.

9. Pour the sauce over the meat and toss well. Serve immediately with soft sandwich buns (I like Francisco-brand Crustini rolls) and barbecue sauce on the side. Leftovers can be refrigerated for up to five days and used in sandwiches and spaghetti (see page 87).

Serves at least 20

DR PEPPER BARBECUE SAUCE

I like bottled barbecue sauce, but if you're going to hover over a haunch of pig for 12 hours, you should make your own. This is a modification of a Bruce Aidells recipe.

Make it or buy it?: Make it.
Hassle: Trivial compared with producing barbecued meat
Cost comparison: Homemade: $0.91 per cup. Sweet Baby Ray's Original: $1.89. Everett & Jones: $3.00.

1 tablespoon neutral vegetable oil
½ cup finely chopped onion (from half a small onion)
1 tablespoon minced garlic
½ cup cider vinegar

2 tablespoons Worcestershire sauce (page 166)
1 cup ketchup
3 tablespoons mustard (yellow, Dijon, homemade—doesn't matter)
1 teaspoon hot sauce (page 81)
⅓ cup Dr Pepper
1½ teaspoons chili powder
Kosher salt
Pepper

Heat the oil in a medium saucepan over medium heat, then add the onion and garlic and cook until soft and translucent, about 8 minutes. Stir in the remaining ingredients and bring to a boil. Simmer gently, stirring occasionally, for about 45 minutes. Serve immediately or store in a covered jar in the refrigerator for up to 2 weeks.

Makes 2½ cups

BARBECUE SPAGHETTI

When you tire of pulled pork sandwiches—or even if you don't—try this easy spaghetti, much loved in my house.

Pinch of kosher salt
1 pound spaghetti
¾ cup barbecue sauce
2 cups pulled pork

1. Heat a large pot of salted water to a rolling boil, then drop in the spaghetti.
2. While the spaghetti cooks, in a large skillet over medium heat, warm up the barbecue sauce and pork, stirring to break up the clumps of meat.
3. When the spaghetti is cooked al dente, add a large ladleful of cooking water to thin the sauce. Drain the spaghetti. Toss the spaghetti with the sauce. Serve immediately.

Serves 4 to 6

BRAISED BEEF

I have to silence myself when someone I'm eating out with orders a braised meat entrée. To braise meat, you put a fatty, inexpensive cut—lamb shank, chuck roast, pork butt—in a big pot, add liquid and maybe an onion and a few herbs. You place a cover on the pot, place the pot in a low oven, and go get a pedicure or prune the pachysandra until the meat is fork-tender and ready to serve.

Make it or buy it? Make it.
Hassle: This cooks itself, though it takes its sweet time to do so. Not a 30-minute meal.
Cost comparison: To make: $2.50 per serving. I once dined at a restaurant where the braised short ribs cost $29.00.

> *3 pounds boneless short ribs*
> *1 tablespoon kosher salt*
> *1 tablespoon freshly ground black pepper*
> *2 teaspoons dried marjoram*
> *3 tablespoons olive oil*
> *2 onions, sliced*
> *2 tablespoons sugar*
> *3 carrots, peeled and sliced*
> *2 celery stalks, sliced*
> *2 bay leaves*
> *1 cup red wine*
> *Horseradish (recipe follows), for serving*
> *Buttered noodles or mashed potatoes (page 222), for serving*

1. Preheat the oven to 300 degrees F. Spread the short ribs out on a flat surface and sprinkle them with the salt, pepper, and marjoram. Be sure to coat all sides.
2. Heat the olive oil in a Dutch oven on the stovetop, and when it's hot, add the short ribs—in batches, if necessary, to avoid crowding. Sear well on all sides. You want the meat to be richly colored all over.
3. With a fork, remove the ribs to a plate. Add the onions, sugar, carrots, celery, and

bay leaves to the fat and drippings in the pot. Cook, scraping up the drippings, until the onion begins to soften and caramelize.

4. Return the ribs to the pot, add the wine, and bring to a boil.
5. Put the lid on the pot and place the pot in the oven. Bake for 3 hours, checking occasionally to be sure the liquid has not evaporated. If it has, add a splash of water. The meat is done when you can break it apart easily with a fork. Remove the bay leaves.
6. Serve with horseradish and buttered noodles, mashed potatoes, or crusty bread.

Serves 6

HORSERADISH

Horseradish sauce—especially this horseradish—is all edge, which makes it the perfect bracing corrective to unctuous meats. You can cut this horseradish with a little whipped cream or mayonnaise if you want to soften its bite, which you might. My biggest challenge was finding fresh horseradish root, which I had to drive 45 minutes to buy. I've since heard it will grow like a weed in the garden, though I'm not sure I want horseradish growing like a weed in the garden.

Make it or buy it? If you can easily get your hands on fresh horseradish, make it. If not, buy it.
Hassle: It takes about twelve minutes.
Cost comparison: To make horseradish: $0.08 per tablespoon. Morehouse horseradish: $0.39 per tablespoon.

6 ounces fresh horseradish
Scant cup cider vinegar
1 tablespoon sugar
Salt

1. Peel the horseradish, trim off the gnarly bits, and put the crunchy white root in a food processor. Grind with the metal blade until the root is finely shredded. Stand back from the feed tube; the fumes could knock you flat.
2. Add ¾ cup vinegar and grind it a bit more. Test to see if the horseradish has a soft,

semisolid consistency. If not, add more vinegar. Stir in the sugar and salt to taste.

3. Store in a jar in the refrigerator, where it will keep about a month, gradually losing potency. That's a good thing.

Makes 1½ cups

BURRITOS

If you cook a lot of Mexican food—pinto beans, savory rice, carnitas, or carne asada—reheat the leftovers, mix some fresh salsa and guacamole, and wrap everything up in extra-large flour tortillas, steamed until soft and pliable. You will be very happy with your burrito dinner.

But if you don't have those leftovers? You have to start from scratch, cooking the beans, the rice, the meat, the salsa, the guacamole. This is a lot of prep work for what is essentially fast food, often eaten by construction workers and kids with incipient hangovers at midnight. There are now taco trucks and taquerias and Mexican restaurants just about everywhere in America where you can buy a splendid burrito for between five and eight dollars. Like the Vietnamese delis, they'll appreciate your business.

Make it or buy it? Buy it.

CRÈME BRÛLÉE

If you like to cook, and you ever mention that you love crème brûlée, someone, someday, may give you a crème brûlée torch. I was glad to get one for Christmas from my father. We promptly fueled it up and made crème brûlée. The first batch was amateurish, but once I figured out to sprinkle the sugar evenly and heavily, then patiently wait for each grain to caramelize, the next batch dazzled, with a glassy, shiny shell protecting the cool cream below. Unless someone gives you a torch, don't make this recipe. I've tried caramelizing crème brûlée under the broiler, as some books advise, and it doesn't work.

Make it or buy it? If you have a torch, make it.

Hassle: It requires a surprising amount of patience and hand strength to torch these crèmes.

Cost comparison: Less than $5.00 to make six crèmes brûlées. I doubt you can buy a single crème brûlée in a restaurant for less than $5.00. (It's not a restaurant, but there *is* a street cart in San Francisco where you can buy crème brûlée for $4.00.)

2 cups heavy cream
5 large egg yolks
⅓ cup sugar, plus more for sprinkling
Pinch of kosher salt
1 teaspoon vanilla extract (page 260)

1. Preheat the oven to 200 degrees F.
2. In a medium saucepan over moderate heat, warm the cream until it is on the verge of a boil. Remove from the heat.
3. In a large bowl, whisk the egg yolks and sugar until creamy and thick. Whisk in the salt and vanilla. Whisk in the cream. Strain the mixture into six 4- to 6-ounce ramekins or crème brûlée dishes.
4. Place on a cookie sheet and slip the sheet into the oven. Cook for 30 to 40 minutes, until the crèmes are mostly firm, with just a little jiggle in the middle.
5. Cover with plastic wrap and chill the ramekins for at least four hours. This is essential: Don't cheat.
6. Sprinkle the top of each crème evenly with granulated sugar. Hold the flame of a propane torch close to the sugar—about ½ inch away—and heat the sugar until it melts and browns. Repeat with the rest of the desserts. Serve immediately.

Serves 6

FLOURLESS CHOCOLATE CAKE

At some point in the 1980s, flour all but vanished from chocolate desserts. Today every restaurant serves some kind of flourless dark chocolate dessert, whether it's called a budino or a decadence or a volcano or a torte. These cakes are quite easy to make. I've made a lot of them. For many years my mother didn't eat wheat flour, and for her fifty-sixth birthday I baked five flourless chocolate cakes and we had a tasting. The winner was a cake from the Italian island of Capri made with walnuts; the loser was a gruesome Spanish cake from a nineteenth-century recipe, made with orange flower water. I've messed with the Capri cake over the years and this is how I make it now, without any walnuts at all. It's probably not even a Capri cake anymore, but it's very easy and you can make a whole cake for not much more than you'd pay for a single slice in a restaurant.

Make it or buy it? Make it.

Hassle: Moderate

Cost comparison: To bake this cake costs about $10.00. To buy a single slice of a flourless chocolate cake at a restaurant or bakery costs at the very least $5.00.

½ pound (2 sticks) unsalted butter, plus more for the pan
All-purpose flour, for the pan
½ pound bittersweet chocolate, chopped
5 eggs, separated
1 cup dark brown sugar, packed
1 tablespoon bourbon
½ teaspoon salt
Whipped cream (page 226; omit the sugar) or crème fraîche
    (recipe follows), for serving

1. Preheat the oven to 350 degrees F. Butter and flour a 9-inch springform pan. Tap out the excess flour.
2. Melt the chocolate and butter together in the top of a double boiler. Cool slightly.
3. Beat the egg whites until stiff. Scoop them into a clean bowl or onto a plate. In

the bowl where you beat the egg whites (you don't need to rinse it), beat the egg yolks until they thicken. Gradually add the sugar, bourbon, and salt and continue beating until the mixture is creamy. Add the chocolate mixture.
4. Fold the egg whites very gently into the batter.
5. Pour and scrape the airy batter into the pan. Bake for 40 minutes, until the cake is puffed and starting to crack. Cool to room temperature.
6. Serve with unsweetened whipped cream or crème fraîche.

Serves 12

CRÈME FRAÎCHE

You can't use powdered buttermilk or soured milk to make crème fraîche; you need real buttermilk, from the carton, which means that you're going to have a lot of buttermilk left over. I suggest pancakes (see page 53). I've never found commercial crème fraîche that's better than what you can make in about 35 seconds—plus a day for the mixture to ripen—at home.

Make it or buy it? Make it.
Hassle: A 4-year-old could do it.
Cost comparison: Under $4.00 to make a cup of crème fraîche. To buy a cup of crème fraîche at Whole Foods: $6.00. At Trader Joe's: $3.79.

1 cup heavy cream
1 tablespoon buttermilk

Pour the cream and buttermilk into a jar, cap, and shake. Leave in a warmish place—like beside the stove—for 24 hours, until thick. Refrigerate. It will keep for up to a week.

Makes 1 cup

NAPOLEONS

My parents did not take my sister and me to restaurants except once or twice a year and it was either Chinese or pizza. Ordering dessert was out of the question. And so my every childhood encounter with the world of restaurant food made a big impression on me. When I was about ten, for my birthday my maternal grandfather took me to lunch at a French restaurant where the maître d' knew his name and sat us at a table in a nook by a window. I ordered soft-shell crabs, which I had never tasted before. For dessert, the waiter brought around a cart displaying the restaurant's pastries. I chose a Napoleon.

It was the first time I had tasted either puff pastry or pastry cream, not to mention fondant, the sticky supersweet white glaze. Together, they blew my young mind. Have you eaten a Napoleon lately? First you get glossy fondant—barely touched with chocolate—that briefly resists the pressure of your teeth, but eventually yields and then you hit a layer of crisp, buttery pastry, which shatters instantly, dropping you straight into the plush, vanilla-scented cream. For years I carried this Napoleon around in my mind as the platonic ideal of a restaurant dessert. I thought I would grow up to wear high heels and silk dresses and go to restaurants where I would eat Napoleons.

But chefs and bakers today treat classical fancywork pastries as if they're as passé as crocheted doilies.

When I put on a silk (well, silky) dress and go to a restaurant, dessert is more likely to be a piece of flourless chocolate cake (page 92) or a thick white bowl of rhubarb crisp. I love rhubarb crisp. But I can make a rhubarb crisp. And even when I see a Napoleon on a menu my heart no longer skips a beat because it is always a riff on a Napoleon, something hip and playful and lazy—like some toasted phyllo dough topped with blueberries and lemon curd. I can toast phyllo and make lemon curd, but I can't make a Napoleon.

It's not all farmstead desserts, of course. Sometimes you get Tinkertoy constructions—shards of this and scoops of something else and never a full bite of anything—which are impressive and interesting, but ego-driven. When I'm done eating these desserts, I can never quite remember what happened.

Anyone can make crisps and simple chocolate cakes and cupcakes and rustic cookies with half an hour and an Easy-Bake oven. And chefs can make random collages of delicious dessert components and scatter them, Jackson Pollock–style, on a plate. But it takes skill and discipline and a severe repression of the ego to make a perfect

Napoleon. I've tried to make Napoleons and I'll probably try again, but my attempts have been multiday catastrophes. Maybe if we all start making our own cupcakes and crisps, pastry chefs will bring back the Napoleon. I am not holding my breath.

Make it or buy it? Buy it. If you can find it.

OYSTERS

I've always perceived eating raw oysters as dangerous, which it certainly can be. But provided you buy them from a reputable fishmonger, keep them chilled, and serve them promptly, the oysters you serve at home are no more or less likely to make you sick than the oysters you order at a restaurant. I have an even harder time paying $3 per oyster at a restaurant now that I've eaten them at home for less than a dollar apiece.

Of course, when you serve oysters at home you have to shuck them yourself—unless you can buy them shucked, which, for a small surcharge, you sometimes can. Ask your fish market. The first time I shucked oysters, I used a butter knife and the shucking was tedious, but totally doable. Shortly thereafter, my mother-in-law sent me a proper oyster shiv, short and sturdy, and that works much more efficiently. If you're worried about gouging your palm while shucking, you can invest in an oyster glove. Choices range from a $5 rubber glove to a $140 mesh oyster glove imported from France.

Make it or buy it? Make it.
Hassle: Not that bad and your guests are so grateful.
Cost comparison: Up to $3.75 apiece in a restaurant; $1.00 at the local fish market, depending on season.

1. With or without a glove, here's what you need to do: Standing over the sink, inspect the oysters carefully. They should all be tightly closed. If an oyster isn't "clammed up" give it a hard tap. If it doesn't close immediately, it is likely dead. Throw it away.
2. Scrub the oysters well with a brush. You'll never get them spotless, but you want to eliminate loosely attached bits of dirt and grit.

3. If you're not using a glove, drape your left hand with a towel to give yourself a firm grip on the oyster. When you look at an oyster, you'll notice it has a flat top and cupped bottom. Place the oyster "cup" side down in your left hand. (You can switch hands, of course, if that's more comfortable for you.) Wiggle the knife into the opening of the shell, trying to find the hinge. Take your time and don't force it. Once you pry your way in a centimeter or two, twist the knife and the shell will pop open. Try to keep the liquid in the cup. Detach the meat from the shell with the knife and wipe away any obvious grit. Then put the oyster on the half shell on a platter. Repeat until the oysters are all shucked or you can't stand it anymore.
4. Serve with mignonette (recipe follows).

MIGNONETTE

½ cup prosecco, Champagne, or white wine
½ cup white wine vinegar
2 shallots, finely chopped
Freshly ground black pepper to taste
½ teaspoon kosher salt

Mix everything together and serve with freshly shucked oysters.

Makes about 1 cup, enough for 10 dozen oysters

PIZZA

A competent *pizzaiolo* with a wood-burning oven that heats to 900 degrees F and cooks a pie in 90 seconds flat can make a better pizza than you can. If you have an authentic Neapolitan pizzeria in your area—and they are just about everywhere these days—give it your business. But it's still fun to make pizza sometimes, especially if you have a baking stone. I thought a pizza peel—the wooden board with a long handle that you use to slide the pizza onto the stone—was silly, until I borrowed my sister's. Now I covet one.

The cheese on a true Neapolitan pizza is always fresh mozzarella. But whether or not that's what you use is entirely up to you. When I taught a sixth-grade cooking class once, I decided to bring in some cheap shredded mozzarella to show the girls the difference between fresh mozzarella—delicate and milky—and factory mozzarella—salty and rubbery. I had them taste the cheeses. To a girl, they preferred the factory mozzarella. They each got to make their own pizza and they fought over the last shreds. One poor girl was forced to use the dreaded fresh mozzarella on her pizza. She looked as if she was going to cry. This recipe calls for fresh mozzarella, but if you like salty, rubbery factory cheese, it's your pizza.

Make it or buy it? Make it.

Hassle: Of course

Cost comparison: To make two 14-inch pizzas costs $15.50, including fuel to heat the oven. Two 14-inch pizzas bought carryout from Domino's: $27.98.

DOUGH

1 tablespoon instant yeast
2 cups warm water (or whey from making yogurt, page 47)
4 cups all-purpose flour
1 cup whole-wheat flour
1 tablespoon kosher salt

BAKING AND TOPPING

Cornmeal, for sprinkling
1 pound fresh mozzarella, homemade (page 201) or store-bought, sliced
½ recipe marinara sauce (page 145), about 1¼ cups
Dried oregano and red pepper flakes, for sprinkling
Olive oil for drizzling

1. The morning of the day you want to eat pizza, mix all the dough ingredients in a bowl, knead for a few minutes, cover with a clean, damp dish towel, and let rise for 2 hours or up to all day.
2. If you have a baking stone, put it in the oven 45 minutes before you want to eat. Preheat the oven to 550 degrees F.
3. Generously sprinkle a cookie sheet or pizza peel with coarse cornmeal.

4. Pat the mozzarella dry and lay on a paper towel for a few minutes so it gives up even more moisture.
5. Divide the dough into two balls. Stretch one ball into a round, about 14 inches in diameter, and place on the cookie sheet.
6. Spread with some tomato sauce—don't overdo it or the pizza will be soggy. Top with half the mozzarella. Sprinkle with oregano and red pepper flakes.
7. Bake for 9 minutes. Drizzle with olive oil. Repeat with the remaining dough and toppings.

Makes 2 pizzas, to serve 8

POT STICKERS

A friend once said, "We live in San Francisco. Why would you try to cook Chinese at home when there are so many great Chinese restaurants?"

I thought this was very wise until I got a Chinese cookbook and became completely obsessed. I smoked ducks and stir-fried live shrimp and steamed breads and made a beggar's chicken complete with the clay sarcophagus. Practically everything I cooked was more delicious than what I'd eaten in restaurants. This is partly because most of the restaurants in San Francisco are Cantonese and I like spicier Hunan and Szechuan dishes. There are a lot of great Chinese restaurants out there, but the place you go "for Chinese" isn't necessarily one of them.

If you have the time and energy, you can do better than a generic Chinese restaurant with a copy of Barbara Tropp's *The Modern Art of Chinese Cooking* or *Mrs. Chiang's Szechwan Cookbook* and supplies from a well-stocked Asian supermarket. These pot stickers are just one example of the extraordinary Chinese dishes you can make at home. I serve these with a sweetened vinegar manufactured by the Pat Chun company of Hong Kong. It's an incredible product, a black, tart-fragrant sauce made from rice wine vinegar seasoned with ginger, orange peel, and cloves. Look for it at Asian supermarkets. If you can't find sweetened vinegar, make a dip by mixing together soy sauce and rice wine vinegar to taste. A dash of sesame oil never hurts.

Make it or buy it? Make it.

Hassle: Wrapping them gets very wearisome and can take an hour or more

Cost comparison: The last time I made these, I priced them to the penny, using ingredients from the Chinese market. This included some very cheap, acceptable $1.29-per-pound fatty ground pork butt. It cost $5.71 to make the entire recipe. Of course, it will cost more if you shop at Safeway, and many times this if you buy pastured hormone-free pork and organic vegetables. But most Chinese restaurants don't do this, so I was simply trying to compare apples to apples when it comes to price. I eked out about 80 pot stickers, but some of them were a little skimpy, so I priced this for 60 pot stickers and came up with a cost of $0.10 apiece. At Young Can Wok, the pleasant Chinese restaurant nearest to my house (as the crow flies), you pay $6.75 for six pot stickers, which works out to $1.13 per pot sticker, not including tip. When we eat there, we always comment on how cheap it is to eat Chinese. Yes, it is, especially if you cook the food at home.

FILLING

1 pound fatty boneless pork shoulder, ground

¾ pound napa cabbage, finely chopped or shredded

1 teaspoon kosher salt

3 tablespoons minced scallion

3 tablespoons minced cilantro

1 tablespoon minced ginger

1 tablespoon minced garlic

Finely grated zest of half an orange

2 tablespoons Chinese rice wine

2 tablespoons soy sauce

1 tablespoon sesame oil

Pinch of red pepper flakes

½ to 1 teaspoon Szechuan peppercorns, toasted and finely ground

*About 80 round dumpling wrappers, homemade (recipe follows)
     or store-bought*

All-purpose flour, for dusting (optional)

Peanut oil, for frying

1. In a large bowl, combine all the filling ingredients and mix well.
2. Fry a tablespoon of the mixture in a small skillet. Taste for seasoning. Add a bit more of anything you think it needs—salt, sesame oil, red pepper flakes.
3. Set up a dumpling wrapping station with the wrappers, the filling, a small bowl of water, and a cookie sheet lined with parchment paper or dusted with flour.
4. Into the middle of each wrapper put about 2 teaspoons filling and, with your fingertips, daub the edges of the wrapper with a bit of water and fold into a half-moon. Pinch and pleat the wrappers. Place on the cookie sheet and repeat 60 to 80 times.
5. Bring a large pot of water to a boil. Drop in about 20 pot stickers and cook for 5 to 7 minutes. Scoop out the pot stickers, drain briefly, and place on a clean cookie sheet. Repeat with the remaining pot stickers.
6. Heat 1 tablespoon of peanut oil in a large skillet. When it's sizzling, add about 10 of the pot stickers. Cook on one side until the skin begins to brown and "thicken." Flip. Cook on the other side. Repeat with remaining dumplings. Serve immediately.

Makes 60 to 80 pot stickers

DUMPLING WRAPPERS

I made dumplings using store-bought wrappers for years until my friend Lisa, who is as fascinated with Chinese cooking as I am, told me that she made her own wrappers and that they were better than any bought wrapper. Right she was. I was horrified both by how hard it is to make dumpling wrappers and by how much better they are. These wrappers are thick and tender. I have never found a commercial dumpling wrapper that is both thick and tender; thick wrappers are usually rubbery and tender wrappers tend to be thin. If I have to choose between thick and rubbery and thin and tender, I choose thin and tender. But of course I'd rather have thick and tender—and homemade. At least if someone else makes them.

Make it or buy it? Buy it.
Hassle: Truly a pain in the ass
Cost comparison: You'll pay about $1.00 to make these, slightly under $2.00 to buy an equivalent number of commercial dumpling skins.

4 cups all-purpose flour, plus more for rolling
½ teaspoon kosher salt
2 cups boiling water

1. Whisk together the flour and salt in a big bowl. Gradually add the boiling water, stirring constantly. (Lisa uses chopsticks, but you can use a mixer for this.) Knead for 5 minutes until you have a tender white dough.
2. Cover with a clean, damp dish towel and let sit for at least 20 minutes and up to 3 hours.
3. Divide the dough into four pieces. Roll one portion into a long snake, about 1 inch thick. Cut the snake into ½-inch segments.
4. On a very large floured surface, with a rolling pin, roll each segment of dough into a rough 3-inch circle.
5. Repeat with the remaining dough. Now you are ready for the joy of stuffing all your wrappers.

Makes 1¾ pounds of dough, about 80 wrappers

SASHIMI

It's a good thing sashimi is expensive, because otherwise we would eat a lot more of it and there would be even fewer maguro in the sea. This did not deter me from trying to undercut our local sushi bar that, like half the Japanese restaurants in America, is called Samurai. How hard could it be to slice raw fish and fan it out on a plate?

At the farmers' market one morning I bought a piece of "sashimi-grade" albacore and a piece of "sashimi-grade" ono. Sashimi grade—which suggests the fish is safe to eat raw—does not appear to be an actively policed designation of the FDA, more like a judgment call made by the fishmonger who may know what he's doing or may not. This fishmonger was charging $15.00 per pound that day, and the two fillets together cost $12.90. Spread out on my cutting board, it looked like a lot of vulnerable, pearlescent fish. I sliced it against the grain into plump, velvety tongues such as I have consumed many times at Samurai. I had to trim away a few raggedy bits of sinew and skin, but there was still a lot of sashimi—eighteen fat slices in all, for which I estimated I would pay $36.00 at Samurai, tip not included.

Food styling is not my forte, but I arranged the sashimi as artfully as I could. The idea, as described in Shizuo Tsuji's *Japanese Cooking: A Simple Art*: "Five or six rectangular slices rest like fallen dominoes against a high bed of crisp shred-cut giant white radish." Mine didn't look like that but it looked okay and the slices of fish did have the "unmistakable bloom of freshness upon them." Then I mixed some powdered wasabi with warm water and put it in glass custard cups. Our chopsticks were being used as gardening stakes at the time, so we had to eat with forks. This detracted.

"How do I know it's not going to kill me?" Mark asked.

"You don't," I replied.

He sighed and began to eat. He quickly cleaned his plate. "Wow," he said, maybe four minutes later. "This was excellent! All you need is some presentation, some pickled ginger, some chopsticks, and you're set."

I was still scrutinizing the tiny red capillaries that threaded through the dense pink-tinged fish flesh. They looked like varicose veins. I prodded the sashimi, which appeared not as a translucent and luxurious delicacy but as something that was very clearly cold and dead.

As with sex, a lot of eating is in the head, and some crucial piece of the seduction went missing for me with homemade sashimi. I know this is irrational, but someone else needs to cut up a fish for me. I ate the sashimi, but without relish. I wouldn't discourage anyone from making sashimi, but it is not something I'll eagerly do again. I feel the same way about steak tartare.

Make it or buy it? Buy it.

STEAK TARTARE

Steak tartare—finely minced raw beef served with various condiments—is a dish I ordered at restaurants. Then I made it at home, and something about chopping that bloody red meat and smooshing it with egg and capers and mustard and then sitting down with a fork took my appetite clean away.

Make it or buy it? Buy it.

CHAPTER 6

FROM BEAK TO TAIL

KILLING CHICKENS

Slaughtering one's own meat has become a rite of passage for Americans who are serious about food, almost an imperative. "You can leave the killing to others and pretend it never happened, or you can look it in the eye and know it," Barbara Kingsolver wrote in *Animal, Vegetable, Miracle* before dispatching a turkey. "The more I'd learned about the food chain, the more obligated I felt to take a good hard look at all of its parts," Michael Pollan wrote in *The Omnivore's Dilemma* as he prepared to annihilate some poultry. "It seemed to me not too much to ask of a meat eater, which I was then and still am, that at least once in his life he take some direct responsibility for the killing on which his meat-eating depends."

No, it was not too much to ask. I entirely agreed.

I should have known that my least favorite chicken—big, rude, handsome Arlene—was a boy. Even as a chick, Arlene (Owen named him after Garfield's girlfriend) was brawnier than the others, and for a while I thought she was just smarter. Then one morning, she proclaimed her manhood. The crowing of a rooster was a sound my neighborhood had not heard for decades, if ever, and there was no question from whose Clampett-like yard it emanated. Since roosters are illegal here, friends suggested that I take Arlene to some cute farm in the country, that I free him in the woods (to be vivisected by raccoons?), or that I return him to the feed store. I knew exactly what I was going to do. "I couldn't butcher one of my pets," a friend reproached. Neither could I. Semiferal Arlene, who swaggered around the yard snarfing up centipedes, was not a pet. Besides, you pay good money for free-range chicken. Why would you just throw it away?

So one afternoon, my father—who put himself through college working at a slaughterhouse—drove over to help with the job. None of us had laid hands on Arlene in weeks and he raced around the yard, squawking furiously, until after a chase, he was landed. A worthy foe, that bird. I held Arlene down on a stump and my father removed his head with a pair of gardening shears.

We took Arlene back to the house and I dunked him in scalding water, holding him by his chalk-green feet. When I pulled him out, he smelled like wet cat. Plucking is no harder than shucking corn and the feathers came off in fistfuls. (I did not save them to make earrings and dream catchers or stuff pillows, but some people do.) After slicing open the body and scooping out the innards, I possessed a fowl that sort of resembled the birds at the supermarket.

Novella Carpenter devotes much of her wonderful book *Farm City* to her adventures raising and slaughtering livestock in the inner city and approvingly quotes Carla Emery, author of *The Encyclopedia of Country Living*: "I don't think much of people who say they like to eat meat but go 'ick' at the sight of a bleeding animal. Doing our own killing, cleanly and humanely, reminds us of our interdependence with other species."

I didn't go "ick." On the other hand, I didn't feel especially humble as I contemplated the dressed carcass. I've eaten a lot of chickens in my life, and they were all dead. There was no epiphany in store for me, no deepening sense of interconnectedness. There are good people who might need to kill a chicken to understand the link between a living bird and a McNugget, but apparently I had grasped and accepted the concept from the get-go. It was good to know this.

The next day I made chicken and rice soup. My children, who knew exactly what was in the pot, to my surprise ate with gusto. "We're honoring Arlene by not wasting her," said Owen. They must teach this in school; I never talk that way. I, on the other hand, could not stop thinking about bugs. I could not look at the meat without thinking about centipedes squirming out from under a brick and Arlene nabbing them. There's a downside to knowing where your food came from.

The very same day that Arlene lost her head, the *San Francisco Chronicle* ran a story quoting K. Ruby Blume, the founder of an organization called the Institute of Urban Homesteading. "The level of appreciation for nature and life when you slaughter your own meat creates a kind of ethic that I think is what we need to save the world," Blume said. "That's why I do this—I want to live with a deep gratefulness and appreciation for what the world provides for me."

Don't we all.

CHICKEN

Make it or buy it? Buy it.

Hassle: Time-consuming and grisly

Cost comparison: Arlene, cleaned and plucked, ended up costing about $2.00 per pound. You can buy a roasting chicken at Safeway for just about that much, and minus the gore. If a factory bird is what you're measuring against, we got rooked. Obviously, though, the Safeway chicken is a piteous and debeaked fowl who never saw daylight and subsisted on antibiotics. A better comparison is a pastured bird from an organic farm, which around here runs $4.79 per pound. And by that yardstick, raising your own meat would seem a good idea. Alas, our backyard chicken was bony and sinewy with stringy, chocolate-colored flesh. You could argue that we have been ruined for "real" chicken by fleecy white supermarket hens. Maybe so. But hard to reverse.

CHICKEN AND RICE SOUP

This is Greek avgolemono—chicken and rice, spiked with lemon and enriched with egg. This soup is truly good food. Campbell's is only okay.

Make it or buy it? Make it.

Hassle: Few soups are easier.

Cost comparison: To make this soup costs $0.62 per cup. Campbell's condensed chicken soup with rice: $0.66 per cup.

One 3- to 4-pound chicken (preferably not killed and cleaned by you)
1 onion, peeled and cut in half
Kosher salt
1 cup rice, long grain or short
2 large eggs
Juice of 2 big lemons—plus more, if desired
Freshly ground black pepper

1. In a large pot, cover the chicken and onion with water and bring to a boil. Skim off any foam with a slotted spoon. Add 1 tablespoon salt and simmer, partly covered, for 2 hours, until the meat is sliding off the bones. Add more water if it seems to boil away too rapidly.
2. Remove the pot from the heat and strain the broth into a large bowl. As soon as the chicken is cool enough to handle, separate the meat from the bones and skin. With your fingers, shred and mash the meat. Discard the onion, bones, and skin.
3. Pour the broth back into the pot and add the chicken and rice. Simmer, adding more water if necessary, until the rice is very tender, about 25 minutes.
4. In a small bowl, beat the eggs and lemon juice until frothy. Add a few ladlefuls of the hot soup, whisking energetically. Pour the mixture into the pot and stir well. Taste for salt and lemon juice and adjust if necessary. Add pepper to taste, and serve immediately.

Serves 6, with leftovers

CHICKEN STOCK

I dread making stock, but dislike wasting food even more, so whenever I have a chicken carcass, I pull out the soup kettle. I put the carcass and any juices from the roasting pan inside, add water to cover, a bay leaf, a sliced onion, and, if I have them, a couple of peeled carrots, a stalk of celery, and a handful of parsley. If I don't have carrots, celery, or parsley, I don't put them in. I bring the mixture to a boil, then turn it down and let it simmer, barely bubbling, for a few hours. I strain it into a big bowl, cool it to room temperature, refrigerate it overnight, lift off the cap of grainy yellow fat, ladle the stock into storage containers, and put them in the freezer. I usually end up with about 2 quarts.

It sounds so frugal and practical and simple—what's not to love? What I dread about making stock is manifold. To start with, I never know what to do with the damp chicken bones and slimy cooked vegetables. I can't put them in the compost and I don't feed chicken to the chickens. If it's not close to garbage day, the bones start to smell in the kitchen trash can—but if I put them in the outdoor can, the raccoons go berserk trying to pry off the lid and sometimes succeed, in which case, what a mess in the morning. Mark likes to stow the bones in a bag in the freezer but then he never remembers to put it out on trash day so we end up with unlabeled bags of bones. And since we have but one small freezer, that means there's nowhere to store the chicken stock.

Vessels for storing the stock present another challenge. Tupperware and yogurt containers work nicely, but they always seem to be either too small or too big or too few. I've tried freezing in canning jars, but sometimes they crack. You can freeze stock in resealable gallon bags and that works great until it doesn't. Once I neatly filled a bag with stock, sealed it, put it in a big bowl for support, and propped it up in the freezer. Sometime in the night, the seal broke, the bag slithered out of the bowl and stock spilled everywhere, freezing in a solid yellow puddle. It's still there. But how can I ever defrost and clean my freezer when it's so full of bones and stock?

On the plus side, it's cheaper to make stock than to buy it, especially if you start with a carcass you would otherwise discard. I estimate that homemade stock, including fuel, costs about $0.25 per cup to make while store-bought canned stock costs about $0.75 a cup. Moreover, if you read the labels of the leading brands, your skin will crawl. It's insulting what Swanson and Campbell put in their soup: among the offenders are corn oil, MSG, and sugar. In fact, the thought of what's in those cans disgusts me so much I can't buy them anymore. I don't enjoy making stock, but I do it.

BAY LEAF

If bay leaf didn't exist, would anyone miss it? I've never tasted something and thought, *This stew is just crying out for bay leaf.* But I keep buying and using it nonetheless. This is another case where it really pays to get out of the big-box supermarket. You can buy a 0.12-ounce jar of McCormick bay leaves at Safeway for $5.19. An equivalent amount from my favorite Chinese market: $0.19.

CHAPTER 7

JUNK FOOD AND CANDY

"Eat all the junk food you want as long as you cook it yourself," Michael Pollan writes in *Food Rules*. "If you made all the french fries you ate, you would eat them much less often, if only because they're so much work. The same holds true for fried chicken, chips, cakes, pies, and ice cream. Enjoy these treats as often as you're willing to prepare them—chances are good it won't be every day."

Oh, Michael Pollan, you underestimate me.

FRENCH FRIES

"How do you get the covering on them?" Owen asked, pulling at the skin of the hot french fry.

"I didn't have to put it on," I said. "It happens naturally when you fry potatoes."

Homemade fries don't taste better than what you can buy at McDonald's, and let's not fool ourselves that they're healthier. But they trounce the frozen competition, like Ore-Ida.

Make it or buy it? Occasionally you want to make fries at home, but this is basically restaurant or road food. If you got in the habit of making these at home you might eventually need to buy a medical scale. Frozen french fries are a last resort.

Hassle: You bet. But it wouldn't stop me. What stops me: fattening.

Cost comparison: It costs about $2.00 to make a pound of french fries—a dollar for the potatoes and another for the oil. (You can and should reuse the oil, so

I've amortized.) For an equivalent amount of inferior Ore-Ida frozen fries, baked in the oven, you'll pay about $2.40. If you deep-fry them: $3.40. From McDonald's, a pound of fries costs between $6.00 and $7.00, depending on who serves you. Not as cheap as you thought, is it?

Neutral vegetable oil or lard (page 155), for frying
2 pounds russet potatoes
Salt

1. Line a baking sheet with paper towels or brown paper grocery bags. Start heating the fat in a sturdy pot.
2. Peel the potatoes and cut into batons, as thin or as thick as you like your fries.
3. When the oil registers 320 degrees F on a deep-fry thermometer, or a bit of potato dropped in sizzles and immediately bobs to the surface, slip in a handful of fries. Turn down the heat so the fries cook gently in the oil but don't darken. You are basically parboiling them right now (albeit in oil, not water) and will fry them again immediately before serving to give them their crust.
4. When the fries are still pale but cooked—you can tell because they will become mealy and tender—scoop them with a slotted spoon onto the baking sheet to drain. Add the remaining fries to the oil and repeat.
5. Immediately—or up to a few hours later—reheat the oil, this time to 360 degrees F. Drop in half the fries and this time let them turn golden.
6. Remove and drain on clean paper. Salt to taste. Repeat with remaining fries. Serve immediately. They're fantastic with mayonnaise (page 39).

Makes 1 pound fries, enough to barely satisfy 4 hungry people

ONION RINGS

An editor once assigned me to review a cookbook by Todd Wilbur, author of the popular *Top Secret Recipes* series, in which he attempts to crack the codes behind classic brand-name foods, like Kozy Shack rice pudding and Krispy Kreme donuts. I was to cook as many of Wilbur's recipes as I could and determine whether he made good on his promise.

The results were shocking and unintentionally hilarious. When Wilbur's recipes failed the test, which they usually did, they failed by producing food that was orders of magnitude better than the originals upon which they were modeled. He aimed low, but he couldn't aim low enough. Intended as an homage to beloved brand-name comestibles, the book inadvertently revealed how truly lousy they are.

The most extreme example in my experiment: the Burger King onion ring. I've eaten Burger King onion rings on road trips and they always hit the spot. But sampling them against homemade offered a lesson in relativity: it is impossible to make a sound judgment about food without a direct comparison, especially when you're hungry.

One night, I made onion rings per Wilbur's commendable recipe and Mark brought home a sack of warm Burger King onion rings. I hope it's obvious that onion rings came to be because sliced onions naturally separate into rings. The Burger King onion ring, however, has moved so far from its origins that it is no longer a natural hoop of onion but ground, rehydrated onions mechanically extruded into a frangible little donut that breaks into crumbs when you bite into it. It tasted musty and tired, and even Mark, who takes pride in his man-on-the-street palate, agreed that you'd feel bad baiting a mousetrap with it. The onion rings I made by separating an actual onion into rings were crispy on the outside, melting and sweet on the inside. Poor Todd Wilbur. Apparently, you need sodium acid pyrophosphate, overworked soybean oil, and underpaid teenagers to make onion rings as awful as Burger King's.

Make it or buy it? If Burger King is your only option, make your onion rings. But a lot of restaurants take pride in their onion rings and they deserve credit and your business. The Outback Steakhouse Bloomin' Onion? Bloomin' delicious.
Hassle: Mighty

Cost comparison: Burger King onion rings cost about $0.62 per ounce depending on who's scooping. Homemade onion rings: $0.15.

1 large white onion, peeled
2 cups milk
2 cups all-purpose flour
3 cups bread crumbs (page 11)
8 cups neutral vegetable oil or lard (page 155)
Salt

1. Slice the onion horizontally into ¼-inch rounds, then separate into rings. Discard any rings that are broken or very tiny.
2. Pour the milk into a large, shallow bowl; pour the flour into another large, shallow bowl; and pour about ⅓ cup of the bread crumbs into a third.
3. Dip a ring into the milk, then into the flour to coat it completely. Dip it back into the milk and then into the bread crumbs. Dip it one last time into the milk and one last time into the bread crumbs. Place on a cookie sheet. Repeat with all the remaining rings, replenishing the bread crumbs as necessary. (If you put all the bread crumbs in the bowl at once, they'll get soggy and stop adhering to the onions.)
4. Line a baking sheet with paper towels or a brown paper grocery bag. In a sturdy pot, heat the fat until it registers 350 degrees F on a deep-fry thermometer, or a pinch of flour that you drop in sizzles on contact.
5. When the oil is hot, fry the onion rings, five at a time, for 3 minutes or so, until golden brown. With a slotted spoon, remove to the baking sheet to drain. Lightly salt and serve immediately.

Makes 1¼ pounds, to feed six

POTATO CHIPS

I love potato chips so much I can't stop eating them and therefore I rarely buy them. Even more rarely, I make them. My father came over once for dinner and we had a few cocktails—we were testing homemade vermouth (see page 234)—and I didn't have anything in the refrigerator to sustain us until the chicken was roasted, but I did have a single sprouting potato from the garden (see page 79) that I peeled and sliced, and twenty minutes later we were eating hot, salty chips. That lowly potato saved the day. Frying potato chips is a useful kitchen trick to have up your sleeve on occasions like this, provided you're not too drunk to handle boiling oil safely.

Chip by chip, homemade chips aren't as tasty as store-bought. Some chips will be dark with bitter, burned edges, some will be a little soft in the middle, some will be blistered and crispy, some will be not quite salty enough, some will be a little too salty, and occasionally you will get one that's perfect. They're fun to eat, but Lay's are better. And Kettle are even better than Lay's.

If you're good with a knife, you can cut the potatoes by hand, but I recommend a mandoline. I once owned an expensive stainless-steel mandoline, but I never touched it again after someone gave me a cheap plastic model made by Benriner. Provided you do not slice your finger off—you must use the plastic safety guard—this product will serve you well.

Make it or buy it? Buy it.

Hassle: I went through a box of Band-Aids and half a roll of paper towels one night because I didn't heed warnings about mandoline safety. It could have been much worse.

Cost comparison: Homemade chips cost about $0.40 per ounce. Lay's classic potato chips: $0.60 per ounce.

Neutral vegetable oil or lard (page 155), for frying
1 pound russet potatoes (approximately 2 large potatoes)
Salt

1. Line a baking sheet with paper towels or a brown paper grocery bag. Start heating 2 inches of fat in a sturdy pot.

2. Peel the potatoes. Cut into paper-thin disks.
3. When the oil registers 350 degrees F on a deep-fry thermometer, or when you drop in a tidbit of potato and it immediately sizzles and bobs to the surface, one by one, drop in a handful of potato slices. (If you drop them all in at once, they'll stick together.)
4. Cook, stirring occasionally, until golden. This should take about 5 minutes. Do not remove the chips when they're still bendable, as chips do not "crisp up" as they cool.
5. As soon as they're firm but before they darken, with a slotted spoon, remove the chips to the baking sheet to drain. Salt the chips. Repeat with the remaining potatoes.
6. Serve immediately.

Potatoes shed a lot of water as they morph into chips—
a pound of potatoes yields only 4 ounces of chips.

ONION DIP

Mixed feelings about this in my household. Using only natural ingredients, I tried repeatedly to replicate the beguiling onion dip that you make by emptying a packet of Lipton onion soup mix into a carton of sour cream and that you serve at Super Bowl parties. The first effort was a failure and everyone—it was tasted by fourteen people—thought mix dip was better. A few weeks later, I tried again, adding homemade Worcestershire sauce and more of all the seasonings. This time, everyone preferred the homemade dip. Everyone, that is, except me. I felt the homemade dip was missing something. Like Lipton onion soup mix. However you make your dip, serve it with potato chips—store-bought.

Make it from scratch or from soup mix? See above.
Hassle: A lot more than the mix
Cost comparison: Lipton: $1.43 per cup. Homemade: $2.05 per cup.

2 tablespoons olive oil
1½ cups chopped yellow onions, from 1 big onion
¼ teaspoon plus ½ teaspoon kosher salt
1½ cups full-fat sour cream
¾ cup mayonnaise (page 39)
¼ teaspoon garlic powder
½ teaspoon onion powder
½ teaspoon freshly ground white pepper
1 tablespoon Worcestershire sauce (page 166)

1. Heat the olive oil in a wide skillet. Add the onions and sauté with the ¼ teaspoon salt until soft and caramelized. Cool completely.
2. In a bowl, mix the remaining salt and the other ingredients. Stir in the onions. Taste for seasoning and adjust. Serve immediately, or cover and store in the refrigerator for up to a week.

Makes 3 cups dip

TORTILLA CHIPS

One night for a party I brought in two different brands of tortilla chips, then cut up some corn tortillas and deep-fried them. Ordinarily polite people became grabby when presented with the hot homemade chips. I became grabby, and I was the hostess. The next day we crumbled up the leftover store-bought chips and fed them to the chickens.

Don't use thick or homemade tortillas for these chips. You want thin, leathery, factory-made tortillas that will fry up crisp and ethereal.

Make it or buy it? Make it on select occasions.

Hassle: Standing over a cauldron of oil gets hot and tiresome and I wouldn't fry chips for a big party.

Cost comparison: A half pound of homemade chips: $1.29. The same quantity of Frito-Lay Tostitos: $2.72.

12 ounces thin corn tortillas
6 cups neutral vegetable oil
Salt

1. Cut each tortilla into eight wedges. (You can put them in a stack and cut them all at once.)
2. Line a baking sheet with paper towels or a brown paper grocery bag. Start heating the oil in a sturdy pot. When it registers 350 degrees F on a deep-fry thermometer, or a wedge of tortilla dropped in the oil sizzles on contact, add a large handful of tortillas.
3. Fry until crisp. With a slotted spoon, remove the chips to the baking sheet to drain. Salt to taste. Repeat with remaining tortillas. Serve immediately.

Makes 8 ounces of chips

CORN DOGS

To make corn dogs: Mix a sweet cornbread batter—Jiffy would work well, though you could start from scratch if you prefer (page 30)—and impale some hot dogs on short skewers. Heat a pot containing 6 to 8 cups of oil to 350 degrees F, swirl the franks in the batter so they're swathed in a thick yellow coat, and drop them in the oil. A few minutes later, when they're puffed and tan, pull them out, drain them on a brown paper grocery bag, and serve. They're much less nsaty than State Fair brand frozen corn dogs (we did a taste test), but it just feels awkward sitting around a dining room table eating deep-fried hot dogs with your family and friends, and you will almost certainly feel a little bit sick afterward. Corn dogs, like cotton candy and Sno-cones, are rodeo food— state fair food, carnival food—and best consumed outside on a sunny day, washed down with Mountain Dew from a coated plastic cup. Corn dogs are a wonderful thing—in context. But Bonita Myers's Wiener Wraps are a better choice for cooking at home.

BONITA MYERS'S WIENER WRAPS

If you want a hot dog recipe that has what vintage cooking magazines called a "fun factor," this is what you should make instead. I first tasted these at my sister-in-law Laura's house and I sat there calculating whether people had noticed how many wiener wraps I'd put away, and how long I had to wait before I could take another. (For some reason, I can say "wiener wraps" with a straight face but not "wiener bean pot." See page 169.) Bonita Myers was the mother-in-law of Laura's mother-in-law, Mary Ann, from whom I requested the recipe. I came home and promptly made them for my sister's fortieth birthday party. I cooked for days—dips, spreads, crostini, dumplings, alcoholic punch—but all anyone talked about afterward were the dry-aged tenderloins my mother brought (expensive) and "those hot dog things" (cheap!).

DOUGH
1 tablespoon instant yeast
8 tablespoons (1 stick) unsalted butter, softened
⅓ cup sugar
1 teaspoon kosher salt

1 large egg
4 cups all-purpose flour, plus more as necessary
1 cup warm water

Neutral vegetable oil, for greasing
1 pound miniature sausages (I use chicken-apple sausages)

1. Mix all the dough ingredients together in a bowl. Knead until smooth. If the dough seems sticky, add a bit more flour.
2. Turn out the dough, oil the bowl, return the dough to the bowl, and cover with a clean, damp dish towel. Let the dough rise for 2 hours at room temperature. At this point you can proceed with the recipe or cover the bowl tightly, and refrigerate for up to 5 days.
3. Grease a cookie sheet or line it with parchment paper. Deflate the dough, roll out to just under ¼ inch, cut into rectangles about the size of playing cards, and wrap the sausages so you have a bit of meat showing from either end. Put the wiener wraps on the cookie sheet, cover, and allow to rise for 1½ to 2 hours, until puffy but not enormous.
4. Meanwhile, preheat the oven to 350 degrees F.
5. Bake the wiener wraps for 12 to 15 minutes, depending on how brown you want them. Serve immediately with saucers of ketchup and mustard for dipping.

Makes about 40

FRIED CHICKEN

One rainy Sunday a few years ago, Isabel, Owen, and I decided to pass the afternoon by watching a DVD of *The Fellowship of the Ring,* that movie about hobbits and elves and Orcs that we'd been hearing about. One hundred and seventy-eight minutes later, during which we neither moved nor spoke, we looked at each other, eyes glazed. We walked straight to the car, drove to the video store, and rented *The Two Towers* and *The Return of the King.* It was getting on dusk when I pulled into the Kentucky Fried Chicken down the hill and bought dinner.

My kids were shocked. Happy, but shocked. What was going on with Mom? KFC? I wondered that myself. But we were hungry and the chicken was hot and we had five more hours of Viggo Mortensen to watch. Fifteen minutes after I pulled into the KFC, we were back on the sofa with the bucket on the coffee table, eating mediocre chicken and mashed potatoes and biscuits and watching *The Two Towers*. It was one of the happiest nights of my adult life and my children get dreamy and nostalgic talking about it.

Not long ago, I cooked a grand fried chicken dinner out of *Ad Hoc at Home* by Thomas Keller. I bought the book based on rave reviews of Keller's chicken, which is brined and air-dried before it is dipped in multiple coatings and fried. The effort paid off; the recipe did not disappoint. To go with that incredible chicken—because you can't serve fried chicken without fixins—I mashed potatoes and baked biscuits. There was a salad in there somewhere, too. Frying chicken is messy and nerve-racking because oil spatters and spits and stings your forearms and you have to do it at the last minute, which is also when you're mashing potatoes and pulling biscuits out of the oven and pouring glasses of water and calling to everyone that dinner is ready. Leave it in the pan too long, and the chicken is ruined; take it out too soon and it's a health hazard. You really have to be up for the logistical challenge.

And fried chicken comes with baggage: You expect fried chicken to be so good that people lick their fingers. Literally. You expect people to linger at the table and loosen their belts, lean back in their chairs, tell stories, pull out a bottle of corn likker. You expect people to somehow recognize that this isn't a meal like all other meals.

Sometimes all of that will happen.

Sometimes it will not.

By the time we sat down, I was bleak with exhaustion, everyone else was ravenous, and we put away that chicken in about ten minutes flat. The coating formed a crispy sheath around meat that, thanks to brining, was juicy and flavorful through to the bone. The potatoes were a celestial cloud of starch and butter; the biscuits, perfection. But I don't remember a thing anyone said; I don't remember anyone lingering at the table or thanking me or recognizing that the meal was special or iconic or hanging around afterward to drink corn likker. Soon I was left with plates of picked-over bones and a ravaged kitchen. One of these days I will forget the evening ever happened. I suspect Mark and our children already have. But that night we ate KFC on the sofa and watched *The Two Towers*? That, we will never forget.

Sometimes I have to remind myself that the symbols of wholesome domestic happiness—hot biscuits, a platter of home-fried free-range chicken, a family sitting around a table—are not domestic happiness. The family sitting in front of the TV with the bucket may be experiencing more joy and grace and love. Or, of course, they may not be.

This is Thomas Keller's recipe, streamlined.

Make it or buy it? There's no easy answer to this one.

Hassle: Epic

Cost comparison: It costs just about twice as much to home-fry your chicken as to buy a 10-piece bucket from KFC—and that's not even factoring in the three large sides they throw in to sweeten the deal.

BRINE

5 lemons, halved
½ cup honey
2 cups kosher salt

Two 3-pound chickens
Neutral vegetable oil or lard (page 155), for frying

COATING

6 cups all-purpose flour
¼ cup garlic powder
¼ cup onion powder
1 tablespoon plus 1 teaspoon sweet smoked paprika
1 tablespoon plus 1 teaspoon cayenne pepper
1 tablespoon plus 1 teaspoon kosher salt
1 teaspoon freshly ground black pepper

1 quart buttermilk (page 53)
Salt and freshly ground black pepper
⅓ cup hot sauce (page 81)

1. Combine the brine ingredients with 2 gallons water in a big pot and bring to a boil. Boil for 1 minute. Remove from the heat and cool completely. Chill.
2. The morning of the day you plan to eat, cut the chickens into 10 pieces each (2 wings, 2 legs, 2 thighs, and 4 breast pieces; put the back in the freezer in a labeled bag for future use in making stock). Drop the chicken into the brine. Soak for up to 12 hours but, says Keller, no longer, lest the chicken become too salty.
3. Remove the chicken from the brine and rinse under cold water. Pat dry, lay out on a rack over a baking sheet, and let sit at room temperature for 2 hours.
4. In a large sturdy pot, start heating the fat; it should reach about 2 inches up the side of the pot.
5. Meanwhile, combine the coating ingredients in a large bowl. Transfer half the coating to a second large bowl. Pour the buttermilk into a third bowl and season with salt and pepper. Set up a dipping station: chicken pieces, one bowl of coating, the bowl of buttermilk, the second bowl of coating, and a parchment paper–lined baking sheet to hold the raw, coated chicken.
6. When the fat registers about 300 degrees F on a deep-fry thermometer, dip the chicken thighs into the first bowl of coating to cover. Dip them into the buttermilk, allowing the excess to run back into the bowl, then dip in the second bowl of coating. Transfer to the parchment-lined pan until all the thighs are coated.
7. When the fat registers 320 degrees F, lower the thighs into the hot fat. Fry for 3 minutes, stirring gently. Cook undisturbed until the chicken is a deep golden brown, about 12 minutes.
8. Meanwhile, coat the chicken drumsticks. You will fry the rest of the chicken just as you did the thighs, starting with the drumsticks, moving to the breast pieces, and finally the wings, letting the fat return to 320 degrees F and adjusting the cooking time so that the smaller pieces fry more quickly. As the pieces are done, remove them to a cooling rack to drain. Serve immediately.

Serves 6 to 8

OVEN-FRIED CHICKEN

Much easier and almost as good.

½ recipe of Keller's brine (page 119)
One 4-pound chicken, cut into 10 pieces (2 wings, 2 legs, 2 thighs, and 4 breast pieces;
    put the back in the freezer in a labeled bag for future use in making stock)

COATING

2 cups all-purpose flour
1 tablespoon garlic powder
1 tablespoon onion powder
1½ teaspoons sweet smoked paprika
1½ teaspoons cayenne pepper
1½ teaspoons kosher salt
½ teaspoon freshly ground black pepper

6 tablespoons (¾ stick) unsalted butter

1. The night before you want to oven-fry the chicken, make the brine. Let it cool on the counter, then put it in the refrigerator.
2. In the morning, drop the chicken pieces into the brine.
3. When you're ready to cook, heat the oven to 400 degrees F.
4. Remove the chicken from the brine and pat completely dry.
5. Combine the coating ingredients in a bowl. In a 12-inch cast-iron skillet, start melting the butter over medium heat.
6. One by one, toss the chicken pieces in the coating, then drop them into the hot butter, skin side down.
7. When all the chicken pieces are in the pan, let fry for 1 minute. Place the skillet in the oven. Bake for 25 to 30 minutes, until the skin is golden brown. Flip the chicken and continue cooking on the other side for another 25 to 30 minutes. Test for doneness by cutting into a piece—it should not have a trace of pink. Serve immediately.

Serves 4

POPCORN

Popcorn wasn't junk food until the twentieth-century miracles of trans fats and the microwave came along. Virtually all brands of microwave popcorn have in recent years eliminated the chemical diacetyl, which gives popcorn the flavor of butter and gives humans who inhale enough of it respiratory disease. However, the microwave bags sometimes contain a chemical—perfluorooctanoic acid (PFOA)—that is thought to be carcinogenic. Home-popped corn remains relatively healthy— fattening if you drown it in butter—but relatively healthy.

Make it or microwave it? Make it.

Hassle: Anyone can make popcorn except, of course, people in an office without a stove. It takes about 2 minutes longer than the microwave.

Cost comparison: Microwave popcorn and standard popcorn cost about the same, though you'll have to shell out a penny or two extra for the salt, and maybe $0.30 for the butter if you pop your own.

3 tablespoons neutral vegetable oil
⅓ cup popcorn
Melted butter (optional)
Salt

1. In a large pot, heat the oil with 5 kernels of the corn. Cover with a lid. When the kernels pop, add the rest of the popcorn and agitate the pan so the kernels don't burn. The kernels will all be popped in a few minutes. You can tell because . . . they stop popping.
2. Toss with melted butter and salt to taste.

Makes about 2½ quarts

CARAMEL CORN

Fresher than Cracker Jack, plus you get to eat it by the greedy fistful from a bowl rather than fishing around in the cramped box with your fingertips.

Make it or buy it? Make it.

Hassle: Easy

Cost comparison: $0.70 per ounce for Cracker Jack. $0.28 for ConAgra's Crunch 'n Munch. $0.16 per ounce for homemade.

2½ quarts popcorn, freshly popped
2 cups skinned, salted, roasted peanuts
1 cup dark brown sugar, packed
½ cup dark corn syrup
8 tablespoons (1 stick) unsalted butter
½ teaspoon kosher salt
1 teaspoon vanilla extract (page 260)
½ teaspoon baking soda

1. Preheat the oven to 250 degrees F.
2. In a wide pan with high sides, such as a turkey roaster, combine the popcorn and half the peanuts.
3. In a medium saucepan, combine the sugar, corn syrup, butter, and salt and bring to a boil over medium heat. Continue to boil for 5 minutes. No need to stir. Remove from the heat and mix in the vanilla and baking soda.
4. While the glaze is still very hot, pour most of it over the popcorn and peanuts, tossing with a buttered spoon until well combined. Add the rest of the peanuts, then the rest of the syrup, and toss.
5. Put the roasting pan in the oven and bake for 1 hour. Cool. Break apart any big clumps. Store at room temperature in a tin or a large resealable plastic bag.

Makes 1½ pounds of caramel corn, about 3 quarts

GLAZED DONUTS

All day long Mother had been baking, and when Almanzo went into the kitchen for the milk-pails, she was still frying doughnuts. The place was full of their hot, brown smell, and the wheaty smell of new bread, the spicy smell of cakes, and the syrupy smell of pies.

Almanzo took the biggest doughnut from the pan and bit off its crisp end.

—*Farmer Boy*

Sometimes I wonder why those *Little House* books had such a powerful hold over me. Everything people did seemed vital and elemental and creative and everyone was all together doing it and when they were done, they sat down to these incredible meals. The books seemed to depict a deeper, richer domesticity than I was experiencing in my own 1970s home, pressed against the heater while my mother refinished a chair and my father watched *Monday Night Football*. Today, I would never turn down a donut from a donut shop, but homemade donuts—hot, yeasty, crispy, and light—are better. As Isabel said, "These take some of the fun out of Krispy Kreme."

Make it or buy it? Make it.
Hassle: Rising. Cutting. Frying. Draining. *Big* hassle.
Cost comparison: Homemade: $0.10 per ounce. Entenmann's: $0.20 per ounce.

2½ teaspoons instant yeast
1¼ cups warm milk
4 tablespoons (½ stick) unsalted butter, softened
3 large egg yolks
3 tablespoons sugar
1½ teaspoons kosher salt
Grated zest of half an orange
3 to 4 cups all-purpose flour, plus more for rolling
Neutral vegetable oil, for deep-frying

GLAZE
1 cup confectioners' sugar
Milk

1. In a large bowl, preferably using an electric mixer, combine the yeast, milk, butter, egg yolks, sugar, salt, and orange zest with 1 cup of the flour. Add the remaining flour in ½-cup increments, stopping as soon as you get a soft but workable dough.
2. Knead for 3 minutes, using a dough hook. Scrape the dough down the sides of the bowl, cover with a clean, damp dish towel, and let rise until puffy, about 1 hour.
3. Turn out the dough onto a lightly floured surface and roll it out thin—to just under ½ inch. Cut as many rounds as possible with a 3-inch biscuit cutter. Then cut out the centers with a 1-inch cutter. Reroll scraps and continue cutting out donuts. Cover the donuts with the towel and let rise for 30 minutes.
4. Heat 3 inches of oil in a large heavy pot to 350 degrees F. When you drop in a pinch of dough it should sizzle immediately and rise to the surface, but not brown immediately. (If that happens, the donuts will emerge crispy on the outside and raw on the inside.) Line a baking sheet with paper towels.
5. Fry the donuts, four at a time, turning with a slotted spoon, until puffed and golden. Drain on the paper towels. Fry the holes. Cool for about 5 minutes.

WHAT TO DO WITH THE OIL?

Dealing with old frying oil is one of the more tiresome aspects of making many of our favorite foods. You can reuse the oil, unless you cooked something particularly messy or smelly. (In fact, according to Nathan Myhrvold, author of the 2,400-page, $625 *Modernist Cuisine*, recycled oil will give a crispier crust to fried foods than fresh oil.) When the oil is cool, strain it into a clean container to reuse four or five times. Use your common sense. I would not, for instance, use oil in which I'd fried fish sticks or onion rings to cook donuts. But I wouldn't hesitate to use donut oil to fry fish sticks. When the oil starts to look grimy and smell stale, get rid of it. (Although according to Myhrvold, you should keep a few tablespoons to inoculate your new oil.)

Don't slosh it down the drain or toilet unless you have a crush on your plumber. Some towns have recycling centers where you can drop off oil to be converted into animal feed or biodiesel. Alternatively, small amounts of oil can be poured into a sealable container (like the bottle it came in) and put out with the trash. I usually pour old oil into the blackberry brambles at the back of the yard. They've seen worse.

6. Meanwhile, mix the glaze by adding milk to the confectioners' sugar and beating until you have a smooth, pourable glaze. Place in a wide, shallow bowl. Dip each donut in the glaze. Place on a rack to let the glaze set. Eat within a few hours.

Makes about 18 donuts and 18 holes

POP-TARTS

One weekend, Mark and I went out to brunch at a kitschy-chic restaurant in San Francisco called Foreign Cinema, where on the menu along with oysters on the half shell and a swordfish confit sandwich, they offered house-made Pop-Tarts for $7.50 apiece.

This Pop-Tart came on its own plate and it was almost twice the size of a Kellogg Pop-Tart. I was disappointed because it was neither frosted nor strewn with colored sugar. It was more like a flaky, buttery jam pie and it was very delicious. I came home and searched for recipes online, found a handful, and set to work. One came from King Arthur Flour via Deb Perelman of the blog Smitten Kitchen. The second was a "pocket pie" recipe from Alton Brown, and the third was a recipe from *Bon Appétit* contributed by none other than Gayle Pirie and John Clark, the chefs at Foreign Cinema. This is a hybrid of the three. When warm (or toasted), the buttery crust shatters between your teeth. These taste very posh but cost less than a "real" Pop-Tart.

Make it or buy it? Make it. Once.
Hassle: Major headache
Cost comparison: Homemade: about $0.40. A Kellogg Pop-Tart: about $0.50.

2 cups plus 2 tablespoons all-purpose flour, plus more for rolling
1 teaspoon kosher salt
1 tablespoon granulated sugar
½ pound (2 sticks) cold unsalted butter, cut into bits
¼ cup cold milk
Neutral vegetable oil, for greasing (optional)
1 egg
⅔ cup jam, any flavor
Sugar, for sprinkling (optional)

½ cup sifted confectioners' sugar
1 to 2 tablespoons milk or heavy cream
⅛ teaspoon vanilla extract (page 260)
A few drops of food coloring (optional)

1. Whisk the flour, salt, and sugar in a large bowl. Add the butter and, using your fingertips, quickly blend until the mixture resembles coarse meal. Add the milk and mix until clumpy. (You're essentially making pie dough.) Form into a ball, then shape into a disk. Wrap tightly and refrigerate for a minimum of 1 hour.

2. Preheat the oven to 350 degrees F. Line two baking sheets with parchment paper, or lightly grease. Beat the egg in a small bowl.

3. On a floured work surface, roll out the dough as thin as you can. If you have a fluted cutter, now is the time to use it. Using a ruler, cut the dough into rectangles 2½ by 4 inches. Reroll and cut the scraps.

4. Brush the perimeter of half of the dough rectangles with some egg. Spoon 2 teaspoons or so of jam into the middle of each egg-brushed rectangle and spread it out, leaving a ¼-inch margin on all sides. Place an unegged dough rectangle on top of each jam-spread rectangle. Seal the edges tightly by pressing with the tines of a fork. Prick the tops of the pastries to release steam. If you are not going to frost the pastries later, sprinkle the tops generously with sugar. Place the tarts on the baking sheets.

5. Bake for 30 minutes, until golden. Let cool completely on a rack.

6. If frosting the tarts, in a small bowl, mix the confectioners' sugar with the milk, vanilla, and food coloring (if using) to make a thick, smooth, spreadable frosting. Frost the tarts. These are best eaten immediately, though you can store them at room temperature for up to five days in a cookie tin. You can toast these in a regular pop-up toaster, but some of the frosting will melt and drip into your toaster. Better to use a toaster oven, if you have one, or an ordinary oven.

Makes 10 to 12 Pop-Tarts

TURKISH DELIGHT

In the neighborhood where I grew up, there's a spice shop called Haig's that has been there as long as I can remember and has always smelled exactly the same, like cumin and coriander and coffee. My mother used to take me there to buy coffee beans from a large, bespectacled man with a bald head like an egg. The old man is gone, as is my mother, but I stop at Haig's every time I'm in the neighborhood. There is never a crowd, never more than one or two other people in the shop, and I dread the day I find Haig's has gone out of business, because I always discover something odd and marvelous there—dried Persian lemons; canned spotted dick from Great Britain; a 1956 paperback copy of *Indian Cookery* by E. P. Veerasawmy which, according to the jacket copy, "should be an important part of any cook-proud housewife's library" and is now a treasured part of mine. You can buy blade mace, which looks like the shavings from a sharpened pencil, or split, peeled fava beans, or fresh halvah. I never leave without buying something and I always, always buy a chunk of the Supreme Turkish delight, which is sold from a big jar on the counter. The pistachios are the bricks, the rose-flavored jelly is the mortar, and I eat it out of the little white sack while walking down the street back to my car. It scatters confectioners' sugar on my fingers and is probably ruining my teeth, but it is too good to resist. If I go into Haig's feeling blue, I come out thinking the world is a big and strange place full of mysterious, rose-scented pleasures, like Turkish delight.

One day, in the throes of my self-sufficiency, I tried to make Turkish delight by simmering a paste of cornstarch, water, and gelatin for an hour. I could not believe how cheap it was going to be! No more would I pay $13 per pound for Supreme Turkish delight from Haig's. I flavored this translucent goo with rosewater, poured in a big handful of pistachios, spread it in a brownie pan, cut it in cubes, and tossed it in sifted confectioners' sugar.

It was gummy and smelled like air freshener.

I collected more recipes from the Internet and planned to continue my quest, and then I asked myself: Why was I boiling cornstarch and gelatin when I could go to Haig's and buy myself a piece—or a pound!—of perfect Turkish delight made by someone who actually knew how to make Turkish delight? What will happen to the expert makers of Turkish delight if people like me stop buying their product? What will happen to Haig's? And where else can I buy a Syrian coffeepot, a jar of Indian lime pickle, or black Dutch licorice?

I quit trying to make Turkish delight.

MARSHMALLOWS

Like most Americans, I grew up thinking a marshmallow was a stiff, eraser-like confection, nominally edible, used in school construction projects involving toothpicks or dropped in hot chocolate. Neither candy nor cookie, a marshmallow was a gummy droid, entirely artificial and not all that enticing. My kids used to eat them only when there was nothing sweet left in the cupboard except raisins. To concoct a marshmallow at home seemed impossible. And to concoct at home a marshmallow that resembles a Kraft Jet-Puffed may be impossible.

After you have tasted a sugar-white homemade marshmallow you will not care. Homemade marshmallows are fairy food, pillowy, quivering, and soft.

Make it or buy it? Make it.

Hassle: Negligible, provided you have a mixer (a handheld mixer is fine if you're strong and patient) and a candy thermometer. If you don't have a candy thermometer, buy one. Cheap and useful.

Cost comparison: The most basic homemade marshmallow costs $0.10. Kraft Jet-Puffed marshmallows: $0.04 apiece. On the other hand, high-end marshmallows like the Whole Foods brand: $0.50.

Three ¼-ounce packets unflavored gelatin
1½ cups granulated sugar
1 cup light corn syrup
2 egg whites
2 teaspoons vanilla extract (page 260)
¼ cup cornstarch
¼ cup confectioners' sugar

1. In a tiny saucepan, over low heat, dissolve the gelatin in 7 tablespoons water. It will be pale beige and viscous. Turn off the heat.
2. In a larger saucepan, heat the granulated sugar and corn syrup with ½ cup water. Bring to a boil, stirring until dissolved. Let it boil until it registers 265 degrees F on a candy thermometer.
3. Meanwhile, in the bowl of a mixer, begin whisking the egg whites. Beat until

firm and glossy. As soon as the sugar syrup registers 265 degrees F, begin pouring it in a slow steady stream into the egg whites, beating constantly. Add the gelatin and continue beating. When you start, the hot liquid will slosh around the bowl and you will think it is hopeless; by the time you are done, the mixture will have swollen into a luxuriant white cloud. Whisk until the bowl is cool to the touch.

4. Whisk in the vanilla.

5. Lightly grease a rimmed cookie sheet. Mix together the cornstarch and confectioners' sugar and sift half onto the cookie sheet. You want a really generous bed of powder. On top of this, spread the marshmallow and smooth the top. Let sit overnight.

6. In the morning, cut the marshmallows into 36 pieces with a sharp knife. If they stick, dip the knife in water. (Damp scissors can also help with the job.) Toss the marshmallows in the leftover powder; you want all the exposed sides of the marshmallows to be lightly coated in powder, which will keep them from sticking to each other.

7. Store in a cookie tin or resealable plastic bag. They keep indefinitely, though they become crustier and less appealing after a week or so.

Makes 36 marshmallows

CHOCOLATES

Few retail experiences are more gratifying than walking into an old-fashioned chocolate shop like See's, studying the array of candies in their frilled paper cups, giving an order to one of the ladies wearing a white uniform, and watching her assemble the selection in a box. If candy can ever be wholesome, candy store candy is wholesome.

Isabel once made cupcakes and had some leftover penuche icing that tasted like the filling of a See's Bordeaux chocolate. She and I spent the better part of a Saturday afternoon making heart-shaped chocolates in cheap plastic molds and filling them with penuche. It was messy and finical and the resulting candies were very cute, but no one liked them as much as See's chocolates. The chocolate shell was too hard and had raggedy edges and it was a little too bitter. There was no selection and there was no box. There was no ceremony. Chocolates are special in part because they are bought.

I think the only reason to make your chocolates is if you're throwing a party and buy some plastic molds in the form of golf clubs, or hula dancers, or whatever your theme might be, and make personalized chocolates with some unique filling, like, I don't know, rose geranium cream. I would love to throw such a party, but even more I would love to be invited to such a party, and I suspect neither is ever going to happen.

Buy your filled chocolates.

Truffles are another story. They're just chocolate ganache flavored any way you like and scooped into little balls.

Make it or buy it? Make it.

Hassle: Actually, yes. These are a hassle.

Cost comparison: A pound of See's truffles costs about $19.00 and you get some variety for that $19.00. To make a pound of homemade truffles, about $11.

1 cup heavy cream

2 tablespoons butter, at room temperature

10 ounces bittersweet chocolate, chopped fine (use a good-quality chocolate, like Scharffen Berger)

2 tablespoons liqueur (Grand Marnier is delicious; so is amaretto)

Cocoa powder, for rolling

1. In a small saucepan over moderate heat, warm the cream until it is on the verge of a boil. Remove from the heat.
2. Stir in the butter and chocolate until they melt. Stir in the liqueur.
3. Scoop into a bowl and put in the refrigerator until the chocolate is firm, about 4 hours.
4. With a teaspoon, scoop the chocolate into small balls. Roll in the cocoa. Store tightly covered in the refrigerator.

Makes 36 truffles, about 18 ounces

RICE KRISPIE TREATS

Invented in the 1930s during the Great Depression, the Rice Krispie Treat could not be easier to make or more delicious. In a saucepan you combine two nutritionally empty packaged foods with melted fat to create, within minutes, a third nutritionally empty food that, when spread in a pan and cut into squares, is outrageously and improbably irresistible. For decades, this was how American children, including me, first acquired an interest in "baking."

Then, in 1995, Kellogg decided to spare us even the trivial effort required to mix the treats and began to market individually wrapped, prepared Rice Krispie Treats. You will pay three times as much to buy your stale-tasting treats premade.

Make it or buy it? Make it.
Hassle: Supervised first graders can make these, though they probably won't scrub the pot.
Cost comparison: Store-bought treats cost three and a half times as much as homemade.

3 tablespoons unsalted butter, plus more for the pan
10 ounces marshmallows (page 129)—though homemade are wasted here
Pinch of kosher salt
6 cups Rice Krispies

1. Generously butter a 9 by 13-inch baking pan.
2. Melt the 3 tablespoons butter in a large saucepan, then add the marshmallows and salt and stir until the marshmallows are creamy and melted. Stir in the cereal.
3. Scrape the mixture into the prepared pan and smooth the top with a rubber spatula or pat down flat with clean hands. Let it rest for 20 minutes until cool and completely set.
4. Cut into 2-inch squares with a very sharp knife. Store in a cookie tin at room temperature, though this is seldom necessary with Rice Krispie Treats.

Makes 24 treats

CHAPTER 8

DINNER

My mother openly and proudly hated to cook and, when I was a child, she rolled out the same sensible meals every week, a never-ending rotation of roasted chicken, bunless hamburgers, steamed broccoli, brown rice, and green salads. I respect people who can do something they dislike that much, every day, year after year. I'm not sure I have it in me. I couldn't understand why she didn't make veal piccata, sloppy joes, cheese soufflé, cannelloni, or nasi goreng. All the fascinating foods I saw when I flipped through cookbooks, as I constantly did starting at the age of seven. If she could make anything for dinner—and why couldn't she?—why wouldn't she?

And here's the thing: I still don't understand. I've struggled with the work-life balance, the time issues, and the kids who won't eat the dal or the vichyssoise or the oxtail stew, but I've never let it stop me. Making something interesting and delectable for dinner is the highlight of my day—if no one else's. I have paid for this small pleasure by enduring much screaming, many tantrums, and dark looks from my spouse. It was worth it, I think.

But, like everyone, there are dishes I've made again and again.

ROASTED CHICKEN

When my daughter, Isabel, was small and I worked full-time at an office, I used to pick her up at day care and rush to get home, where, if I put her in front of *Dragon Tales* and ran straight to the kitchen, I could get the chicken into the oven within fifteen minutes. Then I scrubbed my hands like a surgeon, sanitized everything the raw chicken had come within three feet of, mixed a gin and tonic, set the table, and tossed a salad. We never ate before eight, by which time Isabel was cantankerous and I was a little drunk.

I used to eye the rotisserie chickens, those warm, whiskey-brown birds under the heat lamp near the cash register at the supermarket. They smelled so seductive I wondered how a person could get one home without stopping by the side of the road to eat it with her fingers. My mother, by then a divorcée who was feeding only her footloose self, was always buying rotisserie chickens. I looked down on her for it. Rotisserie chickens were what you ate when you gave up. No, I was going to turn myself into a human pretzel to give my family a proper Norman Rockwell roast bird dinner at least once a week.

But why?

One day not long ago, I bought both a raw chicken and a rotisserie chicken. Every rotisserie chicken was marked 28 ounces and, at checkout, the $3.99-per-pound rotisserie chicken appeared to cost more per pound than the raw chicken. But when we got it home it weighed in at 31 ounces, which brought the price down to more like $3.60 per pound. Meanwhile, the $1.99-per-pound raw chicken weighed 5 pounds at checkout. But after I removed the giblets and roasted it for an hour, it weighed just 3½ pounds, raising the actual price to $2.80 per pound. After accounting for the ingredients—a lemon, a half stick of butter, some herbs, and salt, plus fuel to heat the oven—the cost of the chicken we ate was more like $3.40 per pound. So: $3.60 a pound for a ready-to-eat rotisserie chicken, $3.40 per pound for a chicken cooked from scratch.

The little rotisserie chicken did not look particularly regal, squatting in the middle of the platter, bathed only in the paltry liquids that had collected in the bottom of the heatproof bag. By contrast, the home-roasted chicken was sheathed in golden pepper-flecked skin and reclined in a moat of opulent juice.

I carved the chickens and divided up the portions. We tasted. The breast meat on the home-roasted chicken was bright white and firm; the thigh meat was taupe and also somewhat firm. Except for the crispy seasoned skin, the meat was bland until you sluiced over it the lemony juice, which masked all of its shortcomings.

On the other hand, there were almost no juices to pour over the rotisserie chicken. It didn't need any. The tender meat was fully impregnated with flavor, almost as if it had been braised. Everyone in the family agreed that the rotisserie chicken made better eating. Yet everyone also agreed that the homemade roasted chicken was "better."

Isabel said, "It seems wrong to just bring home a cooked chicken."

I said, "But, why? Why is it more wrong to bring home a cooked chicken than to bring home a box of crackers?"

"I don't know," she said. "But it just is."

It just is. Commentators always mention burgers as the quintessential modern American meal, but I think that sells us short. The roasted chicken is more emblematic of what we're striving for day to day. We want the Norman Rockwell Thanksgiving illustration: a smiling family, a well-laid table, a roast bird. Symbols are important.

Still, if I could go back, I would tell my younger self with the job and the little kid to buy the rotisserie chicken. Norman Rockwell probably never roasted a chicken in his life.

These days, I have more time to roast chickens—but why would I roast a chicken when I have the time to make cannelloni from scratch? Sometimes I roast a chicken anyway. I think the key is to salt the bird the night before, which both improves the flavor of the bird and lets you get the filthy part—touching raw chicken—out of the way ahead of time.

Make it or buy it? Both.

Hassle: Definitely

Cost comparison: Actual cost of home-cooked roasted chicken, starting from scratch: $3.40 per pound. Actual cost of a rotisserie chicken: $3.60 per pound.

1 tablespoon kosher salt
2 teaspoons freshly ground pepper
1 chicken, 3 to 4 pounds
4 tablespoons (½ stick) unsalted butter, softened
2 lemons
Potatoes (optional)

1. The night before you plan to cook the chicken, mix the salt and pepper in a small dish. Sprinkle the chicken all over with the mix, and then gently work the skin free of the breast, keeping it intact, and spread the seasoning on the

meat. Put the chicken in a bowl—no need to cover—and refrigerate for 24 hours.

2. Preheat the oven to 450 degrees F.

3. Put the chicken in a 12-inch black cast-iron skillet, breast side down. Place half the butter in the cavity and smear the rest on top of the bird. Cut the lemons in half and place inside the cavity. Wash your hands with lots of soap.

4. If you are roasting potatoes, peel them and cut them into 2-inch chunks. When the oven is hot, put the chicken in and roast for 1 hour. (The potatoes go in after the chicken has cooked for about 10 minutes—drop them into the melted butter and chicken fat that's beginning to accumulate in the pan.) The chicken is done when a leg moves easily in its joint. If you have an instant-read thermometer, stab it deep in the bird's thigh. It should register 165 degrees F. If it doesn't, return the chicken to the oven and test it again 5 minutes later.

5. Take the bird out of the oven and if you have time, let it sit for 10 minutes so the juices settle. If you don't have time, go ahead and carve. The pan sauce is really good, so be sure to spoon some on each serving.

Serves 4

SALAD

How much do you dislike washing lettuce? I dislike it a lot. I used to sometimes buy a plastic box of "triple-washed" lettuce just so I didn't have to wash it. I know some people wash it anyway, but what was the point of buying "triple-washed" lettuce if I was then going to wash it? What is the point of the "triple washing"?

One day I bought a 10-ounce head of organic red leaf lettuce for $1.99 and brought it home. It lost about 2 ounces when I chopped off the core and pulled off some ratty outer leaves. Cost of edible lettuce from the head: $4.00 per pound.

Meanwhile, a 5-ounce plastic box of prewashed organic mixed baby greens cost $4.99. Cost of edible lettuce from the plastic box: $16 per pound. I don't hate washing lettuce *that* much.

People will eat more salad if there's a chance the next bite will contain a toasted nut. Pine nuts are great, but they currently cost more than $30 per pound.

Almonds are an affordable substitute, as are pumpkin seeds. They all are better toasted.

Another way to add crunch to your salad and upcycle stale bread at the same time: croutons.

CROUTONS

It's ludicrous to the point of heartbreaking that factories are devoted to manufacturing pellets of stale-tasting bread that trucks then ferry all around the country. If factory croutons tasted good all that trucking might be worth it, but croutons from the box could double as packing peanuts, and vice versa. Moreover, they are often spiked with partially hydrogenated oils and high-fructose corn syrup. Corn syrup has a place in pecan pie, but in croutons?

Make it or buy it? Make it.

Hassle: Enough that you're not going to make croutons for every salad or bowl of soup

Cost comparison: Homemade croutons will cost you pennies to make and use up stale bread you would otherwise throw out. At my local safeway, Mrs. Cubbison's Caesar Salad Croutons cost more per pound than lamb chops.

A few pieces of bread, fresh or stale
Olive oil or unsalted butter
Minced garlic, herbes de Provence, red pepper flakes, saffron, etc. (optional)
Salt

1. Preheat the oven to 325 degrees F. Cut the bread into cubes, as large or as small as you like.
2. Heat a few tablespoons of olive oil or butter in a skillet. At this point you can add a few pinches of minced garlic or any herb or spice you choose. Sauté for 30 seconds.
3. Add the bread cubes and stir them around in the hot oil for a couple of minutes until they're well coated and starting to form a crust. Sprinkle lightly with salt to taste.
4. Spread on a cookie sheet and toast in the oven for 10 to 15 minutes. They're done when they're crunchy and look like croutons. Good luck not eating them all right

off the cookie sheet. If you have any left over, put them in a cookie tin, where they'll keep for a few weeks.

VINAIGRETTE

The first ingredient in Wish-Bone Italian dressing: water, which explains the lack of body. The second ingredient: soybean oil—a cheap, comparatively unhealthful fat. The fifth ingredient: sugar, which is unnecessary in a vinaigrette. But the biggest problem with Wish-Bone is that it doesn't taste very good.

Make it or buy it? Make it.
Hassle: Slight. Triple or quadruple the recipe and store in the refrigerator until it runs out.
Cost comparison: Homemade: $0.60 for a half cup. Wish-Bone: $0.63.

3 tablespoons vinegar (your choice)—red wine, white wine, sherry, blackberry
1½ teaspoons Dijon mustard
7 tablespoons olive oil
Kosher salt and freshly ground black pepper

In a small jar, mix the vinegar and mustard. Add the olive oil, cap tightly, and shake until blended. Season to taste with salt and pepper, then shake again.

Makes a generous ½ cup

FRUIT VINEGAR

The first vinegar I tried making was fruit vinegar, using the fascinating recipes I found in Diana Kennedy's *From My Mexican Kitchen*. To make banana vinegar, you put collapsing, blackened bananas, unpeeled, in a colander over a bowl, cover with a towel, and let the fruit disintegrate and drip and drip and drip into the bowl for many days. "Lots of little flies will swarm around because of the fermentation," Kennedy writes. And they did. Midway through the banana vinegar project, we invited some prospective friends to dinner and a few hours before their appointed arrival time, I took the vinegar outside. I hoped the flies would follow. They did not. Moreover, the disappearance of the bananas seemed to throw the flies into confusion, and as we sat there in the living room, the little flies zoomed around at eye level. I apologized once, and then tried to maintain my poise. We had a good time with these new friends but it's been two years and they still haven't called to invite us back so I guess we should now call them "acquaintances." Was it the flies, or was it us? Which is worse?

In any case, when the bananas had given their all, they left behind an inky fluid that I mixed with brown sugar, decanted into a jar, and capped. It was sweet and rich and complex and scant. Three pounds of bananas ultimately yielded a cup of vinegar. Between the small quantity, the effect on our social life, and the fact that you can use blackened bananas to make banana bread, which is better, I crossed banana vinegar off my list.

To make pineapple vinegar, in a big jar you combine the peelings from a pineapple with water and sugar and let them ferment. No flies. However, writes Kennedy, "If things don't go according to order, small white maggots will float on the top." Fortunately, things went according to order and I ended up with about a quart of honey-gold vinegar that smelled like pineapple. Alas, it was barely tart. It was a feeble vinegar, incapable of standing up to oil in a dressing, however lovely its fragrance.

BERRY VINEGAR

No, the best vinegar I've made is simply wine vinegar infused with berries. I once made raspberry vinegar and it was stupendous, but since raspberries cost a fortune, for the next batch I used the wild blackberries that grow all along the road to my house and produce many pounds of jammy fruit every July. The spicy berries balanced out the acid and made one of my all-time favorite vinegars.

Make it or buy it? Make it—but only with free wild berries.
Hassle: None
Cost comparison: If you have to buy raspberries, it can cost $5.00 per cup to make raspberry vinegar. Store-bought: $2.55. Blackberry vinegar made with wild fruit: between $0.50 and $2.00 per cup depending on whether you use cheap red wine vinegar or really cheap red wine vinegar.

1 pound blackberries or raspberries
2 cups red or white wine vinegar

1. Combine the vinegar and berries in a clean glass jar. Cap tightly and let macerate for 6 weeks at room temperature.
2. Strain the vinegar and discard the berries. Store in a jar or bottle, tightly capped in the cupboard.

Makes 2 cups

BURGERS

When I was growing up we ate hamburgers once a week, served bunless with a side of steamed broccoli and a green salad. My mother made memorable burgers, moist and salty and flavorful. And rare. But that was then. I would choose a rare hamburger as my last meal, but I've read *Fast Food Nation*, and my children have never eaten a rare hamburger and may never know the primal pleasure. I cook burgers until they are thundercloud gray all the way through.

My husband thinks I am neurotic. Once, early in our marriage, he bought a bag of premade beef patties. I flinched when I came across the sack in the freezer. I think packaged beef patties resemble Gaines-Burgers and I suspect that they're made from the worst of the worst scraps of meat and gristle and cartilage swept from the slaughterhouse floor at the end of every shift.

I said, "These are the burgers that give people *E. coli*."

"Once every ten years," he said. "I've never gotten *E. coli*."

"How hard is it to just shape your own burgers?"

"Well, you make it hard," Mark said. "Before I met you I didn't realize you couldn't mix the hamburger meat on the same cutting board where you slice the tomatoes. And you have to wash your hands. I used to like making hamburgers but now it's a pain in the ass."

About that he is correct. But I am not the reason. Industrialized food is the reason.

One day I decided I would try grinding my own hamburger from grass-fed Whole Foods beef so I could serve the burgers rare. I bought a chuck roast that cost more per pound than the house-ground beef, which made me feel silly, but a rare hamburger is worth it. First, I tried to chop the meat in the food processor and the result was an unevenly ground amalgam of smeary beef paste and sinewy chunks. I pulled out the meat grinder. Always a mistake. The meat was extruded from the die in a pinkish goo and emitted a bloody aroma. The cooked patties were simultaneously chewy and pasty and no one liked them at all.

I probably would have given up on burgers entirely, if Isabel hadn't asked to make dinner one night. She took a twenty out of my wallet and walked to the supermarket where she bought ground beef, and while I sat on the sofa reading magazines, she cooked. She told me she had decided to "be creative" and had mixed seasonings into the meat, and, being Isabel, she had written down precisely what she did so it could be repeated in case it worked out well, which it did. These are the only burgers we make anymore, and they are fabulous even when cooked to a uniform thundercloud gray and served bunless with a side of steamed broccoli and a salad.

For every pound of ground chuck:

1 tablespoon Worcestershire sauce (page 166)
Pinch of cayenne pepper
⅓ cup bread crumbs (page 11)
¼ teaspoon kosher salt
Pinch of freshly ground black pepper
1 large egg

1. Mix all the ingredients together with your hands. Form into patties. Wash your hands with lots of soap.
2. Fire up the grill or heat a skillet over medium-high, then add the patties. Brown on one side, then turn down the heat to cook for about five minutes. Flip and cook for about 10 minutes more. You can tell a burger is done by breaking into one with a knife—these burgers are supposed to be gray inside.

A pound of ground chuck serves 4

PASTA

My mother was an Italophile and one year for Christmas she gave me a pasta machine. Thereafter, every Wednesday night she came over and we made pasta. In almost all the photos I have of her from the last five years of her life she is posed with one of my children, triumphantly draping a swale of pasta through the machine. Sometimes she has hair, and sometimes she is bewigged; sometimes she is thin and sick, and sometimes she is plump and radiant. But on Wednesday nights, we made that pasta.

The great, imperious Italian cookbook author Marcella Hazan writes: "There is not the slightest justification for preferring homemade pasta to the factory-made. Those who do deprive themselves of some of the most flavorful dishes in the Italian repertory."

With all due respect, I think Hazan is mistaken. Far from preferring homemade pasta, most Americans have never even tasted homemade pasta. I have cooked hundreds of pounds of store-bought pasta, and it is very convenient and very good, but to say Barilla spaghetti is no less glamorous and delicious than homemade pappardelle is like saying an Old Navy sweater is every bit as glamorous as a Diane von Furstenberg wrap dress.

Don't make this if you're in a hurry and don't make it if you're alone. It's possible, but not advisable, at least for beginners. The last time I made pasta I called to Isabel, who was in her room doing homework, to come down because the strips of pasta were getting too long and I needed another set of hands. She came down, sighed heavily, and said, "Be sure you write in the recipe that you need two people." And so I have. Also, you really need a machine. Some cookbooks will tell you that the wood grain in a rolling pin makes for a "pebbly" textured noodle that better holds the sauce. I tried hand-rolling pasta once and was so tired of all that rolling, rolling, rolling, that by the time we ate, many hours later, I almost wished Marco Polo had never gone to China.

Make it or buy it? Both.

Hassle: If you aren't in the mood for a hassle, don't make pasta.

Cost comparison: A cheap luxury. You can make a pound of pasta for a dollar. Dried pasta: between $1.00 and $3.00 per pound—or much more if you buy a premium imported Italian brand. Supermarket fresh egg fettuccine, such as Buitoni: $6.00 per pound.

2 cups all-purpose flour
2 large eggs
2 large egg yolks

1. Put the flour in a large bowl, make an indentation, and crack in the eggs. Drop in the egg yolks.
2. Beat in the eggs and yolks. Knead the dough until well combined, about 2 minutes. It will look lumpy and a little craggy. It should be dry to the touch, but there should be no visible flour—a dough that is too dry is harder to fix when you start rolling than a dough that is a bit too moist. If the dough looks too dry, add a few drops of water.
3. Roll out with a pasta machine, starting on the widest setting. If the dough tears, it is possibly too wet. Simply dust it with flour, fold it over itself, and start again. Roll twice at each setting before moving to a narrower setting. Cut as desired.
4. To cook, heat a pot of salted water to a rolling boil, drop in the pasta, and cook for about 2 minutes, until tender and silky. Drain.

Makes 14 ounces of pasta, to serve 4

PESTO

It's curious that children like pesto, as pesto is intense green and garlicky—so clearly vegetable. And yet they like it. I don't think I've met a child who didn't.

One night we tested three supermarket pestos—Buitoni, Safeway Select, and the Monterey Pasta Company. I found them horrid, each in its own distinct way. The flavors of real pesto are strong and clean, but these were all murky. The ingredient lists suggest possible reasons why: cream powder (Monterey Pasta Company), sugar (Buitoni), reduced lactose whey (Buitoni).

Out of season, basil is pricey, but if you grow basil, or can buy it cheaply in the summer, make a lot of pesto and freeze it in jars. Pine nuts have recently been selling for upward of $30 per pound, which makes them more expensive than filet mignon. I made pesto with walnuts and tasted the end product side by side with pine nut pesto. The walnut pesto lacked a certain *je ne sais quoi,* but it was very, very subtle. If you don't want to shell out for pine nuts, try walnuts or experiment with other nuts.

Once, a long time ago, my daughter, Isabel, and I went to a French restaurant and since they didn't have chicken fingers, the only thing on the menu she wanted was pasta with pesto, which isn't even French. This particular pesto was creamy and pale jade green and she loved it and told me she wanted me to make pesto like that. I don't usually have crème fraîche (page 93) in the house, but when I do, I put a spoonful in the pesto.

Make it or buy it? Absolutely make it.

Hassle: Nothing to it

Cost comparison: The price for a 7-ounce container of pesto averages $6.50. If you use walnuts, your homemade pesto will cost about $1.00 less. Made with pine nuts, the price jumps to $7.50.

2 packed cups fresh basil, leaves only, washed and dried
3 garlic cloves, peeled
½ cup olive oil
3 tablespoons nuts (pine nuts or walnuts)
½ cup grated Parmesan cheese
Kosher salt to taste

1. Place the basil in the bowl of a food processor with the garlic cloves, olive oil, and nuts. Blend until smooth and creamy.
2. Scrape down the sides of the work bowl and add the cheese. Blend to combine. Taste and adjust for salt. Use immediately, or store in the refrigerator for 1 day. Freeze for longer storage.

Makes a generous cup, enough to sauce a pound of pasta

PARMESAN: GRATED OR BY THE CHUNK?

At Whole Foods, you pay exactly the same amount whether you buy your Parmigiano-Reggiano grated in a tub or in a brick from the cheese counter. Either way, it costs a pretty penny: $21 per pound. I know that you're supposed to always grate Parmesan by hand just before you serve it. For years, that is what I did. Then I stopped, and no one noticed. There are few kitchen jobs, including squeezing limes, that I dislike more than grating hard cheese. I would rather learn to make Parmesan than grate it—except if I made it, I would eventually have to grate it myself. I sometimes buy chunk Parmesan to shave over special dishes, like Caesar salad, but otherwise, like for adding to pesto? Pre-grated. Always.

MARINARA SAUCE

I like food with bite and this hearty sauce has plenty, unlike most bottled sauces. Many major producers such as Classico, Barilla, and Newman's Own add sugar to their marinara and it tastes unwholesome and overly sweet. Plus, the routine sugaring of savory food is annoying.

Make it or buy it? Make it.
Hassle: Slight
Cost comparison: Homemade costs about $1.50 per cup. Classico: $1.60. Rao's: $3.86.

2 tablespoons olive oil
1 onion, thinly sliced
4 garlic cloves, chopped
1 teaspoon red pepper flakes
One 28-ounce can crushed tomatoes
Kosher salt

1. Heat the olive oil in a large saucepan over low heat. Add the onion, garlic, and red pepper flakes and cook, stirring occasionally, until the onion is tender.
2. Add the tomatoes and their juice. Simmer for 30 minutes over medium heat. Add salt to taste. Use immediately, or cool to room temperature and store in a jar in the refrigerator for up to a week. Freeze for longer storage.

Makes about 2¾ cups

QUESADILLAS

This is my default dinner, default lunch, default snack, default breakfast. To make one, put a flour tortilla in a skillet over medium heat, top with sliced or grated cheese (Jack or cheddar), fold it into a half-moon, and let the cheese melt.

How hard could it be to make a tortilla?

FLOUR TORTILLAS

Not hard at all, as it turns out. These homemade tortillas taste elemental, more floury than what you buy. I had always liked store-bought tortillas, but now they taste suspiciously slick, like flour spiked with monoglycerides, amylase, and calcium propionate. Not bad—but not as staff-of-life satisfying.

> **Make it or buy it?** Both. Even though they taste inferior and cost more, packaged tortillas are so convenient. I can't give them up. When possible, make your tortillas. As necessary, buy them.
> **Hassle:** Minimal
> **Cost comparison:** Under $0.10 to make a medium tortilla; about $0.25 to buy one.

3 cups all-purpose flour
¾ teaspoon kosher salt
5 tablespoons neutral vegetable oil, shortening, or lard (page 155)

1. Combine the flour and salt. Add the fat, mixing until the flour forms clumps. Add ¾ cup water and mix until the ingredients come together and form a dough.

Knead briefly, until smooth, springy, and tender. Divide into 12 balls, each just a little larger than a golf ball, cover with a clean, damp dish towel, and let rest on the counter for 20 minutes.

2. Heat an ungreased skillet until very hot. With a rolling pin, roll each ball of dough into a rough circle 6 to 8 inches in diameter. Don't worry about rolling it out as thin as you possibly can; this isn't strudel dough.

3. Place a tortilla on the skillet and cook for about 30 seconds to 1 minute, until it starts to blister and turn brown in patches. Flip, and cook on the other side. Wrap in a clean napkin or dry dish towel and proceed with the rest of the tortillas. These do not keep well, probably because they do not contain 14 ingredients, most of them unpronounceable, so eat them as soon as possible.

Makes 12 tortillas

CORN TORTILLAS

Thin, leathery store-bought corn tortillas make the best quesadillas. In my experience you can't make good quesadillas with homemade corn tortillas—they're too thick and soft. However, they're deeply satisfying eaten all on their own, earthy and grainy, and they make the ideal starchy accompaniment to chili, carnitas, and posole.

Make it or buy it? Depends on what you're using the tortillas for.
Hassle: No big deal
Cost comparison: Homemade tortillas cost about $0.05 per ounce. Store-bought: between $0.06 and $0.22 per ounce.

2 cups masa harina
1¼ cups warm water

1. In a bowl, stir together the masa and water. Shape into rounds the size of golf balls.
2. If you have a tortilla press—cheap and often sold at Mexican markets—sandwich the ball between two pieces of plastic wrap, place in the press, and press down hard. (If you have sandwich bags, they work even better than plastic wrap.) Peel back the wrap and put the flattened tortilla on the counter while you finish pressing the rest.

(If you don't have a tortilla press, pat the dough out as flat as you can between your palms, going back and forth, hand to hand. My maternal grandmother, who is Guatemalan, says this is the only proper way to make tortillas—which may be why, in 45 years, I have seen her make tortillas only once. It is definitely harder this way.)

3. Heat a skillet as hot as you can get it. Three at a time, cook the tortillas until they're starting to blister and color, about 3 minutes. Flip, and continue cooking on the other side. Eat while they're still warm.

Makes 10 tortillas

KIMCHI

Kimchi is a pungent, garlicky fermented pickle, typically made with cabbage, that is served at most Korean meals, including, I have read, breakfast. Supposedly, there are as many recipes for kimchi as there are Korean cooks and I once found a recipe that calls for a "small octopus."

I first tasted a kimchi quesadilla from a Kogi truck in Los Angeles, one of the locally beloved armada of vehicles that sell Mexican-Korean fast food—kalbi burritos, tofu tacos, kimchi quesadillas—to Angelenos willing to wait in line forty-five minutes for their fix. The kimchi quesadilla satisfied a craving I'd never even known I had—for capsicum, sour cabbage, strarch, and rich oozing cheese, all together.

To make a kimchi quesadilla you need to ferment some kimchi, as home-fermented kimchi puts the store-bought products I've tasted to shame. There's a bit of a fermentation revival happening in the United States now, inspired largely by a delightful and idiosyncratic book called *Wild Fermentation* by Sandor Ellix Katz. Katz has fermented almost everything, including a goat: "As it cooked, an overwhelming odor enveloped the kitchen. It smelled like a very strong cheese suited to only the bravest gastronome. There was some swooning and near fainting, and several folks were nauseated and had to leave the room."

Start with kimchi.

Make it or buy it? Make it.

Hassle: Involves a little engineering

Cost comparison: To make a quart of kimchi costs just over $2.00. A quart of supermarket kimchi costs at least $10.00.

1 small head cabbage finely shredded, about 1½ pounds before trimming

1 tablespoon fine sea salt

2 teaspoons fish sauce

¼ cup whey from making yogurt (page 47), optional

4 red radishes, trimmed and quartered

3 scallions, chopped

5 garlic cloves, finely chopped

1 tablespoon grated peeled ginger

2 tablespoons hot sauce (page 81), or you can use any heat source
you prefer: Tabasco, sriracha sauce, chopped jalapeños,
supermarket red pepper flakes, kochukaru, etc.)

1 cup applesauce (page 151) or 1 apple, peeled and grated (unconvential but good)

1. Mix all the ingredients in a bowl with your hands, massaging the salt into the cabbage. Let sit, covered, at room temperature for 1 hour.

2. Pack the kimchi into a glass quart jar. Find a smaller jar that will fit inside the rim of the quart jar—a jelly jar, for instance—and fill it with water. Cap it tightly. Place it on top of the cabbage and press down so the juices are forced up and over the vegetables. Cover the whole contraption with a clean apron or T-shirt and tie tightly around the middle. You want the kimchi able to breathe, but inaccessible to flies.

3. Let the kimchi ferment at room temperature for 3 to 5 days, tasting daily. When you like the flavor, dismantle the contraption, cap the jar, and store in the refrigerator.

Makes 1 quart

CHAPTER 9

FRUIT

For the chickens, for the $163 seed bill, for the whole ramshackle barnyard that I can see from my bedroom window, I blame an apple tree. Or credit an apple tree. I still don't know which. That apple tree, it gave me ideas.

When Mark and I were first married, we rented a house in the foggiest neighborhood in San Francisco, a famously foggy city. Whole summers went by and we did not see the sun. As the puckish *San Francisco Chronicle* columnist Herb Caen once put it, "There wasn't a sky in the cloud." Rather than sod lawns in front of their houses, people in our neighborhood sometimes just poured cement and painted it pink or green. It was like living on the moors of Great Britain with painted concrete instead of heath, the desolation punctuated by Chinese grocery stores instead of taverns. For a long time, we wanted to live nowhere else. Then, when we had two children, we decided we wanted to buy a house. Our decision to move to the suburbs had nothing to do with crime, home prices, parking spots, or family values. I thought, *If we stay here inside the cloud with the pink and green concrete, we will never, in our entire lives, grow a garden.* I had no reason to believe that I would even like gardening, but as we all know, the Garden is symbolic.

We decided to move to Mill Valley, a sunny town just north of San Francisco where Cyra McFadden set her 1970s satiric classic *The Serial*, about the misadventures of some spouse-swapping, pot-smoking, middle-class men and women who aren't quite as groovy as they want to be. The realtor who sold us our house was named George, and Mark and I thought George had probably enjoyed some wife swapping and pot smoking in his day. We underestimated his cunning. He took us in at a glance—pale, anxious young city people in search of their Garden—and drove us straight to a house well outside of our price range. He looked me in the eye and, standing there in front of a too-small 1960s faux Tudor on a steep hill, pointed out the apple tree that grew against the cement stucco south wall. I didn't see the cement stucco, only the tree. He twisted an apple off a bough and sank his teeth into it. I realize now that the apple could not have been ripe—it was midsummer and those fruits don't mature until September—but George betrayed nothing. Although it stretched our finances thin as phyllo dough and I had to persuade, cajole, seduce, and bully Mark into the purchase, and later take the blame whenever anything broke or rattled or leaked, which it did, we bought that apple tree.

Our tree is a Melrose apple—a cross between a Jonathan and a Red Delicious—and its branches weep under a load of red-striped fruit every September. There's a reason Shel Silverstein did not call his book *The Giving Pea Vine*, or *The Giving Turnip Plant*. We do nothing for this tree, and it gives us more apples than we can eat, autumn after autumn. One year, we had to saw off a limb and the next year the tree produced two apples. I thought, *The gig is up; the tree is done with us.* But the year after that the tree generated hundreds of pounds of fruit—more than ever before. Nothing else has ever been so easy.

APPLESAUCE

Commercial applesauce is a hospital staple, good for people who are sick or toothless. Aromatic and spicy, homemade applesauce is like pie without crust.

Make it or buy it? Both. My mother used to can applesauce in the fall for us to eat year-round, and it's the noble thing to do. But I am not so industrious. I make small batches once or twice in the fall when we have too many apples, and I buy it (or don't eat it) the rest of the year.

Hassle: Peeling apples

Cost comparison: If you have your own apple tree, making applesauce is practically free. Making 5 cups of applesauce cost me less than $0.50. If you buy apples, it costs slightly more to make your own applesauce than to buy a jar of Mott's.

4 pounds apples
½ to ¾ cup sugar
1 teaspoon ground cinnamon

1. Peel, core, and slice the apples. Place in a saucepan with enough water to just about cover. Bring to a boil over medium heat. Stir in ½ cup sugar.
2. Simmer the apples for about 25 minutes, until they are very soft. Stay close; if the liquid evaporates, the applesauce will quickly scorch. If necessary, add a splash more water.
3. Mash. If you want the applesauce extremely smooth, run it through a food processor or food mill. I like mine chunky. Add cinnamon and more sugar to taste. Store in the refrigerator for a week. For longer storage, freeze.

Makes 5 cups

APPLE CRISP PIE

Homemade is the point of pie. While it's acceptable to eat pie in a café called Grandmom's where you can actually see an old woman in an apron—if she has a bun even better—to buy pie from a supermarket is like ordering salad in a barbecue shack. If you're going to bring home dessert from Stop & Shop, bring home Klondike bars.

My father and sister have always contended that crisp is easier and tastes better than pie, and they're right, but I remain staunchly pro pie. Crisp doesn't signify the way pie does. Sukey doesn't give Johnny Tremain a piece of apple crisp, she gives him a piece of pie. Early in her marriage, Laura Ingalls Wilder doesn't ruin a crisp by forgetting to add sugar, she ruins a pie. Mildred Pierce doesn't make her fortune selling crisps.

This pie is really two desserts in one, an overstuffed hybrid of crisp and pie that I bake to please everyone in my family. There's a short bottom crust that establishes it as a pie, but the top sags under the crunchy streusel of a crisp.

Make it or buy it? Make it.
Hassle: Again with the apple peeling
Cost comparison: If you have an apple tree, baking this pie costs about $3.00. If you buy apples—Melrose work well, if you can find them, but so would Gala or Gravenstein—you will pay about $8.00 to bake this pie. Whether from the in-house bakery or the freezer, a streusel-topped apple pie at Safeway costs just under $9.00.

About 8 apples, peeled, cored, and cut into ½-inch chunks (about 6 cups)
½ cup sugar
1 tablespoon fresh lemon juice
1 teaspoon ground cinnamon
1 unbaked 9-inch pie crust (recipe follows)

STREUSEL

¾ cup granulated sugar
¾ cup dark brown sugar, packed
1¼ cups all-purpose flour
½ teaspoon kosher salt
12 tablespoons (1½ sticks) cold unsalted butter, cut into tablespoons

1. Preheat the oven to 350 degrees F.
2. Toss the apples with the sugar, lemon juice, and cinnamon. Scrape into the pie shell, being sure to capture all the juices that cling to the bowl.
3. Mix the streusel ingredients with the paddle attachment of a mixer, with your fingers, or with a pastry cutter, until clumpy. Heap on top of the apples. This will seem like a lot of streusel, but try to pack it all on there. You can do it.
4. Place the pie on a cookie sheet and put the cookie sheet in the oven. Do not skip this step unless you enjoy cleaning the oven. Bake for 1 hour and 15 minutes, or until the pie is bubbling and the apples yield easily when pierced with the point of a steak knife. Serve warm or at room temperature. To store, cover and keep at room temperature for 1 or 2 days. After that, store in the refrigerator for up to a week.

Makes one 9-inch pie, to serve 8 to 10

PIE CRUST

People are unnecessarily intimidated by pie crusts. Your first ten crusts may look like kindergarten art projects, but so long as the edges are presentable—so long as there are edges—no one who eats the pie will know or care. Many recipes are very specific about what type of fat to use. Cooks swear by all-butter crusts, Crisco crusts, lard crusts, even vegetable oil crusts. My favorite is this butter-lard crust, which has the most flavor and shatters when you bite into it. But use whatever fat you want; the crust will be better than anything you can buy. Homemade crust tasted against Safeway's frozen shell was delicate and rich, as opposed to brittle and bland. Likewise, it outperformed Pillsbury roll-out dough, which is oversalted and contains suspected carcinogens BHA and BHT. Not that a trace amount will give you cancer. It's the principle.

Make it or buy it? Make it.

Hassle: A pie crust can be mixed in 4 minutes, but you really do have to chill the dough, especially this dough, which is more fragile than some. Also, rolling takes practice and can be frustrating until you've done it twenty or thirty times.

Cost comparison: Homemade: just under a dollar. A Safeway-brand frozen pie crust: $1.70.

1⅓ cups all-purpose flour, plus more for rolling
½ teaspoon kosher salt
2 teaspoons sugar
4 tablespoons (½ stick) cold butter, cut into bits
4 tablespoons cold lard (recipe follows), cut into bits (if you have time, freeze the lard bits)
¼ cup ice water

1. Sift the flour, salt, and sugar into a large bowl or a food processor.
2. Add butter and lard, a few bits at a time, blending with your fingers or pulsing in the processor, until the mixture forms a coarse meal.
3. Add the water, a tablespoon at a time (you probably won't need all of it and should use as little as you can get away with), and mix just until the dough begins to form a ball. Shape it into a disk, wrap tightly, and refrigerate until very cold, at least 3 hours.
4. Flour the work surface and roll the dough into a rough circle, ¼ inch thick or less. The circle doesn't have to be perfectly round—ragged edges are fine. This recipe makes a little extra dough in case of mistakes. Lift the dough and place it in a 9-inch pie plate. (If you fold the dough in half and then in half again, it's easier to place in the pan.) Don't stretch the dough. You should have a lot of overhang. Tuck the edges over and pinch decoratively. I like to squeeze the dough between the side of my middle finger and my thumb to create a tall, fluted crust,

like a garland. It will collapse during baking, but the ruins of its beauty endure. You can also crimp the pie crust by pressing it against the rim of the pie plate with the tines of a fork. That's easier, if not as pretty.

5. To prebake pie crust: Preheat the oven to 425 degrees F. Place a piece of foil in the shell and pour in enough rice, dried beans, or pie weights to keep it from puffing.
6. Bake for 15 minutes. Carefully remove the weights and foil and return the dough to the oven. Bake 5 minutes more. Cool before filling. If you're not using the crust immediately, cover and store at room temperature for up to a day.

Makes one 9-inch crust

LARD

Try to avoid Armour and other brands of hydrogenated lard. They contain the preservative BHA, a carcinogen in rats and potentially humans that is probably safe in small quantities, but why consume any at all? You want freshly rendered lard. This, alas, is hard to find. Once a kitchen staple, in the early and mid-twentieth century lard was replaced by Crisco, which Procter & Gamble touted as a clean, modern alternative. We now know that Crisco is a heart attack in a bright blue canister, while lard—by no means a health food—contains mostly monounsaturated fats, just like olive oil. Moreover, the saturated fats that lard does contain have a neutral effect on cholesterol.

Yet even today, lard has a backwoods taint to it, not helped by epithets like "lard ass" and "tub of lard." Rendering your own lard is easy, but it takes all day and will lend your house a unique perfume that some people won't appreciate. Even so, I recommend doing it. You will probably have to ask your butcher for pork fat and this might entail a special order. I also recommend rendering a lot all at once and storing it in the freezer.

You want the fat from the back, kidneys, or belly. The highest-quality fat is called leaf lard, and usually comes from around the kidneys—it is brittle and will break into little pieces. But take whatever fresh fat you can get. This is one case where you really should seek out organic pork, because toxins accumulate in animal fat, and lard is nothing but.

Make it or buy it? Make it. You may not have a choice.
Hassle: Acquiring the pork fat is the hardest part.

Cost comparison: Organic pork fat costs about $3.00 per pound, and a 10-pound hunk yields 12 cups of ivory lard. Very few shops carry freshly rendered lard these days, but I found one high-end butcher an hour away that sells it for $5.00 per pound. I'd buy it if I lived within easy driving distance.

Massive hunk of fresh pork fat

1. Choose a day when you aren't going anywhere or expecting company. In the morning, preheat the oven to 250 degrees F.
2. Cut the fat into chunks the size of your hand and place in a wide Dutch oven or deep skillet with a cup or so of water. (The water keeps the lard from burning in the early stages of the process and will eventually evaporate away.) Place the pot in the oven and let the fat melt for 6 hours.
3. Midway through the afternoon, take out the pot and ladle some of the luminous golden liquid into a cheesecloth-lined sieve set over a large bowl. When you've extracted as much liquid as you can, return the pot to the oven where the diminished chunks of fat will continue to melt and shrink for a few more hours.
4. Remove the pot again, and pour the contents through the sieve, pressing down on the the greasy, shriveled bits. Throw away bits of fat that remain. They look as if they might be tasty with salt and lime juice—like chicharrónes—but aren't. Pour the liquid lard into containers to cool and solidify, then store in the refrigerator for use in the next few months, or in the freezer, for longer. In addition to pie crusts, you can use lard to make tamales and fry chicken.

CHAPTER 10

HONEY

Happy is the man with a bit of land. To work with living and growing things is to work in partnership with the creator and have a part in shaping the forces that move the world.

—Frank C. Pellett, *A Living from Bees*

A hundred years ago, small diversified farms across America typically had a beehive or two, the same way there were a few chickens running around the yard, a hog, and some fruit trees. On my grandparents' ranch in Wyoming, the bee boxes were fenced off with barbed wire so the cattle wouldn't knock them over. One day when I was about fourteen, I was riding my pony near the boxes and a bee got caught in my hair and couldn't get out. I shook my head and started kicking the pony, who started trotting, and as the bee buzzed louder, I kicked harder and the pony ran faster. I started to cry, and my parents looked at me with amusement, concern, and—I'm guessing now—shame. It was just a little bee. I've read that the worst place to be stung is on the tip of the nose, but until that happens to me, I'm going to stand by the scalp. My mother, who patted baking soda and water on the sting, told me the bee could have escaped if I kept my hair combed.

This is just to say, I was not born a bee whisperer. Bees make me nervous. But they also fascinate me. They are utterly mindless and yet brilliant, fundamentally gentle and communitarian, but capable of swarming, terrorizing and stinging. They vibrate with purpose, fertilize crops, make one of the loveliest foods you'll ever eat.

My primary worry about getting bees was that we were going to offend or injure our neighbors. As Frank C. Pellett, the author of my favorite beekeeping book, put it in 1943, "When the bees sting the neighbors, it leads to annoyance which is unpleasant."

And so when I finally screwed up the nerve to get bees, I followed Pellett's advice and chose the most secluded location on our lot: smack up against our house, invisible from the street, sheltered by our majestic California buckeye tree. There I set up a pair of wooden boxes the same color as our house, for camouflage.

One spring day, shortly after we had acquired our chickens, I drove up to Sonoma County and picked up our bees. They came in two mesh-lined crates. The queens were confined to tiny cages affixed to the sides, each queen cage the size of a pack of Dentyne gum. Mark and I put on veiled hats and gloves and embarked on moving the bees from their temporary crates to their permanent home in the boxes. With a screwdriver, I removed a screw from each tiny queen cage and plugged up the hole with a miniature marshmallow. Over the course of a week, as the workers nibbled away at the marshmallow, they would gradually get to know the queen and by the time the marshmallow was gone and she was free, they would all be ready to welcome her to the colony. We rubber-banded each queen's box to a frame within the hives, and poured the bees into the boxes. They gushed out in a vibrating mass, some of them moving straight into the boxes, some of them forming a cloud around us. It was exhilarating and alarming and as easy as that.

You can't identify with a bee, or intuit what it needs, or hug it. Sometimes bees' energy seems more electrical than biological and you have to learn about bees the way you have to learn physics or calculus. In high school, I was very bad at both. But I was not in high school anymore. I read my bee books and I read beekeeping websites and I liked to observe the bees who, on warm days, dive-bombed in and out of the hive, shooting toward the horizon like guided missiles. I sat outside and watched them come and go, their legs covered with bright orange pollen.

And every few weeks, for the first several months, I pulled out my hat and gloves and went to check inside the hives. I lifted the lid and pulled out the frames and found them loaded with eggs and larvae. Then more eggs, more larvae. Then the frames began to fill up rapidly with honey. What would it taste like? Because our bees lived beside that great, flowering buckeye tree, I Googled buckeye honey. I had heard of orange blossom honey and tupelo honey and eucalyptus honey, but never buckeye honey. We'd have our very own varietal!

There was a lot of literature about bees and buckeyes, but none of it was devoted to delicious honey. The native California buckeye turns out to be toxic to bees, who eat the pollen and feed it to their young, who grow up wingless. "Just make sure your colonies of bees are at least 3 miles away from any buckeye trees," one California beekeeping site warned—one California beekeeping site I had somehow not been following.

For a while, the bees seemed fine living three feet from a poisonous tree. Then, in the late fall, I noticed a sharp decline in activity around the hives. A few weeks later, there was no activity whatsoever. I didn't even put on gloves when I went out and lifted the lid off of the first hive, so certain was I of what it contained: nothing. As I had suspected, not a single bee flew up to greet me or sting me, not in the first hive, and not in the second. I tested the hive for American foulbrood, and it wasn't that. It could have been varroa mites. And it could have been the buckeye. No one could tell me for sure.

Now that the bees didn't need it, I could harvest all the honey, and there was a lot. Capped honeycomb is one of the most extraordinary objects in the natural world, on a par with a full-blown rose or a conch shell. The honey is sticky and liquid and yet immaculately suspended in wax hexagons. Man could not invent such an ingenious container; the best we can do is a jar.

The easiest way to harvest honey is to get your hands on an electric centrifugal extractor, a metal canister into which you insert the frames of honey. Flip a switch, the frames spin around, and the honey flows into the tank and down through a spigot into the waiting jug. Lacking an extractor, I harvested our honey the old-fashioned way: I turned on the stove, stuck the blade of a large knife into the flame until it was hot, scraped all the comb off the frames into a large strainer, and crushed it with a pestle. The honey flowed abundantly from the wax, sticky and slow. Our honey was the color of cognac and we got almost three gallons from that first—and last—crush.

I melted the wax in an "old" pot, as directed by the *Honey Handbook*. It was scummy and dirty and I scraped out roughly a half pound of greasy wax, which is still sitting in a plastic bag in the cupboard. Perhaps one day I will make soap with it. Perhaps not.

The next year I got more bees and watched them closely. One hive failed within weeks. The other failed after six months. Until we move, or until the buckeye falls over in a storm, my beekeeping career is on hiatus.

HONEY

Make it or buy it? Don't get bees for the honey. You can buy honey. Moreover, flavors vary widely from region to region and when you buy honey, you can choose the flavor you like best. The honey from our hives is rich, robust, and a bit heavy, derived from eucalyptus, Himalayan blackberries, sage, lavender, buckeye, and all the sundry plants that thrive in our Mediterranean microclimate. It's good, but if I could choose I would choose the straw-colored alfalfa honey from the high plains of Utah and Wyoming.

You also have to ask yourself: how much honey am I really going to eat? In a bad year—a year when all our bees died—I harvested three gallons of honey. That could last us a decade, and doesn't begin to pay for the hives. I spent about $1,200 on our bee folly. That works out to $25 per cup of honey.

Here is why you should consider getting bees: they are strange and wonderful creatures and they are good for plants and trees and crops. And although our beekeeping experiment was an expensive catastrophe in the end, I'm not at all sorry we tried it.

HONEY CANDY

A few years ago I became infatuated with a brand of imported Italian candies called Honees—hard amber drops that taste, as the name suggests, like honey. But they don't taste as much like honey as my grandmother's honey candy, which I hadn't made or tasted since I was a child. Spray the measuring cup with oil (see page 26) and the honey will slide right out.

Make it or buy it? Make it.
Hassle: A short, simple project—fun and tactile.
Cost comparison: Sweet deal. Honees cost about $0.86 per ounce. Homemade: about $0.18 an ounce for a superior candy.

Butter, for the pan and your hands
1 cup honey
1 cup sugar

1. Generously butter a 9 by 13-inch metal baking pan.
2. Pour the sugar and honey into a heavy-bottomed saucepan. Over high heat, bring to a boil. No need to stir. Let the mixture boil until it registers 300 degrees F on a candy thermometer, at which time it will appear to be nothing but a mass of frothy golden bubbles. Immediately pour the hot mixture into the buttered pan.
3. Let it cool just enough that you can handle it—about 10 minutes. It should still be quite warm and malleable. Butter your hands well, and keep a little butter ready to re-grease as necessary. Scoop the mass of warm honey into your hands and begin to stretch and fold it. Stretch and fold the candy and watch as it turns pale and begins to glisten. It's beautiful—the color of a palomino horse. Keep stretching and pulling until the candy is cool and starts to stiffen.
4. Now, working quickly—you don't want it to harden before you've cut it—put the honey on a clean work surface and roll it into a skinny rope, 4 to 5 feet long. With a clean pair of kitchen shears or scissors, snip it into pieces about ¾ inch long. Let cool completely now.
5. Store the candy, the pieces not touching, in a cookie tin or plastic storage container. You can layer the candy if you use waxed paper, though the candy gets stickier after a few days and may eventually stick even to that.

Makes about 80 pieces of candy

HONEY GRAHAM CRACKERS

Sylvester Graham would be appalled by the "cracker" that today bears his name. Born in Connecticut in 1794, Graham was a Presbyterian minister who preached that people should avoid meat, highly processed grains, and feather beds in order to quash the sex drive. Even married couples were to resist. Graham: "Sexual excess within the pale of wedlock is really a very considerable and an increasing evil." In nineteenth-century American cookbooks you'll find recipes for Graham "wafers" that go something like this: "Beat flour with cold water. No salt. Bake in a hot oven." Such a cracker might quash not just the sex drive, but the life drive.

How we got from there to Honey Maid is a good question, but I'm not sorry we did. Every American child knows that the contemporary graham cracker is a cookie in the guise of a wholesome snack, as does every American parent. Most of us respect the code of silence. This homemade graham cracker is adapted from Karen De Masco's *The Craft of Baking*. It is definitely a cookie.

Make it or buy it? Depends. If you want to reminisce about mediocre childhood snacks but don't want to eat a mediocre childhood snack, make these. If you are serving small children, I recommend Honey Maid Cinnamon Grahams.

Hassle: Mixing these is effortless; cutting them into perfect rectangles, a headache.

Cost comparison: Homemade graham crackers: $0.18 per ounce. Honey Maid Cinnamon Grahams: $0.23 per ounce. Annie's organic graham crackers shaped like bunnies: $0.53 per ounce.

1½ cups all-purpose flour, plus more for rolling
¾ cup whole-wheat flour
¼ cup wheat germ
1½ teaspoons kosher salt
½ teaspoon baking soda
½ teaspoon ground cinnamon
½ pound (2 sticks) unsalted butter, softened
¼ cup light brown sugar, packed
¼ cup granulated sugar
¼ cup honey

1 tablespoon granulated sugar
¼ teaspoon ground cinnamon

1. Sift together the flours, wheat germ, salt, baking soda, and cinnamon. Pour anything that remains in the sifter back in with the other ingredients.
2. In the bowl of a stand mixer, beat the butter, sugars, and honey until fluffy. In two installments, add the dry ingredients, fully incorporating the first before you add the second. Turn the dough onto the counter, knead once or twice, then flatten into a disk. Wrap and refrigerate for at least 30 minutes. (You can refrigerate the dough overnight, but it will need to sit at room temperature for about 20 minutes before you roll it out.)
3. Preheat the oven to 350 degrees F. In a tiny bowl whisk together the topping ingredients.
4. Cut the dough into two portions. On a lightly floured work surface, roll one chunk of dough into a rectangle about ⅛ inch thick. Using a ruler and a rolling pizza cutter, if you have one (a knife works if you don't), cut the dough into 3½ by 2-inch cookies. Transfer to an ungreased baking sheet. Prick with a fork to simulate the dimples in a graham cracker and sprinkle with cinnamon sugar. Repeat with the remaining dough.
5. Bake until slightly colored, about 12 minutes. Remove to a cooling rack. The cookies will still be bendy, but will harden as they cool. They are best after a few hours, but for longer storage, you can keep them in a cookie tin at room temperature for about a week.

Makes approximately 28 crackers

CHAPTER 11

CURED MEATS

Curing your own meat at home raises a host of questions about food safety: Is jerky technically cooked, or is it raw, and therefore can it harbor salmonella? What about *E. coli*? Can you get trichinosis from a naturally cured prosciutto? It takes some of the joy out of the experience when, after eating a slice of prosciutto, you start wondering if your vision is blurring and muscles weakening as you manifest early symptoms of botulism poisoning. Trust me on this.

But there's a risk in everything we do and eat, and you can minimize these risks. Trichinosis—once a serious problem—is now very rare in the United States. Irradiation kills *Trichinella,* as does prolonged freezing, and proper cooking.

Botulism can be prevented with the use of so-called pink salt during the curing process. Pink salt also goes by the names Prague Powder #1 and Insta-Cure #1, and it is ordinary salt that has been spiked with sodium nitrite, which, in addition to killing *Clostridium botulinum,* keeps meat pink. Sodium nitrite is a known carcinogen and you should therefore eat cured meats in moderation, whether made by you or anyone else. You can order pink salt from butcher supply companies (see Appendix), and unless you plan to open a smokehouse, three dollars will buy you a lifetime supply.

BEEF JERKY

How people made beef jerky in 1864: "First, all the bones are taken out; then the flesh is cut into sheets, or thin pieces, put into a strong pickle, or rubbed with dry salt, and packed away for two or three days . . . then spread out in the sun to dry hard."

The following recipe uses the oven, rather than the sun, and makes a spicy-sweet snack that, unlike many commercial jerkies, contains no MSG. The USDA recommends cooking jerky prior to dehydrating it, but the oven temperature in this recipe should be high enough to kill any bacteria. As an extra precaution you can heat the meat for ten minutes at 275 degrees F after it has been dried.

Make it or buy it? Make it.

Hassle: Minimal

Cost comparison: Homemade jerky: $0.93 per ounce. Store-bought jerky: $1.00 to $1.89.

1 pound lean boneless steak, such as sirloin
1 teaspoon kosher salt
½ teaspoon freshly ground black pepper
½ teaspoon red pepper flakes
½ teaspoon onion powder
½ teaspoon garlic powder
2 tablespoons honey
2 tablespoons Worcestershire sauce (preferably homemade; recipe follows)

1. Trim the steak of fat and sinew, then slice into thin strips. Mix the remaining ingredients in a bowl that can accommodate the steak. Taste the marinade and adjust the seasonings as you wish. Add the meat and mix so that every piece is coated with the marinade. Cover and refrigerate overnight.
2. Preheat the oven to 155 degrees F. Place a metal cooling rack on a rimmed cookie sheet, and spread the steak out on the rack. Bake for 6 to 8 hours, until the meat is dark, shriveled, and completely dried.
3. Store airtight in a tin or resealable plastic bag for up to 2 months.

Makes 6 ounces

WORCESTERSHIRE SAUCE

I'm aware that it sounds obsessive to make your own Worcestershire, a condiment you probably use only occasionally, in minute quantities. But wait until you taste this stuff. It's black and shiny, almost iridescent, with so much umami you'll want to eat it with a spoon. Credit goes to Emeril Lagasse for this knockout recipe.

Make it or buy it? Make it.
Hassle: You babysit the sauce all day, but it's not a needy baby.
Cost comparison: A pint of homemade costs about $8.00. Lea & Perrins: $9.50

3 tablespoons olive oil
2 large onions, chopped
2 serrano chiles, chopped, with seeds
2 tablespoons minced garlic
1 teaspoon freshly ground black pepper
Two 2-ounce cans anchovies, drained
¼ teaspoon ground cloves
1 tablespoon kosher salt
1 lemon, peel and white pith removed and discarded
2 cups dark corn syrup
1 cup molasses
1 quart distilled white vinegar
¼ pound fresh horseradish, peeled and grated

1. In a heavy pot over high heat, combine the oil, onions, and chiles. Cook, stirring, until the vegetables are soft, about 3 minutes. Add the garlic, pepper, anchovies, cloves, salt, lemon, corn syrup, molasses, vinegar, 2 cups water, and the horseradish. Bring to a boil.
2. Reduce the heat and simmer, stirring occasionally, until the mixture barely coats a wooden spoon, about 6 hours.
3. Strain through a fine-mesh sieve into a bowl and let cool to room temperature. Store in a bottle, preferably one with a spigot. Keeps in the refrigerator indefinitely.

Makes about 1 quart

SALT PORK

Almanzo ate the sweet, mellow baked beans. He ate the bit of salt pork that melted like cream in his mouth.

—*Farmer Boy*

There was no food I fantasized about more as a child than salt pork, except maybe watermelon rind pickle. But since no one I knew ate salt pork and I had never seen it at the grocery store, I assumed it was extinct, a food we left behind in our sod homes on the prairie, along with the dandelion wine, corncob jelly, and chokecherry jam.

Then, in my twenties in a grim New York City Food Emporium, I came across a square brick of Hormel salt pork in the refrigerator near the baloney. I carried it home to my apartment and unwrapped it reverently. I could not believe how seductive it was, a garish pastrami pink generously striped with white fat that really did look as if it would melt "like cream" in my mouth. I immediately sliced it and fried it and took a bite. I spat it out. It was more mineral than meat. I couldn't believe that this was what I had been pining for all those years.

Maybe it was, maybe it wasn't. We'll never know exactly how salt pork tasted in days of yore. Pigs were different, preserving methods were different, and tastes were different. Today there's interest in salt pork among hard-core Civil War reenactors, but recipes are not in heavy rotation on the Food Network. Salt pork recipes in antique cookbooks, like the 1830 *Frugal Housewife* ("Dedicated to those who are not ashamed of economy"), generally involve layering the pork with salt in a barrel, putting a stone on top to weight it down, and sticking it in the cellar. From the *Frugal Housewife*: "Look to it once in a while, for the first few weeks, and if the salt has all melted, throw in more. This brine, scalded and skimmed every time it is used, will continue good twenty years."

She was a very frugal housewife. There are other methods for salting pork today, like the one in *Charcuterie* by Michael Ruhlman and Brian Polcyn. It's worth making your own salt pork just to flavor baked beans.

Make it or buy it? Make it.
Hassle: Not bad
Cost comparison: Homemade salt pork: $3.00 per pound. Hormel: $5.85 a pound.

One 4-pound chunk pork belly, skin on
¾ cup kosher salt
6 tablespoons sugar
4½ teaspoons pink salt (see Appendix)

1. Cut the pork belly into chunks the size of your fist. In a small bowl, mix together the salt, sugar, and pink salt. Toss and coat the pieces of pork with the cure. Pack the pork in a crock and store, covered, in a cool place, like the cellar. Alternatively, you can put the meat in a resealable plastic bag in the refrigerator.
2. After seven days, remove from the refrigerator. I mean cellar. Unlike store-bought 7 pork, it will be flabby and a dusty, dispirited pink, but what it lacks in beauty it makes up for in succulence. Rinse the meat, pat dry, and wrap tightly. Store in the refrigerator for 2 weeks. Freeze for longer storage.

Makes 2½ pounds

Pork belly—a luscious and fatty cut from the midsection of a pig—typically requires a special order from the butcher and will cost between $5 and $8 a pound if you shop at a Western supermarket. If you want it cheaper and sooner and happen to live in an area with a large Asian population, Chinese supermarkets stock pork belly as routinely as Western supermarkets stock boneless, skinless chicken breasts. I've bought a lot of $2.99-per-pound pork bellies from a local Chinese market, no special order required. I'll warn you, though: not only are these pork bellies never organic, once I bought a skin-on pork belly from a Chinese market and it came with big, fleshy nipples. Easy to detach, but disconcerting.

BAKED BEANS

In Western novels and movies, cowboys are always stabbing open cans of beans and spooning them up cold by the fire while telling stories. So I suppose canned beans are traditional in their way. My paternal grandmother—the daughter, wife, and mother of cattlemen—was modestly famous for her baked beans, which she ladled from a richly glazed brown ceramic bean pot. "Would you like another bean, Bob?" she would ask my grandfather, and then spoon a pint or so of beans onto his blue-and-white Poppytrail china plate. *Would you like another bean, Bob?* My sister and I got a big laugh out of the way she talked.

After she died, I inherited my grandmother's bean pot, as well as the Poppytrail china and her bulging recipe file. During a fit of nostalgia a few years ago, I pulled out her famous recipe for beans. I sighed. Here it is verbatim: "Wiener Bean Pot: 2 1 lb. cans pork & beans, 1 envelope dry onion soup mix, ⅓ c catsup, ¼ cup water, 2T brown sugar, 1 T mustard, 10 frankfurters (sliced)."

I can't empty a packet of onion soup mix into a recipe (with one exception—see page 114) without cringing, just as I can't say, "Mark, would you like another bean?" or speak the words "wiener bean pot" without a disrespectful smirk. I've used the bean pot constantly over the years since my grandmother's death, but I use my own recipe. There's nothing wrong with canned beans, but they don't have as much personality as these do.

By the way, you need to eat the jelly-like salt pork, skin and all. Like cream, it melts on your tongue.

Make it or buy it? Make it.
Hassle: Harder than stabbing open a can
Cost comparison: Homemade: $0.92 per cup. Van Camp's: $0.86 per cup. Bush's: $1.65.

1 pound dried navy beans
1 tablespoon neutral vegetable oil
½ pound salt pork, cut into 1½-inch cubes
1 onion, chopped
1 tablespoon Dijon mustard
⅓ cup maple syrup

⅓ cup dark brown sugar, packed

1 teaspoon freshly ground black pepper

½ teaspoon cayenne pepper

1 apple, peeled and cut into ½-inch cubes

2 teaspoons kosher salt, plus more to taste

1. Soak the beans overnight in water to cover.
2. Drain the beans. Preheat the oven to 300 degrees F.
3. Heat the oil in a Dutch oven and brown the salt pork. Add the onion and cook, stirring occasionally, until the onion is translucent. (You can use a bean pot to make this, but it generates fewer dishes to use the Dutch oven in which you fry the pork.)
4. To the fried pork, add the beans and all the other ingredients. Stir well and add 6 cups of water.
5. Bake for 3 to 4 hours, replenishing water as necessary. Midway through the cooking, taste for salt and adjust. When they're done, the beans should be very soft, but not falling apart. Serve immediately or cool and store for up to 5 days in the refrigerator.

Makes 2½ quarts beans, to serve 10

CANADIAN BACON

Canadian bacon isn't actually Canadian; it's what the British call "back bacon," and it consists of lean pork, brined and smoked. Store-bought Canadian bacon is watery and flabby and typically cut too thin. If I'd known how to smoke my own Canadian bacon at the time, I would have lasted a lot longer on the South Beach Diet. This recipe makes a sweet, substantial bacon that is a lovely seashell pink.

Make it or buy it? Make it.

Hassle: It's a whale of a hassle when your house burns down, so heed warnings about smoking (see page 172).

Cost comparison: Homemade Canadian bacon: $4.00 per pound. Supermarket Canadian bacon such as Land o' Frost: $10.00. Jones Canadian bacon: $13.00.

1½ cups kosher salt
1 cup light brown sugar, packed
8 teaspoons pink salt (see Appendix)
1 tablespoon vanilla extract (page 260)
One 4-pound pork loin

1. Combine the kosher salt, sugar, pink salt, and 1 gallon water in a large pot and bring to a boil. Remove from the heat and cool to room temperature. Stir in the vanilla and chill overnight.
2. Place the pork in the cold brine and weight it down with a plate to keep it submerged. Let rest in the refrigerator for 2 days.
3. Remove the loin from the brine, rinse well, and pat dry. Place on a rack in the refrigerator to air-dry for 24 hours.
4. An hour before you plan to smoke the pork, take it out of the refrigerator to bring to room temperature.
5. Smoke the pork until it registers 150 degrees F when tested in its thickest part with an instant-read thermometer. (See page 172 for smoking details.) You can slice and fry the bacon immediately, or wrap tightly and store in the refrigerator for a week. For longer storage, wrap tightly and freeze.

Makes 3¾ pounds

SMOKING

Even if you don't have a dedicated smoker, you can still smoke just about anything short of a whole pig in a Weber kettle grill or in a pot on the stovetop. Here's how.

SMOKING IN A CHARCOAL GRILL

1. Soak two large handfuls of wood chips (mesquite, applewood, etc.) in a pan of water for half an hour.
2. Remove the grate from the grill and place a handful of unlit charcoal in the belly of the grill, pushing it over to one side. Top with a handful of the soaked chips. Light some additional charcoal in the chimney and when the coals are smoldering, dump them on top of the chips. Top these hot coals with the rest of the damp wood chips.
3. For a drip pan you can use a foil pan from the supermarket or a metal bread pan from your kitchen, preferably one you don't care about. Place it in the belly of the grill opposite the wood chips and charcoal. Put the grate on the barbecue. Fill another pan with water, which will help keep the temperature down inside the grill, and put this next to the drip pan. (Ultimately, you want the temperature to hover around 250 degrees F.) Close the grill and pop a long-stemmed thermometer through the vent. Give it some time to get really hot and smoky in there—you want it somewhere between 200 and 300 degrees F.
4. When the temperature is within range, put the piece of meat on the grill directly over the drip pan and under the vent. (If the vent is right above the heat source, the smoke will shoot straight up without wafting around the meat and imparting its flavor.) How long you smoke depends on the size of the piece of meat; I always check the internal temperature after about 20 minutes, just to see how things are going.

SMOKING ON THE STOVETOP

Before you start, you need a working exhaust fan and a fire extinguisher or a full carton of baking soda handy. I've done a lot of smoking on the stove and had only one near disaster, but it was harrowing. Here's what I did wrong. First, I didn't soak the wood chips—I was in a hurry and just dipped them in the water for a minute. Then I dumped the barely damp chips into the pot, added the pork belly, and cranked the heat up to high. I left the room for half an hour, enjoyed a lively phone conversation, and forgot about the meat. When I returned and lifted the lid of the pot, the chips spontaneously ignited. I very carefully carried the whole pot outdoors, where it flamed lustily for a few minutes before the dregs of a box of baking soda and an entire sack of flour ended the excitement. Bacon and pot were ruined, but the house still stands. Soak the chips for the full amount of time, keep the heat moderate, don't leave the room, and know exactly how you'll extinguish a fire in the unlikely event you set one.

1. Soak some wood chips in water for at least half an hour. You want them to smolder, not ignite.

2. Choose a large metal pot that will easily accommodate the meat with plenty of room for smoke to circulate. Line the pot with foil.

3. In the bottom of the pot, place a handful of your damp wood chips, and on top of them place a double-layered piece of foil to serve as a drip pan. You do not want fat and meat juices dripping on the smoking chips.

4. Set up a metal rack so that it straddles the drip pan. I use a small stainless-steel platform with long legs that cost $0.69 at a Chinese kitchen supply store.

5. Place the meat on the rack. Cover the top of the pan with more foil and put a lid on top of that, slightly ajar. Turn on the exhaust fan full blast and the heat to high. As soon as you see wisps of smoke snaking out of the pot, turn the heat down to medium-low. You do not want an inferno; you want a long, leisurely smoke. You don't need to hover over the pot, but you should stay near to monitor the situation. Check the temperature of the meat after about 20 minutes with an instant-read thermometer.

6. When the meat is done, turn off the stove. Take the pot outside, as a lot of smoke will gush out. Lift out the meat and cool on a rack to room temperature.

BACON

I came of age in the 1980s believing that bacon was an evil force in American culture, right up there with cigarettes, malt liquor, and J. R. Ewing. Virtuous people didn't eat bacon; they got up in the morning, went for a jog, and ate a bowl of muesli or an egg white omelet. They were all about the Pritikin diet.

Times have changed. At some point in the last few years, bacon became everyone's naughty best friend. Even vegetarians love bacon. Dieters love bacon! There's a bacon-of-the-month club and I went to a trendy restaurant where cake was served topped with candied bacon. It was insanely delicious and also insane. People wear T-shirts silkscreened with strips of bacon and get tattoos of pigs on their biceps. Bacon, bacon, bacon, enough with the bacon. I feel about bacon the way I do about Tina Fey. Sometimes I get sick of the adulation and want to dislike bacon.

Except, of course, I can't. It's bacon.

I was intimidated by the prospect of making bacon, but it's extremely straightforward. You jacket a piece of pork belly in salt and spices, let it sit for a few days, rinse it, then smoke it (see page 172). There's almost infinite flexibility in the spicing, which is the fun of making it yourself. My favorite bacon is coated in fruity—almost plummy—Aleppo pepper, and is inspired by a recipe in *Ethan Stowell's New Italian Kitchen*. This bacon is sweeter and meatier than any supermarket product I've tasted. Plus, you can slice it as thick as you want. Alas, you may be unable to slice it as thin as you want. When I serve homemade bacon it appears in either scraggly little scraps or chunky slabs, often on the same plate.

One final reason to make bacon is that people will think you're rad. I was standing in line at the Chinese butcher one day and pointed to an enormous slab of pork belly. A young man said, "What are you going to do with that?" I said, "I'm making bacon." He began salaaming and said, "I revere you." It was embarrassing, and more evidence of the esteem in which people currently hold bacon.

Make it or buy it? Try it! Decide for yourself.

Hassle: Easier than you'd expect, but not precisely "easy"

Cost comparison: Using cheap pork belly from the Chinese market, homemade
    bacon costs about $3.50 per pound. Supermarket bacon ranges from $4.99 to

$11.00 per pound. If you're just trying to lowball the Piggly Wiggly, you can, though not by much.

¼ cup kosher salt
2 teaspoons pink salt (see Appendix)
½ cup light brown sugar
⅓ cup ground Aleppo pepper (see Appendix)
One 2-pound slab skin-on pork belly

1. Mix the salts, sugar, and pepper in a small bowl. Rub the seasoning over the entire surface of the pork belly. Try to work it into every cranny. Place the belly in a bowl that will hold it snugly. Cover tightly. Refrigerate for 7 days, turning every 1 or 2 days to ensure the pork is covered in cure.

2. Remove the belly from the refrigerator and rinse well. Pat dry. Place the belly on a cooling rack over a baking sheet in the refrigerator and air-dry, uncovered, for 2 days.

3. Smoke the bacon until an instant-read thermometer inserted into the thickest part of the meat reaches a temperature of 140 degrees F. You can use a smoker, a kettle grill, or a large pot on the stovetop (see page 172).

4. When the bacon is smoked, remove it from the smoking vessel and cool for a few minutes. With a sharp knife, ease off the skin.

5. Cool to room temperature, then wrap and chill until firm. Slice to eat now, store in the refrigerator for up to 2 weeks, or freeze for up to several months.

Makes about 1½ pounds

PANCETTA

The only trouble with making American bacon is that you have to smoke it. Not so pancetta. Pancetta is unsmoked Italian bacon and it's the killer app in countless pastas, soups, and Italian braised dishes. If you're used to buying your pancetta from the deli counter, expensive skinny slice by expensive skinny slice, the day you unwrap your stout chunk of easy, cheap homemade pancetta you'll think you're super-clever. This is adapted from the recipe that appears in Michael Ruhlman and Brian Polcyn's *Charcuterie*, an indispensable guide to curing your own meat.

Make it or buy it? Make it.
Hassle: Easier than bacon; one of the simpler curing projects
Cost comparison: Homemade: $4.00 per pound. Primo Taglio: $29.00 per pound.

CURE
4 garlic cloves, minced
2 teaspoons pink salt (see Appendix)
¼ cup kosher salt
2 tablespoons light brown sugar
2 tablespoons black peppercorns
2 tablespoons juniper berries
1 tablespoon coriander seeds
1 teaspoon blade mace or freshly grated nutmeg

5 pounds fresh pork belly, skin removed, cut into 3 pieces
2 tablespoons coarsely ground black pepper, for sprinkling the cured meat

1. Place all the ingredients for the cure in a spice grinder and process for 1 minute until combined.
2. Rub the cure all over the pork belly, trying to work it into every cranny.
3. Place the pork belly in a snug container, cover tightly, and refrigerate for 7 days, checking occasionally to make sure it's covered in cure. If not, redistribute the cure.
4. After 7 days check to make sure the belly feels firm at its thickest point; if it does, you are ready for the next step. If not, leave it in for a couple of days more.

5. Remove the belly from the container and rinse well under cold water. Pat dry. Sprinkle the meat all over with the cracked pepper.
6. Wrap in cheesecloth, tie like a package, and hang it in a cool place for 1 week. I hang it from a pipe in the crawl space.
7. Unwrap the meat and cut it into 4-ounce chunks. Freeze what you won't be using in the next couple of weeks.

Makes 4 pounds

PROSCIUTTO

Over the course of nearly 400 days, prosciutto undergoes a maturation process that comes to fullness in the remarkable bloom of aroma when the ham is later opened. That moment each year is like a birth, a long season's waiting for the revelation of what can only be imagined by looking from the outside. Prosciutto is an act of patience and a stunning transformation, raw flesh to rose-colored, mildly salted delicacy that nearly melts on the tongue. Your own prosciutto is likely to taste like none that you have ever tasted before.

—Paul Bertolli, *Cooking by Hand*

DUCK PROSCIUTTO

I started with duck prosciutto. It sounded easier than pig prosciutto and you can't buy it at the grocery store. I found two straightforward recipes, one from the chef Gary Danko and one from *Charcuterie*, then married the two.

2 cups kosher salt
One 8-ounce duck breast
2 teaspoons ground fennel
Grated zest of 1 orange

1 tablespoon freshly ground black pepper
1 tablespoon ground coriander

1. Put the salt in a bowl and roll the duck in it. You want the duck completely jacketed in salt. Cover and refrigerate for 24 hours.
2. Remove the duck from the salt, rinse, and pat dry. Coat with the remaining ingredients.
3. Wrap the duck in cheesecloth and tie up with a string, like a present. Hang the duck breast for 2 weeks in a cool place, like from a sturdy pipe in a crawl space, or from a hook in a closet.
4. Unwrap the breast, which will now be firm and wizened. Vigorously brush off any mold with a clean toothbrush, place the breast in a plastic bag, and put it in the freezer.
5. When the prosciutto is frozen solid, with a very sharp knife slice off as much meat as you want to serve, cutting it very thin and letting it come to room temperature before eating. Store the remaining prosciutto in the freezer and slice as needed.

Makes 1 duck prosciutto

The duck prosciutto was port-colored and capped with a thick layer of creamy fat and a thinner layer of very chewy skin. Each slice was too small and stiff to drape over a piece of melon, but on its own terms it was delicious or I thought so, anyway. I gave a tidbit to my husband and he grimaced, saying, "What *is* this?"

I understood his distaste. It was delicious—but chewy and the duck skin was cold, flabby, and pimply. It was delicious—but not something I badly wanted to eat, though I did, almost every night until it was all gone, a few little shards with a glass of wine.

There were two other problems with this prosciutto. First, it was expensive. No one in my family hunts, and although by that time we had acquired some ducks, I was done with slaughter. At $18.99 per pound for duck breast, after shrinkage my duck prosciutto cost about as much as real prosciutto di Parma, which we all liked a lot better. And that was the second problem with duck prosciutto: we all liked prosciutto di Parma a lot better.

And so one morning I drove to Marin Sun Farms in Point Reyes, California, and bought a $97, fourteen-pound pork leg. I paid extra for a pastured pig because, as Ruhlman writes, "The quality of the end result is entirely dependent on the hog, where it lived, what it ate, how fat it grew." The pigs at Marin Sun Farms supposedly feed on wild acorns, and what could be more toothsome than wild acorns? I have no idea, but wild acorns sounded right. I brought the haunch home and promptly submerged it under five pounds of kosher salt.

"You're wasting a lot of salt," Owen said, looking up from *Archie and Veronica*. "We don't have an endless amount of salt in the sea."

"I think we might," I said.

"We do?"

I thought for a minute. "I don't know."

"What are we going to do with all that?" Mark asked.

"Eat it," I said. "We're going to save buckets of money."

He watched me for a minute. He said, "It's like we need a ride and you've decided to build a car."

After I had refrigerated the salted meat for a few weeks, I brushed it off, slathered it in lard and peppercorns, wrapped the meat in cheesecloth, tied it with twine, and hung it from a pipe in our crawl space. Every few weeks, I would go check on the prosciutto to make sure it hadn't been chewed down by a rat or attacked by flies. It was always just hanging there peacefully. After six months, I cut it down one afternoon, laid it out on the kitchen counter, unwrapped its bandages, and beheld a monstrosity: a bulbous hunk of what might have once been meat, covered with luxuriant chalk-green mold and cracked peppercorns that resembled small black beetles. It was too odd to be disgusting. It now weighed nine pounds, some of that bone, some of it mold. I put it on the dining table and there it sat, worrying me, until the next morning, when after several cups of coffee, I recklessly sawed off a hunk.

Inside, the flesh was beautiful, camellia pink swathed in plush white fat. I took a bite. It tasted exactly like prosciutto. Spectacular. I had done it.

About a minute later, I began Googling "botulism homemade prosciutto" because Ruhlman's recipe does not, like some, include pink salt. After forty-eight hours, when it was clear I was not going to die of botulism, I began Googling "trichinosis homemade prosciutto." A few weeks later, when I showed no symptoms of trichinosis, I began serving the prosciutto.

It was wonderful—once I got past my fears. Let's say that buried inside that rind I can slice out six pounds of prosciutto. Including the price of salt, pepper, lard, and cheesecloth, I'll have paid about $17 per pound for prosciutto. A deal, given that even the mediocre supermarket brand prosciutto sells for $31 per pound. There are problems, though. This is a lot of prosciutto and I suspect it will be hulking in our already overcrowded refrigerator for months to come. Moreover, I cannot slice it neatly and I do not plan to buy a slicer. When I cut the prosciutto, the slices resemble slices of Christmas ham—thick. All things considered, unless you are a staunch and serious hobbyist and also a pig farmer, I think you should buy your prosciutto.

Make it or buy it? Buy it.

REUBEN SANDWICH

As with a lot of iconic American dishes—the martini, the French dip sandwich, Crab Louie—the history of the Reuben sandwich is widely disputed. Was it invented in New York City in 1914? Or in Omaha in the 1930s? In Lincoln in 1937? Disputed as well are its components. A Reuben can be made with corned beef or pastrami. I prefer pastrami. To make a Reuben, thinly slice pastrami, enough to make at least three layers on the bread, and heat in a skillet until the fat in the meat starts to soften. The bread must be rye (see page 12) and you should butter the *outside*—it gives the sandwich a nice crust. Now drain a scoop of homemade sauerkraut (see page 183) and mound it on the unbuttered side of a slice of bread. Top this with a generous quantity of Russian dressing (see page 184). Top the dressing with the warm meat, and top the meat with a slice of Swiss cheese. Close the sandwich with the other slice of bread, unbuttered side down. You can cook the sandwich in the hot skillet in which you warmed the meat, weighting the sandwich down with a smaller heavier skillet before flipping and cooking on the other side. If you have a panini press, that will also do the job and leave ridges in your bread. The sandwich is done when the crust is toasted and crunchy, and the cheese is melted and oozing out. It's a big mess and really delicious.

PASTRAMI

Under the entry for "pastrami," *The Oxford Companion to Food* quotes a traveler through nineteenth-century Romania who commented on the "thin, black, leather-like pieces of meat dried and browned in the sun, and with salt and squashed flies."

While there are no squashed flies on the pastrami at Ralph's, that is about the best that can be said of it. Thinly sliced and flattened into aseptic plastic packets, supermarket pastrami is sweet, flaccid, and watery. Real pastrami is fatty, rich, and peppery, but unless you live near a delicatessen, it's hard to get your hands on any. Fortunately, though labor-intensive, it's quite possible to make.

I made my first pastrami using a five-pound brisket and a recipe from Michael Ruhlman and Brian Polcyn's *Charcuterie*. We carved away at this immensity of pastrami for weeks, used it in cold sandwiches, and scrambled it with eggs. It tasted fabulous, but there was so much of it and it was very, very lean. I subsequently pastramied some short ribs, another *Charcuterie* suggestion, and ended up with fist-size chunks of meat that were deliciously fatty, but that shredded rather than sliced, sort of like pulled pork (see page 84).

Then one day there was a bargain on lamb shoulder so I bought one and pastramied that. Lamb pastrami turns out to be slightly musky, with the perfect ratio of meat to fat. And it is very traditional. In *The Book of Jewish Food*, Claudia Roden writes that the original old-style Romanian pastrami was made with mutton. This recipe uses Ruhlman's pastrami technique, with a spice rub inspired by a recipe from Marcus Samuelsson's *Aquavit*.

(LAMB) PASTRAMI

Make it or buy it? Make it.

Hassle: Prodigious

Cost comparison: Homemade beef pastrami costs about $4.00 per pound. Super-market pastrami: $10.00 to $15.00 per pound.

BRINE

1½ cups kosher salt

1 cup granulated sugar

8 teaspoons pink salt (see Appendix)

1 tablespoon pickling spice

½ cup dark brown sugar, packed

¼ cup honey

1 tablespoon garlic powder

One boneless 4- to 5-pound lamb shoulder, or beef brisket, short ribs, or chuck roast

3 tablespoons black peppercorns

1 tablespoon coriander seeds

¼ cup mild paprika

2 tablespoons Chinese five-spice powder

1. Combine all the brine ingredients with 1 gallon water in a pot large enough to later hold the lamb. Bring the brine to a simmer, stirring until the salt and sugars dissolve. Remove from the heat, allow to cool to room temperature, and refrigerate until well chilled.

2. Put the meat in the brine and place a plate on top of the meat to keep it completely submerged. Refrigerate for 3 days.

3. Remove the meat from the brine, rinse well, and pat dry.

4. In a dry skillet, toast the peppercorns and coriander seeds until fragrant but not burned. Cool and grind in a spice grinder. Combine with the paprika and five-spice powder. Coat the meat.

5. Smoke to an internal temperature of 150 degrees F. (See sidebar on smoking, page 172.)

6. Preheat the oven to 275 degrees F.
7. Place the smoked meat in 1 inch of water in a Dutch oven and bring the water to a simmer over high heat. Cover, place in the oven, and braise for 2 to 3 hours, until tender. Cool to room temperature. Pat dry. Wrap tightly and store in the refrigerator for 1 week. For longer storage, freeze.

Makes about 5 pounds

SAUERKRAUT

You can use purple cabbage or green; you can add dill, fennel, or mustard seed and omit the apple and caraway. You can add shredded beets, pineapple, grapes, or quince, though the minute you add chiles and garlic you're not making sauerkraut, you're making kimchi (page 148). I always disliked sauerkraut until I made it. It's an essential component of the Reuben but also works wonders on a grilled cheese sandwich.

Make it or buy it? Make it.
Hassle: Engineering challenges
Cost comparison: Homemade will set you back $2.00 per quart. Bubbies: $5.70.

1 small head green cabbage, about 1½ pounds untrimmed
1 tablespoon fine sea salt
1 tablespoon caraway seeds
1 apple, peeled and grated
¼ cup whey (page 47), optional

1. Slice the cabbage thin and chop into pieces about 1 inch long. In a large bowl, toss with the other ingredients, massaging the salt into the shreds. If you have time, let the cabbage macerate for 1 or 2 hours at room temperature.
2. Pack the cabbage tightly into a wide-mouth quart canning jar. Find a smaller jar that will fit inside the rim of the quart jar—a jelly jar, for instance. Fill it with water and cap it tightly. Place it on top of the cabbage and press down so the juices are forced up and over the vegetables. Cover the whole contraption with

a clean apron or T-shirt and tie tightly around the middle. You want the kraut able to breathe, but inaccessible to flies.

3. Place the contraption on a tray on the counter. (Occasionally, the jar will overflow.) Let the kraut ferment at room temperature, tasting daily. When you like the flavor—for me, it takes about 5 days—dismantle the contraption, cap the jar, and store in the refrigerator.

Makes 1 quart

RUSSIAN DRESSING

Russian dressing—that thick, coral-hued salad bar staple—may once have been made with caviar, which may be how it acquired the name. One 1923 recipe for Russian dressing called for mayo, chili sauce, green pepper, onions, pimientos, and "if liked, add one tablespoon caviar."

Don't like. Caviar would be wasted in a Reuben, for which you want a basic Russian, like this one. Wish-Bone is too sweet. This dressing is plenty sweet, but the horseradish and Worcestershire push back hard.

Make it or buy it? Make it.
Hassle: Mixing is all
Cost comparison: Homemade: $1.00 per cup. Wish-Bone: $2.20 per cup.

½ cup mayonnaise (page 39)
2 tablespoons ketchup
1½ teaspoons horseradish (page 89)
½ teaspoon Worcestershire sauce (page 166)
½ teaspoon onion powder
1 tablespoon pickle relish (page 241)
Salt and freshly ground black pepper

Stir everything together and taste. Adjust seasoning with salt and pepper. Store in a jar in the refrigerator, where it will keep for months.

Makes a scant cup

DILL PICKLES

Juicy and refreshing. Hard to go back to Vlasic.

Make it or buy it? Make it.
Hassle: Simple
Cost comparison: $2.00 per quart for homemade. Close to $6.00 for Vlasic.

4 pickling cucumbers, 1½ to 2 pounds
2 garlic cloves, peeled
1 teaspoon coriander seeds
2 teaspoons red pepper flakes
1 bay leaf
A few sprigs of fresh dill
1 teaspoon yellow mustard seeds
Peel of 1 lemon, removed with a vegetable peeler in strips
2 fresh grape leaves (optional, but the tannin keeps the pickles crisp)
2 tablespoons fine sea salt

1. Cut the tips off the cucumbers. Place the spices and lemon peel in a 1-quart canning jar. Add the grape leaves and pack the cucumbers in vertically.
2. Dissolve the salt in 2½ cups water and pour over the cukes, making sure the vegetables are submerged in the brine. Find a smaller jar that will fit inside the rim of the quart jar—a jelly jar, for instance. Fill it with water and cap it tightly. Place it on top of the cucumbers and press down so the juices are forced up and over the vegetables. Cover the whole contraption with a clean apron or T-shirt and tie tightly around the middle. You want the pickles able to breathe but inaccessible to flies.
3. Place the contraption on a tray on the counter (occasionally, the jar will overflow). Let it ferment for 5 days.
4. Dismantle the contraption, cap the jar, and store in the refrigerator.

Makes 4 pickles

APPLE-SAGE BREAKFAST SAUSAGE

While bacon is very in, sausage is still kind of out. Maybe it's just the way it looks—like stubby fingers on a fat little man—or the fact that "how sausage gets made" is code for "disgusting." With reason. I hate grinding meat and stuffing sausage, but this particular sausage can be ground in the food processor and served in patty form.

Make it or buy it? Make it.

Hassle: Moderate

Cost comparison: Homemade: $3.20 per pound depending on the price of pork. Jimmy Dean: $6.10 per pound.

3½ pounds untrimmed boneless pork shoulder, cut into ¾-inch chunks

2 tablespoons kosher salt

4 tablespoons fresh sage, finely chopped

1 tablespoon minced garlic

¼ cup light brown sugar, packed

1 teaspoon freshly ground black pepper

1 large apple, peeled, cored, and chopped

1. Mix all the ingredients until the seasonings are evenly distributed. Chill.
2. Grind the mixture in a meat grinder, or pulse very small handfuls in a food processor.
3. Mix well, with either a wooden spoon or the paddle attachment of a mixer.
4. In a small skillet, fry a small portion of the sausage and taste for seasoning. Adjust.
5. Form the sausage into patties and fry immediately, or roll into a log and slice as needed. Store in the refrigerator for up to 3 days. Freeze for longer storage. It's a good idea to divide the sausage into small packets, so you can take one at a time out of the freezer. This recipe makes a lot of sausage.

Makes 3½ pounds

HOT DOGS

I was pretty sure homemade hot dogs were a bad idea. But I had also once thought this about hot dog buns, bagels, Worcestershire sauce, and bacon and I had been mistaken. So I decided to give the hot dog recipe in *Charcuterie* a try. The results:

Day 1. I buy the meat. Ruhlman calls for boneless short ribs in his hot dogs. I think that this is a very choice cut for a sausage ordinarily made with "parts," and I'm not sure how I feel about that. I chill the meat. (Chilled meat: the prerequisite to any non-disastrous sausage-making venture.)

Day 2. I assemble the grinder and feed the meat into the machine. It always sounds very easy when people describe grinding meat. It ordinarily occupies a sentence in a recipe. In my kitchen, grinding meat always occupies at least an hour. Every minute or so I disassemble the grinder with fat-slicked hands and remove, with the point of a steak knife, the web of membrane that blocks the holes in the die. By the time I am done, the meat is no longer chilled, but slimy and warm. I mix in the salt and pink salt (see page 164 and Appendix) and put the meat in the refrigerator for a resting period that Ruhlman writes will "develop the myosin protein that helps give the hot dog a good bind and a good bite." I lie down on the sofa for my own resting period.

Day 3. I retrieve the meat paste from the refrigerator and stir in dry mustard, paprika, ground coriander, pepper, garlic, and two spoonfuls of corn syrup. From the bowl now wafts the unmistakable perfume of hot dog. This is exciting! I know that fennel seed makes Italian sausage taste like Italian sausage and sage makes breakfast sausage taste like breakfast sausage, but I have never paused to wonder what makes a hot dog taste like a hot dog. Perhaps because I was afraid of what the answer might be. But now I know. You could rub this simple spice mixture on a piece of flounder or chicken and people would be very confused—*Why, this chicken tastes like hot dog!* You could spread it on buttered toast, you could toss it with pasta.

I spread the wiener sludge on a cookie sheet and pop it into the freezer. Forty-five minutes later, I prize off gelid shards of eraser-colored paste and ease them back inside the grinder. The meat is now fine and slippery and obsequiously spurts from the grinder's apertures in squiggly worms the texture of liverwurst. Meat paste flies and oozes in all directions. As directed, I spread what paste I manage to extract from the machine on the cookie sheet once again, and back in the freezer it goes.

Meanwhile, I decide to clean the mess on the grinder. Raw pink hot dog paste has worked its way into every crevice of the machine, and to get it out I have to probe delicate orifices with a bit of damp paper towel wrapped around a toothpick. Thirty minutes later, when I have almost finished detailing the grinder, it is time to remove the meat from the freezer again. I put it in the food processor to whip it to a "uniform paste."

Because I dislike stuffing sausages, I momentarily consider making hot dog patties, but unlike breakfast sausage hot dogs by definition are tubular. So I pull out the tub of sheep intestine casings—limp, translucent, and packed in salt—and soak them briefly in cool water. Then I affix an intestine to the end of the grinder's sausage-stuffing attachment. I feed the mixture through the grinder one last time to midwife eight stubby, phallic wieners.

I pull out the bag of hickory chips, rig up the stovetop smoking apparatus (see page 172), and smoke the dogs for 45 minutes. They shrink and torque and I plunge them briefly into a bowl of ice water to chill. Then they go back into the refrigerator.

Day 4. I grill those hot dogs for dinner.

How are they? Good! No better or worse than the usual, but good. I have achieved the fine-grained, baloney-like texture of hot dogs you might buy at a baseball game, minus the disconcerting stray cartilage chips. Cosmetically they don't quite measure up—they are squat and bulbous—but all in all, I am proud.

But they have been an expensive endeavor. Ruhlman estimates that his recipe yields two and a half pounds of hot dogs from two and a half pounds of short rib meat, but I end up with a scant pound and a half of stuffed dogs. Short rib meat costs six dollars a pound and hot dogs, on average, cost five dollars a pound. This means I had made ten-dollar-per-pound hot dogs. With a tremendous amount of work, I had been able to turn a respectable cut of beef—so delicious braised and served with potatoes and a glass of zinfandel—into very expensive wieners.

They are, on the other hand, despite the dose of pink salt, comparatively healthful hot dogs, frankfurters that a person can eat without any squeamishness. And most people I know feel squeamish about hot dogs.

This is rational. The vast majority of commercial dogs are made of industrial meat scraps, which often include animal skins. In a typical mass-market hot dog, the percentage of fat—including, in some cases, trans fats—is almost twice as high as the fat naturally enrobing a beef short rib. Big food companies make hot dogs with mechanically separated meat (msm) that, as described matter-of-factly by the United States Department of Agriculture, is "a paste-like and batter-like meat product produced by forcing bones with attached edible meat under high pressure through a sieve or similar device to separate the bone from the edible meat tissue." I read that and I wanted to unread it. I bet you do, too. Beef franks no longer contain this "batter-like" substance because of the risk of bovine spongiform encephalopathy (mad cow disease), but chicken and pork hot dogs do.

Yet however nauseating the concept of "msm"—and it is very nauseating—should we really use short ribs in hot dogs? If we make our sausage from good cuts like the short rib, aren't we eliminating a vehicle for the less alluring bits and therefore being even more wasteful than we already are?

I will probably continue to eat store-bought hot dogs occasionally and squeamishly.

Make it or buy it? Buy it.

MUSTARD

The first time I made mustard, it was so pungent my eyes watered and my nose ran. I packed the jar in the refrigerator and forgot about it until a month or so later. When I tasted it again, I discovered that the flavor had both blossomed and mellowed, and there was a great caviar-like "pop" when I bit into the mustard seeds. This is a grainy mustard.

Make it or buy it? Make it.
Hassle: Very slight
Cost comparison: French's yellow mustard: $0.07 per tablespoon. Homemade: $0.22 per tablespoon. Grey Poupon Country Dijon: $0.33 per tablespoon.

½ cup yellow mustard seeds
2 tablespoons dry mustard
⅓ cup vinegar (berry vinegar, page 139, is nice though your mustard will be redder)
*   plus 1 tablespoon*
1 tablespoon sugar
1 teaspoon kosher salt
2 garlic cloves, peeled

1. In a spice grinder, grind the mustard seeds—they won't totally break down—with the dry mustard. It will look a little like wheat germ.
2. Scrape the mixture into a small bowl and stir in ½ cup water. Cover and let rest at room temperature overnight.
3. Scrape the mixture into a blender or food processor and add the vinegar, sugar, salt, and garlic. Liquefy. Scrape down the sides. Taste the mustard and add more vinegar if necessary to form a spreadable condiment.
4. Store in a jar in the refrigerator and wait at least a week before eating.

Makes 1¼ cups

CHAPTER 12

DUCK EGGS

April is the cruelest month for the spouses of animal lovers. On a sunny April afternoon, a year after I brought home the chickens, I went to buy them some cracked corn at the feed store. There, on the floor, sat a deep bin lit by an orange heat lamp and inside, quivering and twitching, was a mass of tiny downy ducklings. Some were black and some were yellow, like Ping, and they all had exquisite miniature rounded bills. I went to the cash register and asked for a cardboard box.

I brought four ducklings home and put them in a cage on the office floor.

"I can't believe we have ducks!" cried Owen when he got home.

Isabel raised her eyebrows and disappeared to her room.

Mark stood looking down at the cage.

"I know," I said. "But supposedly they lay a lot of eggs."

"They are very cute," he said.

Cute. And slovenly. It should have come as no surprise that ducks like water. Within hours they had splashed the contents of their drinking bowl around the cage and onto the wood floor. I moved them to the laundry room and replaced the shredded newspaper bedding. I came back after another hour to find the bedding soaked once again, and exuberantly soiled. By the end of the day it was papier-mâché. By the next morning, it reeked. Animal cages smell bad enough when they're dry; they smell worse when they're wet. I changed the feculent bedding in that cage daily, and each time, the ducklings scrambled into a corner, squealing, piling one on top of the other to avoid me. Ducks may be domesticated, but they aren't friendly.

Soon the room smelled so noxious, I didn't want to do laundry anymore. When we'd had them only ten days, I filled a plastic baby pool with water, and put the ducklings out in the yard with the chickens.

Three of our ducks turned out to be Indian Runners, a skinny, flightless bird from Java, tall and upright with a long neck that almost resembles a snake. Beatrix Potter's Jemima Puddle-Duck is thought to be an Indian Runner. They were very weird looking and they were, unfortunately, all boys. The fourth duck, and only female, was a brown Rouen duck. "They make fine roasting ducks and have abundant, delicately flavored flesh," reports the American Livestock Breeds Conservancy. I was done with slaughter, and this duck's abundant, delicately flavored flesh was useless to me.

Rouen ducks are not known for their egg production, but ours proved herself a champion layer. When she was about five months old, she delivered her first egg—long and heavy with a very hard, waxy white shell. Thereafter, she produced an egg almost every day and I scrambled them and fried them and they tasted like chicken eggs, except they were slightly richer and higher in cholesterol, and the yolks were the lurid orange of a California poppy.

Just as there are cat people and dog people, I think there are chicken people and there are duck people. We soon figured out that we were chicken people. A hen might one day take it into her tiny skull to climb a tree all by herself to see what's on the other side of the fence. Or she might become so fixated on plucking every last centipede from under the woodpile that she loses track of her companions. Chickens squabble. Chickens have pet projects. Chickens have minds of their own, however small. Not so the ducks, who waddled in lockstep formation around the yard, wing to wing, all day, every day, muttering. They were like Hare Krishnas, always chanting in a gang. And they started their chanting just before dawn. I would lie there in the dark, listening to them.

"Those ducks are not right," Mark said one morning as we lay in bed. I had thought he was asleep.

"It's like in *Rosemary's Baby* when she hears the devil worshippers in the apartment next door."

"Do you think they're harassing the chickens?"

"Probably."

"I guess it's better than having a dog," said Mark, rolling out of bed.

"I don't want you to remind me of this because I'll take it all back later," I said, getting up to join him, "but sometimes I hate having animals."

One day I heard a hen shrieking and ran outside to find two of the ducks jabbing at her with their blunt bills. It would have been pathetic, like stabbing someone with a butter knife, but the ducks were working as a team. A few days later, I caught them attacking another hen, but they had now figured out how to use their bills like clamps and had grabbed her neck feathers and were shaking her.

"Just say the word and I'll drive them out to the woods and leave them there," Mark said.

"We can't do that."

"Why not?"

"A raccoon will just eat them. It would be inhumane."

"We're going to keep them forever?" said Mark.

"We could put an ad on Craigslist, I guess."

We did. No one answered. A week later we posted the ad again and received a single reply. Apparently, only one person in all of Northern California wanted to adopt our "chatty gang of flightless ducks." We did not ask what this person intended to do with them.

A few days later, Owen and Mark took the ducks in a box down to the Safeway parking lot to meet their new owners. Twenty minutes later, with an empty box and downcast expressions, the two of them returned.

"I have no idea if we just gave them over to some satanic cult," Mark said. "I have no idea about those people. They had stringy hair and they say they keep their ducks in a hot tub."

"They were teenagers," said Owen contemptuously.

"A hot tub," said Mark.

We did not miss their chanting or the screams of the hens or the fetid baby pool, but I still feel guilty when I think about those weird, helpless ducks. And I miss those big orange-yolked eggs.

DUCK EGG RAVIOLI

This glamorous dish is broadly adapted from *Ethan Stowell's New Italian Kitchen*. The egg yolks poach inside the ravioli and glow golden through the gossamer skin. When you break them, they meld with the Parmesan and butter to form a rich sauce. It's almost worth keeping ducks just so you can make this, though chicken eggs will also work.

1 bunch asparagus, as skinny as you can find
4 tablespoons (½ stick) unsalted butter
1 garlic clove, minced
Kosher salt
1½ cups ricotta, homemade (page 198) or best-quality store-bought
1 teaspoon sweet smoked paprika
1 recipe pasta (page 141)
All-purpose flour, for dusting the work surface
12 to 14 duck egg yolks
Grated Parmesan cheese, for serving

1. First, prepare the asparagus. Snap off the tough stems at the natural breaking point. Finely slice the asparagus, leaving a few of the delicate buds intact.

2. Melt the butter in a skillet and add the garlic, cooking until it softens. Add the asparagus and cook over medium heat for 5 to 10 minutes, until just tender. Salt to taste.

3. In a medium bowl, mix the asparagus with the ricotta and smoked paprika. Taste again. It should be gently spicy and salted to your taste.

4. Using a machine (see page 143), roll out the dough to the thinnest setting. The strips should stay wide, but they should be thin, almost translucent. Cut the pasta strips into 4 rectangles, each about 18 inches long. Dust the work surface with flour and then lay out one strip of pasta. Place 2 tablespoons of the ricotta mixture on the dough, centering it a few inches from one end. Put 3 more on that first strip of pasta, each mound about 4 inches from the last. Make a slight depression in each mound and then gently place 1 egg yolk in each depression. Brush the dough with water and cover with a second sheet of pasta. Press down

gently around the filling, eliminating any air and sealing the dough. Cut between the ravioli with a knife. These are big, rustic ravioli with wide skirts. Repeat with the remaining pasta sheets. You should end up with 12 to 14 ravioli.

5. Fill a pot with water and bring to a low boil. Gently slip the ravioli, four at a time, into the water and poach gently, about 4 minutes. You want the pasta just shiny and cooked, but the yolks must remain bright and barely poached. Repeat with the remaining ravioli.

6. Melt the remaining butter in a skillet, add ⅓ cup of the pasta cooking water, and swirl to combine. Add the ravioli and *gently* push them around in the butter to coat. You don't want the yolks to break before you serve them.

7. Place 2 ravioli on each plate. Sprinkle with Parmesan and serve immediately.

Makes 12 to 14 ravioli, to serve 6

CHAPTER 13

CHEESE

I did not expect to become a cheesemaker any more than I expected to become a chicken fancier. I had read a book about cheesemaking once and was put off by all the rules and temperatures and humidity readings and pieces of special equipment. I was discouraged by the repeated use of the word "sanitize." When on a whim I signed up for a Camembert-making class at a co-op grocery, my expectations were low. The idea that I could make Camembert—the soft, mold-ripened French cheese—struck me as amusing and unlikely.

There were two teachers that day at the Camembert workshop. Sacha Laurin, an expatriate Australian cheesemaker, announced right off that she kept her distance from certain ingredients, such as animal-based rennet and calcium chloride, an additive that can help milk form a curd. (They are both probably harmless, but frowned upon by purists.) Sacha was lovely and articulate and orderly, a believer in rules of hygiene and timing, the precise, principled artisan I imagined all cheesemakers to be.

The other teacher was Steve Shapson, a cheesemaker from Wisconsin, who ignored the clock and used calcium chloride with abandon. He never let tending the cheese get in the way of telling a story, and he was a fount of stories.

The pair of them—together—taught me the most important and liberating lesson I've learned about making cheese, and it is one that applies to cooking more broadly: there are as many ways to make good cheese as there are cheesemakers. At the end of the class Sacha and Steve arrayed some of their Camemberts on a platter, maybe a dozen in all. Some of them were coated in herb, some in ash, some in dried lavender; some were made by perfectionist Sacha on a warm day and some on a cold day and some were made by Steve, perhaps while he was answering e-mail and simultaneously brewing a batch of beer. Each cheese was recognizably Camembert and each was entirely different, sometimes dramatically, sometimes subtly so, and there was not a single one that I did not want to eat. Cheese is made differently by different people all over the world. The rules are constantly bent and disregarded and religiously adhered to, depending on the cheese-maker. You do not need a stopwatch in your pocket and a clipboard in your hand—unless you work better that way. The cheese you make will reflect your choices and personality, as well as the weather and the conditions in your house and the milk you started with.

"Is it milk season?" Mark asked when he saw the quantity of milk I had bought on my way home. Yes, it was milk season. I made Camembert the next day and for the next six weeks I made cheese almost every day. The crawl space behind my closet became a ripening area, and it gave me immense satisfaction to watch the pots and plastic storage containers proliferate, each of them containing a dairy experiment. There were outright failures, like a slimy feta, and some pleasant mediocrities, like a farmhouse cheddar, and there were some horrendous, noisome mistakes.

Once I neglected to flip some cheese, the mold grew over the matting, and when I tried to separate the two the rind came off and molten ivory fluid flowed out all over the ripening container. On another occasion, I went down to check on a batch of Camembert and noticed some of it looked a bit frowsy. I leaned closer to inspect and discovered that the snowy rind was crawling with maggots. I carried the cheese out the back door and dumped it on the ground for the chickens, who raced over and set to work plucking out the worms one by one, the way children pick the marshmallows out of a bowl of Lucky Charms. Sardinians make a sheep's milk cheese that they intentionally infest with maggots and call *casu marzu*, but to be surprised by maggots in your Camembert is exactly as much fun as finding your child's hair crawling with lice. You don't go rushing to the computer to Tweet about it. You *must* keep your cheese covered at all stages of production. Just one fly can ruin everything.

But mostly there were hits. You can absolutely start with Camembert, but it makes more sense to begin with an elementary cheese, like ricotta.

RICOTTA

You can use vinegar, lemon juice, citric acid, or buttermilk to coagulate ricotta. I've tried them all and the results are indistinguishable. What makes a difference is the milk you use. Ordinary milk makes a ricotta that is fresher and sweeter than anything you can buy at Stop & Shop, but unhomogenized organic milk yields a velvety ricotta reminiscent of very soft mozzarella.

Make it or buy it? Make it.

Hassle: Minimal

Cost comparison: Homemade ricotta: $1.70 per cup. Precious: $2.50. To make ricotta with organic, unhomogenized milk: a little over $3.00. But, in my opinion, worth it.

1 gallon milk
¾ cup distilled white vinegar or 1 teaspoon citric acid or 6 tablespoons
fresh lemon juice or 1 quart buttermilk (from the carton)

1. Combine the milk and vinegar (or any one of the alternatives) in a big pot. Gradually heat until the mixture is on the brink of a boil. It should look curdled. Turn off the stove and let the ricotta settle for about 20 minutes.
2. Meanwhile, line a colander with a piece of cheesecloth or white cotton, such as a clean old pillowcase, and place over a large bowl.
3. Gently ladle the ricotta into the cloth-lined colander and let drain for 20 minutes or so. (Save the whey in a jar in the refrigerator for up to 10 days to use in bread and bagels.) Store the ricotta, tightly covered, in the refrigerator. The sooner you use it the better, as fresh ricotta picks up refrigerator odors quickly. I wouldn't plan to keep this fresh for more than a week.

Makes 2½ cups

MASCARPONE

This is one of the most delicious "cheeses" I've ever made, and one of the most temperamental. It helps if you use a very tight weave of cheesecloth, doubled over. When you're draining off the whey, you want to give the cheese as little chance to escape as you possibly can.

Make it or buy it? Make it.

Hassle: Easy, but heartbreaking when it doesn't work

Cost comparison: You can make a cup of mascarpone for less than $1.50. Mascarpone from Whole Foods: $7.00 per cup.

1 quart heavy cream or half-and-half
¼ teaspoon tartaric acid

1. Put the cream in the top of a double boiler over medium heat and warm to 196 degrees F, stirring. Remove the cream from the heat and add the tartaric acid, stirring for 1 minute.
2. Remove the top from the double boiler and continue stirring until the cream begins to look thick and custardy. If it doesn't seem to thicken at all, add the tiniest pinch more tartaric acid.
3. Let it sit at room temperature to gather itself for about 30 minutes. Line a sieve with very fine-weave cheesecloth, doubled over. Place it over a small bowl and pour the cheese into the sieve. Cover tightly with plastic wrap—otherwise the cheese will pick up refrigerator flavors. Place in the refrigerator for 12 hours or more. Store, tightly covered, and use to make tiramisu or semifreddo (recipe follows).

Makes 2 cups

ESPRESSO AND MASCARPONE SEMIFREDDO

This world-beating dessert comes from Lynne Rossetto Kasper's *Splendid Table*, a splendid cookbook full of opulent dishes from the Italian region of Emilia Romagna that I like to read recipes for, even if I never cook them. The only changes I've made to this recipe are to replace the rum with bourbon, and to change the garnish from shaved chocolate to chopped toasted hazelnuts. This semifreddo is a little like tira-misu, without the soggy sponge cake. It's an ideal dessert for parties because you can make it a few days ahead. Actually you *must* make it ahead.

CUSTARD

3 tablespoons instant espresso powder

4 large egg yolks

4 tablespoons sugar

2 tablespoons bourbon

2 teaspoons vanilla extract (page 260)

1 pound mascarpone (see page 199)

¼ cup heavy cream

MERINGUE

4 large egg whites, at room temperature

¾ cup sugar

¼ cup water

GARNISH

1 cup hazelnuts, toasted and chopped

1. Pour the instant espresso granules into a glass measuring cup and add enough boiling water to make ⅓ cup. Stir to dissolve. Let cool.
2. In a large bowl—metal or glass—whisk together the coffee, yolks, sugar, bourbon, and vanilla. Put the bowl over a pan of boiling water and whisk for a few minutes until thick. The mixture should reach 165 degrees F on a thermometer. Scrape it into a smaller bowl, cool to room temperature, cover, and chill in the refrigerator for 4 to 6 hours.
3. When the custard is cold, make the meringue. Place the egg whites in the bowl of an electric mixer. Pour the sugar and the water into a small saucepan and set over medium heat. Cook until the sugar has just melted and the syrup is clear. Turn the heat to high and put a thermometer in the pan. When the syrup is at about 240 degrees F, turn on the mixer and beat the egg whites until they are moist, just starting to stiffen—you don't want them dull or clumping. When the

syrup reaches 250 degrees F, start pouring the syrup very slowly into the mixer as you beat. Turn the beater to medium and continue mixing until the bowl cools to room temperature.

4. As the egg whites are beating and cooling, in a small bowl mix the mascarpone and the heavy cream. Fold this into the cold custard.

5. As soon as the meringue is cool, fold that, too, lightly into the custard. You don't want the semifreddo homogeneous—some streaks of meringue add interest. Scoop the mixture into a storage container, cover tightly, and freeze.

6. Three hours before you plan to eat, move the semifreddo to the refrigerator. Serve in individual dishes, topped with the chopped hazelnuts.

Serves 12

MOZZARELLA

You can make most cheeses—Camembert, cheddar, Gouda—with generic supermarket milk. Not mozzarella. To make mozzarella, you need minimally processed milk. Local organic unhomogenized (i.e., expensive) milk is your best bet. This isn't a gratuitous "local and organic is always better" lecture. If you use ordinary supermarket milk, your mozzarella may not set and you will have to pour it down the drain. This happened to me and it could put you off mozzarella making forever.

And that would be sad. There are few more thrilling kitchen moments than when you hold in the palm of your hand a ball of homemade mozzarella, tender, springy, and still a bit warm. This recipe comes from Ricki Carroll, founder of the New England Cheesemaking Supply Company, a peerless source of ingredients and information.

Make it or buy it? At least try it once.

Hassle: It's no picnic, all that stretching and pulling and hot whey sloshing around.

Cost comparison: If you have a good source for the proper milk (like a couple of goats) this is a bargain. But the only cow's milk I've successfully used to make mozzarella costs $8.00 per gallon. This yields $9.00-per-pound mozzarella. You can buy acceptable fresh mozzarella for $6.00 per pound.

1 gallon whole milk (see headnote)
1½ teaspoons citric acid
¼ teaspoon liquid rennet
¼ cup kosher salt

1. Pour the milk into a large pot and stir in the citric acid.
2. Heat the milk to 90 degrees F. This is just barely warm, not even close to hot. Remove the pot from the heat and slowly stir in the rennet, using an up-and-down motion. Cover the pot and let it sit for 5 minutes.
3. Gently probe the curds with the side of a spoon. They should look like broken custard or tofu, with a clear separation between the thick curd and the watery whey. If you don't see well-defined curd, put the top back on the pot and let it rest a few more minutes.
4. When it is ready, with a long knife, gently break the curd into 1-inch cubes.
5. Place the pot back on the stove and heat to 110 degrees F, gently swirling the curds around with a spoon. Remove from the heat and continue to stir gently for 2 minutes.
6. Scoop the curds into a sieve set over a large bowl. Return the whey to the pot and heat to 175 degrees F. Add the salt.
7. Put on rubber gloves. Divide the curd into two rough balls, give them each a good squeeze, and drop them both into the hot whey. Knead, stretch, and pull the mozzarella balls, one at a time, folding each ball over on itself and working it like taffy. If it starts to tear instead of stretch, dip it back in the whey. Keep kneading and stretching until you have a smooth, shiny, cohesive cheese. Form it into a tight ball and drop it into a bowl of ice water for a few minutes. Remove. Eat immediately. You can refrigerate the cheese and keep it for up to a week, but it will never be more delicious than it is right now.

Makes 1 pound

BURRATA

One night a decade ago I first tasted burrata, a close cousin of mozzarella, at an Italian restaurant in Berkeley. It was bouncy like mozzarella, but also suave and creamy like . . . well, it was unlike anything I'd ever eaten before. I looked for it in vain over the next few months and then years, and never stopped thinking about it. Invented in Italy in the early twentieth century, burrata is one of the world's stranger cheeses. If you watched much television circa 1978, you may remember a brand of gum called Freshen-up in which a tablet of ordinary gum enveloped an inner kernel—a "burst"—of flavored gel. Burrata is the cheese version of Freshen-up. It's an all-mozzarella dumpling: mozzarella that has been stretched into a skin and then wrapped around a "burst" of more liquid mozzarella curd.

Ten years later, suddenly I cannot escape burrata, or at least what passes for burrata. I went out to dinner one night and there it was on the menu of the trattoria in my suburban town. It arrived on a plate the shape of a long canoe, six small piles of semisolid white curd. This was not quite how I remembered it. It was as if I had ordered a dumpling, but received only filling. In any case, it was delicious—salted, peppered, and served with fresh tomatoes.

The very next day I met my friend Debra for lunch at a café and there it was on the menu again. It arrived on a round plate, a few inert slices of chalk-white cheese. This was not quite how I remembered it. It was as if I had ordered a dumpling, but all that came was the wrapper. I remarked to Debra that I thought the restaurant was passing off ordinary mozzarella as burrata, and Debra said I should complain to the waiter. Debra will politely stop people who have just littered and inform them that they just littered, while I am someone who will watch someone litter and think, *Wow, he just littered, that's weird, why do people litter?* I ate the mozzarella, which was delicious—salted, peppered, and served with fresh tomatoes. A few days later, I was shopping at Whole Foods and there it was, burrata again, this time in its proper, bulging dumpling form. I took it home and dissected it, analyzed it, then served it, salted and peppered, with fresh tomatoes.

Because the Whole Foods burrata, made by the Gioia company of Southern California, cost $12 for a dumpling the size of a peach, I wondered if I could hack it. The answer is yes. But it was no walk in the park.

Make it or buy it? Both.

Hassle: You bet it's a hassle, and it provides many opportunities for frustration and failure.

Cost comparison: To make this burrata costs about $10.00. To buy an equivalent amount at a supermarket you'll pay between $18.00 and $34.00.

1. Start by preparing the recipe for mozzarella on page 202, up through step 6. This is the point at which you find yourself with a sieve full of soft mozzarella curd and a pot of almost-boiling-hot whey. Proceed as follows:
2. Divide the curd into three portions and drop one portion into a medium bowl. Pour ½ cup heavy cream into the bowl, perhaps more, and with your fingers, shred and mash the curd. This is going to be the filling and you want the mixture as soft, homogeneous, and milky as you can get it. Salt to taste. The filling is now ready. Set it aside.
3. Put on rubber gloves, squeeze the two remaining portions of mozzarella into rough balls, and drop them into the whey. Let them sit there a minute. Take one of the portions in your hands and stretch it like taffy. When it's extremely plastic and pliable, stretch it very thin, into a square about 7 by 7 inches—or bigger if you can. In a way, it will resemble pizza crust. If it breaks, dip it into the hot whey and start again, or patch it the best you can. As soon as you have a skin of stretched mozzarella, place it on a clean surface and into the middle drop a good dollop—about half—of the creamy curd mixture. Now draw the skin up around the filling and twist and pinch the mozzarella at the top so you have a little sack. Visualize it in the shape of a sloppy Hershey's kiss. Repeat with the remaining mozzarella curd.
4. Serve within the hour with salt, pepper, olive oil, and fresh tomatoes.

Makes 1 pound, 5 ounces

CAMEMBERT

To make Camembert, you don't need special equipment except Camembert molds and cheese matting. Both can be bought (see Appendix) or improvised. I recommend improvising. For molds, you can use soup cans (preferably BPA-free) or PVC pipe from the hardware store sawed into 6-inch lengths. Ideally, your molds would have holes punched in the sides like a colander to allow maximum drainage of whey, but I have never had such holes and have made superlative cheeses. You need four molds, each 3 to 4 inches in diameter. If you are using soup cans, remove the bottoms and the tops, wash the cans well, then run them through the dishwasher.

Cheese matting can be any perforated surface that will elevate the cheese very slightly to allow the whey to drain. A sushi rolling mat is ideal, if you have one. I've used the plastic screen from our gutters which I cut into squares and sterilized, though I've since begun to suspect that gutter plastic is not "food grade." The bottom of a plastic pint strawberry basket, also sterilized, is a better option.

Now you have the equipment, you need the ingredients. The four that you can't buy at the supermarket: mesophilic culture, *Penicillium candidum* powder, calcium chloride, and liquid rennet. If you have a computer and a credit card, in five minutes you can order them all from a cheesemaking supply shop. These are cheap. Once these magical ingredients arrive, there is nothing standing between you and Camembert.

Make it or buy it? If you think this sounds fun—which it is—give it a try.

Hassle: Is fishing a hassle? Is golfing a hassle? Whittling? Cheesemaking is a hobby, an art, an obsession, and a pleasure, and if you don't feel this way about it, you shouldn't do it. Because it's also definitely a hassle.

Cost comparison: This recipe makes 2½ pounds Camembert and costs about $9.00. To buy that much Rouge et Noir, a widely available brand of Camembert made in California, would cost you about $50.00. Even if you blow it, and lose your whole investment in this cheese, it's not a big one.

2 gallons whole milk
¼ teaspoon mesophilic culture
⅛ teaspoon Penicillium candidum *mold powder*
¼ teaspoon calcium chloride (optional)
¼ teaspoon liquid rennet
4 teaspoons kosher salt

1. You don't need to sterilize everything the cheese touches, but pot, spoon, molds, mats, and hands should definitely be extra clean. In a large pot, "warm" the milk to 85 degrees F. This is not actually warm, simply less cold than milk straight out of the refrigerator. Turn off the heat.

2. Sprinkle the mesophilic culture and mold powder over the surface of the milk. Using a slotted spoon and an up-and-down motion, gently draw the culture and

mold into the milk without breaking the surface. (Obviously, you have to break the surface to get the spoon into the milk, but once it's there, try to keep it submerged.)

3. If you're using calcium chloride, dissolve it in ¼ cup cold water. Add to the milk using the same up-and-down motion.

4. Dilute the rennet in ¼ cup cool water. Add to the milk and stir, again with the up-and-down motion. Cover the pot and leave on the stove. You want it to remain at 85 degrees F for 1½ hours. (Maintaining this temperature sounds more complicated than it is; residual heat from the burner should be enough to keep the lidded pot at around 85 degrees F. If your kitchen is very cold, you can fill a larger pot with barely warm water and place the pot of milk inside to bring the temperature up. I've never needed to do this.)

5. After 1½ hours, check for what cheesemakers call a "clean break." This means that when you probe the contents of the pot with a spoon, it separates into custardy curd and watery whey. It will look a bit like packaged soft tofu. If the curd is still fragile—if the mixture doesn't separate cleanly into those two components—let it sit for a few minutes longer.

6. When you get a clean break, it's time to cut the curd. This is hard to explain, but easy to do. Imagine the contents of the pot as a Rubik's cube that has not yet been separated into the smaller component cubes. You want to make those cuts. Working parallel to the sides of the pot, using a long-bladed knife or thin spatula, cut a series of straight parallel lines through the curd, 1 inch apart, reaching all the way to the bottom. Now turn the pot 90 degrees. Make a second series of cuts, 1 inch apart, at a right angle to the first. From the top it now looks like a sloppy checkerboard. Next you need to make horizontal cuts through the curd. Simply reach your knife blade down to about 1 inch from the bottom of the pot and make a horizontal cut, the knife edge parallel to the bottom. Clearly you can't cut perfect cubes this way, and you don't need to. You're just trying to cut the contents of the pot into relatively even pieces. Continue making these cuts at 1-inch intervals all the way to the top of the pot. Let stand for 5 minutes.

7. Very gently lift and agitate the curds with a slotted spoon for 10 minutes until they start to shrink. You are encouraging them to give up even more of their whey. If you see any large curds—these are called "lemons"—cut them in two.

8. Let the curds settle to the bottom of the pan and rest for a few minutes. Mean-

while, set up the molds. On a rimmed cookie sheet, place a cooling rack. On top of that, place the cheese mats, and on top of the cheese mats, set the soup cans or molds.

9. Using a ladle, dip off whey until you see the surface of the curd. Gently ladle the curd into the molds, filling them all the way to the top. You will think this is a mistake, that these Camemberts will be much too tall. Don't worry. They shrink. Drape the cheeses with a clean dish towel to keep out flies and let the curds drain for 2 hours at room temperature.

10. Carefully flip the molds so that the whey now drains from the other end for another 2 hours.

11. Flip again, and 2 hours later, repeat.

12. Let drain at room temperature overnight without flipping.

13. In the morning, slip the cheeses out of their molds. Sprinkle the top of each with ½ teaspoon kosher salt. Flip and salt the other side.

14. The cheeses can ripen in any capacious lidded container such as a Chinese sand pot, a cake carrier, a large plastic storage container, or a Dutch oven. Put a doubled-over piece of paper towel in the bottom, put the piece of cheese mat on top of that, and put the cheese on top of the mat. Cover with the container's lid.

15. Ideally, you will now place the ripening container in a location where the temperature ranges from 50 to 55 degrees F and the humidity is about 90%. If you have a thermometer and hygrometer, good for you. If you don't, just pick a cool spot, like a basement crawl space. If there's no cool spot in your house, the refrigerator will do.

16. Flip the cheeses daily, replacing the damp paper towels with dry ones. When you reach in one day and the paper towel is dry, you can stop changing the towels. But you should continue to flip the cheese daily. The soft white mold is the penicillin mold you sprinkled on the milk, expressing itself as a blooming rind. In about 3 weeks, the cheeses should be soft and ready to eat. If they're still firm, give them a few days. To store, you can just put them in a small lidded plastic container or plastic bags in the refrigerator. They last a long time—months.

Makes 2½ pounds

CHAPTER 14

GOATS

If rather than a lush green garden, you want your outdoor space to resemble a Third World village, I suggest getting some chickens, who will methodically denude the landscape of every blade of grass, low-lying weed, and wildflower. And if you want to rid yourself of shrubbery and small trees as well, get goats. Very soon you will have the adobe patio of your dreams.

When you start making cheese, it's a matter of days, perhaps hours, before you "idly" look up the local municipal code to see if you are permitted to keep a couple of goats, East Friesian sheep, maybe even a cow. While you can produce surprisingly good cheeses with supermarket milk, unhomogenized fresh milk is the coin of the realm.

Cows were out of the question for our suburban lot, and goats, I soon learned, are illegal, as are sheep. I was not about to let this deter me. I took Jennie Grant as my role model. A few years ago, Grant was quietly and illegally keeping two goats in her Seattle backyard when some neighbors complained to the authorities. She launched a petition and won a city council member to her cause, and in 2007, goats were legalized as pets in Seattle, an eminently sensible change.

I can see both sides of almost every issue, but I can see no reason whatsoever that goats should be illegal anywhere that dogs are permitted, which as far as I can tell is everywhere. I wrote a note to our supervisor inquiring why this law remained on the books. As I pointed out in my letter, goats do not bark, they do not smell. They do not (usually) bite and *never* rampage through the neighborhood killing chickens. They eat invasive, flammable brush and poison oak, and they actually produce something useful—fertilizer and milk—which dogs do not.

The supervisor responded that he was surprised at this law, that he had always assumed two small goats were permissible, that his very own brother-in-law kept goats in Mill Valley. Although this was as legally relevant as a bubble gum wrapper, I printed out the e-mail, pinned it to my bulletin board, hopped onto Craigslist, and began shopping for goats.

The Nigerian Dwarf supposedly descends from the miniature goats that were brought over in the 1930s on ships from Africa to feed lions and tigers heading for American zoos. A few lucky goats survived, the ancestors of today's Nigerian Dwarves. As the name suggests, these goats are small. A full-size Swiss dairy goat is the size of a Great Dane and can produce a gallon of milk a day. A Nigerian Dwarf is the size of a border collie and gives a quart or two of milk per day. This is the tricycle of goats and this was the goat for us. Owen and I picked up our first goat from a Sonoma County farm when she was ten days old. She was smaller than a cat and had a Yoda profile and a splotchy calico coat. I put her on the passenger seat of the car and looked over at this tiny mammal, who let out a petulant scream. *Oh, my God,* I thought. *What have I just done?*

"Let's call her Peppermint," said Owen, hanging over the front seat. "I just thought of it out of my head."

On the way home, we stopped at Target and I bought a baby bottle and, since Peppermint would be living in the house with us until we found her a companion, a packet of Huggies, sized for a newborn.

"You're crazy," Mark said when Peppermint tottered out of the car and down the driveway in her diapers.

"I know," I said.

"Well," he said, "she is very cute."

She was very cute. For almost a month, Peppermint lived in the house with us. She slept in Owen's bed, sat on the sofa while we watched *Lost,* and rode around in the car with me when I ran errands. While I never carried her in my purse like a Chihuahua, it did cross my mind. She was very clean, cleaner than any dog. Like tiny high-heeled shoes, her hooves click-clicked on the wood floors as she followed me from room to room. If she couldn't find me, she wailed until I called her and then she would scamper over and leap into my lap. Three times a day, she drank milk from a bottle, slamming down each meal in under a minute, the milk frothing at her mouth like foam on a latte. We were all besotted.

Goats are herd animals and must have goat friends. Given Peppermint's happy and instant integration into our lives, I decided that for her companion we could handle a full-size breed, like a Nubian. Now that I'd mastered the tricycle, I was ready for a Peugeot ten-speed. Moreover, I wanted a full-grown doe this time. It would be a year before baby Peppermint gave milk, and I wanted to ramp up the cheesemaking right now.

I answered an ad posted by a 4-H girl named Wyone who had a Nubian doe that was milking at slightly over a gallon a day. This goat's name was Pastry and she was a beauty. The supermodel of the goat world, the Nubian is a leggy breed with a Roman nose and long, floppy ears. I had to have one. I bought a $200 molded plastic calf hutch that looked like a cross between a tent and a Porta-Potty and dragged it into the middle of our yard.

One morning, Owen and I drove an hour north to Wyone's farm. She led us back around the house to a paddock where lovely Nubian goats of all sizes and colors perched on hay bales and spools.

Owen squeezed my hand.

"You love goats," I said.

"I also love ducks and chickens," he corrected. "Don't leave them out."

Pastry had an auburn coat and white ears that resembled the pigtails on Cindy from *The Brady Bunch*. I gave Wyone a $100 check and led Pastry into the back of our minivan, where she rode home, completely silent.

When we pulled into our driveway, none of the neighbors was out raking or retooling mountain bikes, which seemed a good omen. A few neighbors had met tiny Peppermint and responded amiably, but I was unsure how they would react to a goat the size of a motorcycle with a giant, bulging udder. Owen and I coaxed Pastry out of the van and led her down the stairs to the yard. There, surveying her new home, suddenly she balked, locked her bony knees, and uttered an agonized cry that emanated from deep inside her chest. She turned and looked me in the eye with a wild expression and I looked back at her, puzzled, and then she bellowed again.

The shout of a miserable Nubian goat bears no relationship to a bleat. Pastry sounded like a sick, anguished human. "You're okay," I told her. She bellowed again and established her rhythm, which was to bellow every twenty or thirty seconds. When I attempted to briefly leave her side, she chased me and upped her tempo to constant, frantic screaming.

This is fine, I thought in those first minutes, patting her back. *I can wait this out. I'll just sit here in the yard and keep her company. All will be well.* Owen brought out his copy of *LEGO Star Wars: The Visual Dictionary* and sat on a hillock of ivy near me.

The minutes and then the hours passed. Owen read. Pastry bellowed. Our neighbor's Geek Squad van pulled up and his head popped up over the fence a few minutes later. "What's that noise?" he asked.

"Oh, it's just a goat," I said casually. "She's having a bad day."

Owen read. Pastry bellowed. I began to worry.

"I need to go inside for just a little while," I said to Owen.

"You can't leave me here alone with her."

"I won't be gone long and you'll be fine."

"I really, really don't want you to go," he said.

"I'll buy you any LEGO in the store if you sit out here."

"Which one?"

"Which one do you want?"

He thought. "The AT-TE Walker, it's like a car with legs and it brings around clone troopers."

"How much does it cost?"

"You said any LEGO, Mom."

"Whatever," I said.

I went in the house and called Mark. "Could you please, please come home? This goat is a problem."

When I went back outside, Pastry was bellowing and Owen was no longer reading, he was weeping. "Mom," he said. "This is so embarrassing. We should have *never* gotten this goat. The neighbors are going to hate us. They're going to get really angry."

"It's going to be fine, honey," I said. I fed Pastry a dried leaf, which she crunched like a potato chip.

"Oh, that's not so bad," shouted Mark as he strode up the hill an hour later. "She just sounds like an elephant!"

Night fell. I poured myself a glass of wine, grabbed a sleeping bag, and walked down to the hutch to spell Mark. "Enough of this nonsense, right, girl?" I said. I found a patch of clean straw and sat. Pastry looked at me, searching my eyes. *You seem like a very nice person, but what is happening? Who are you? Where is my baby? Where are my sisters? Where is Wyone?* Then she bellowed again.

I lay down in the sleeping bag, holding Pastry's collar to keep her from bolting the hutch. She stood, staring out warily into the dark, bellowing only occasionally now. The wine had made me thirsty, and I thought of our sofa lit by the glow of a reading lamp, the clean sheets on the bed, a glass of water.

The suburbs fall eerily silent at night, the sounds of children and leaf blowers suddenly and completely absent. I could hear the furtive snapping of twigs as the cats made the rounds, and probably the skunks, rats, and raccoons as well, though I preferred not to think about them. Through the cut-out window in the plastic hutch I could see our house with the one light in the bedroom lit late into the night, where Mark was reading. The house looked insubstantial, the walls we lived inside thin and provisional. Cars howled far in the distance on the highway.

At dawn, I crawled out of the hutch, dry-mouthed and stiff, hoping that Pastry might greet the day with serenity. But she tore out of the hutch after me and gazed around in what appeared to be renewed horror. She broke the silence with a bellow. Straw clung to my jeans and I smelled, even to myself, like goat. I looked up and saw Mark on the patio, staring down at me with an expression on his face so thunderous it required all my bravado just to meet his gaze.

I went into the house, sat on the sofa, and listened to Pastry. Neighbors were eating their Puffins and tying their ties, listening to Pastry. If we got busted, I would not blame them. If we got busted, I'd lose not just Pastry, but Peppermint. My heart would break. At 6:58 a.m. I called Wyone. Fifteen minutes later, Pastry and I were in the van driving north.

"Nubians, as a breed, are well known for their repertoire of vocal skills," I read in *Dairy Goat Journal* a few days after the Pastry fiasco. *No kidding*, I thought. Had I merely chosen the wrong breed? Could I try again with a grown doe from a more timid breed? The Oberhasli is everywhere described as a calm and quiet caprine. It is also the handsomest of the dairy breeds, with a walnut brown coat, a black dorsal stripe, and black boots. According to *Dairy Goat Journal*, the coloring should resemble "the wood on the back of a violin." Goats bring out the poet in everyone.

Jennie Grant, the Seattle goatherd, had recently acquired an adult Oberhasli whom she described in her blog as "graceful, docile, and has something of the wilds about her, like a deer." She did not mention any noise. I wrote to Jennie, introduced myself, and asked whether her Oberhasli had cried much when she brought her to her new home.

"Funny you should ask," Jennie wrote back.

That was not what I wanted to hear. "How loud is she?" I wrote.

"I'd say she is about as loud as a non-power lawn mower, maybe a bit louder, but not nearly as loud as a gas-powered mower," Jennie replied.

I read the e-mail to Mark. "That doesn't sound so bad," I said.

"We don't have a lawn," he said. "And I don't see why we need any mower at all."

I found an Oberhasli breeder four hours away in Fresno, made an appointment, and drove down one morning. I willed myself not to look at the paddock of grown does. I pointed to a coltish two-week-old beauty. And that is how we ended up with Natalie.

When Natalie arrived, both she and Peppermint moved into the yard, where they have stripped every last leaf from every last shrub and tree and started in on the bark, peeling it away in strips. I had a few small fruit trees growing there and one day I watched Natalie put her feet up against the side of a plum and push and push until the crown bowed to the ground under her weight and she could eat all the tender leaves. Before I could get to the hardware store for wire to protect the other trees, she had moved on to the chocolate persimmon and the Bartlett pear. There is no longer a trace of the would-be orchard.

They were a lot of work, especially in the beginning. I tried, with moderate success, to enlist my human kids to pitch in. One afternoon a few days after school let out for the summer, I heated the milk for the goats and filled their baby bottles. "Would you please take these out and do the feeding?" I asked Owen, who was lying on the floor, drawing a Transformer.

"You do it," he said.

"You do it?" I replied.

"Yes, you do it."

"Did you just say, '*You do it*'?"

"I always do it," he said.

"That is not true."

He said, "I did it last night."

"And I did it this morning."

"Because I was sleeping. Besides, you like getting up early."

"I do not like getting up early."

"Then why do you do it?"

"So I can feed the goats! So I can do the laundry! So I can make you breakfast!"

"You like to cook," he said. "Making breakfast is fun for you."

"JUST GO OUTSIDE AND FEED THE GOATS!"

Owen stared at me in shock. He shouted, "You want me to be a SLAVE for you! Summer was not invented so kids could be SLAVES for their parents."

"Actually," I said wearily, "it was."

There were no exchanges like this in the *Little House* books, ever. Owen went outside. A few minutes later, I heard him singing.

But for all the hassles, goats have been the most rewarding of pets. We have only to step out the back door, for the two of them to come running, bleating jubilantly. "They're like paparazzi with us," said Owen. They don't want to sleep in their molded plastic goat hutch, they want to sleep jammed up against the house, under the eaves, right beside the door in case one of us might open it and they can push their way in and join us on the sofa to watch *Fringe*. I built a barrier to keep them out of the vegetable garden and they broke through. I reinforced. That very afternoon I was leaving to take Isabel to her dance class and the goats came racing toward us as we stepped out the back door. Their eyes were shining, and they were nickering. *"Hi, guys, we are so glad to see you. The weirdest thing happened, after we got through the hole in the gate last time? Well, it's blocked now! But we figured out how to get past it anyway so everything's okay. What's up?"*

But what about the milk? When they were eight months old I took our goats back to the farm where I bought Peppermint to be bred. You learn something about the earthy roots of the English language when you spend time around livestock. You're idly observing chickens one day and suddenly a lightbulb goes off about some phrase you've thoughtlessly used all your life: rules the roost, pecking order, henpecked, flew the coop, clipped her wings.

When you watch a goat after a good meal start kicking her heels up in the air, you think, "She's feeling her oats!" And when you see a big, hairy buck goat start grunting and sticking out his tongue when he meets a couple of cute does: "Wow, what a disgusting old goat." As I write, Natalie is due in six days. If Peppermint got knocked up, she's sure carrying it well.

GOAT MILK

Make it or buy it? Goats are wonderful, but if it's just their milk you're after, buy it.

Hassle: Like having a dog you don't have to walk

Cost: Peppermint cost $350; Natalie cost $100; I paid $200 for the hutch and $100 to rent the truck to transport it to our yard. I bought the goats vaccines and a currycomb and a nail clipper, and $300 of hay and grain. I paid the vet

$250 when Natalie got sick. Each goat incurred a $50 stud fee. And then there was all the mileage. We will ignore the cost of the espaliered pear tree and my decimated orchard. So far I estimate that we have spent $1,600 on our goats and acquired not a drop of milk. I don't see how this is ever going to pencil out. But we love our goats the way people love their Labradoodles and if they one day give us some milk? Well, that will be nice.

FRESH CHÈVRE

This cheese is fluffy and feathery, all the flavors bright and clean and new. It's also easy and cheap.

Make it or buy it? Make it.
Hassle: Easy
Cost comparison: Homemade, using store-bought goat's milk: $8.00 to $9.00 per pound. Laura Chenel goat cheese: $14.00.

1 gallon goat's milk (preferably not ultrapasteurized)
¼ teaspoon mesophilic culture
1 drop liquid rennet
Kosher salt

1. In a very clean, large pot, heat the milk to 77 degrees F, just to take the chill off.
2. Sprinkle the culture over the top of the milk. Using a slotted spoon, with an up-and-down motion, stir the milk to draw the cultures down into the liquid.
3. Add the rennet. Again, stir the milk with an up-and-down motion.
4. Cover the pot and leave at room temperature to rest undisturbed for 24 hours.
5. Set a colander or sieve lined with cheesecloth over a large bowl. Pour the cheese into it. Let drain for 8 hours at room temperature. Stir in salt to taste. Store in a bowl in the refrigerator, tightly covered. It will keep for 10 days.

Makes 2 pounds, 1 ounce

CHAPTER 15

TURKEY

A few weeks before Thanksgiving, I began pondering where to buy a turkey. A local farm known for its humane practices and environmental sensitivity had been advertising heritage turkeys—old-fashioned breeds that, unlike factory-farmed birds, can fly and mate unassisted. According to the farm's website: "Their flavor is spectacular, the meat succulent and rich—they are, without a doubt, the best-tasting turkeys you'll ever eat." I wanted in! The price was $6.89 per pound and I needed a fifteen-pounder. I did the math: that's a $103.35 bird.

This gives a person pause. Meanwhile, Lucky had been advertising a free turkey with just $99.99 in purchases. In other words, a perfectly edible bird plus yams, marshmallows, cranberry sauce, brussels sprouts, and potatoes, with enough left over for wine and after-dinner mints, for less than the price of a single heritage turkey. Of course, Lucky's turkeys were flightless Frankenbirds who had endured sorry lives sucking up antibiotics in sordid factory farms. Still, it was tempting.

But I was trying to be a better person. Since I now followed the farm section of Craigslist the way other crazy ladies follow QVC, I noticed within minutes when an ad for a live tom turkey popped up one afternoon. Someone was selling a bird for ten dollars to "a good home or whatever." Or whatever. You would think I would have learned my lesson with Arlene, but I promptly called to reserve this turkey who had spent his happy days waddling around with goats and chickens on a small farm. We'd house the turkey in our yard for a few weeks, treat him royally, then slaughter him. My daughter rolled her eyes, my husband rolled his eyes, but Owen was psyched. Over the next few days, he and I read about turkeys, looked at turkey web pages, and became generally carried away with the awesomeness of turkeys, who are handsome, varied, and supposedly much smarter than people think.

But when I called to arrange to pick up our turkey, the owner had changed his mind, perhaps after pricing his own Thanksgiving feast. What a blow. We needed a turkey! By expanding my search on Craigslist, within five minutes I'd tracked down a thirty-five-dollar bird in an unfamiliar Central Valley town several hours away. No trip is too far when you have a turkey in your sights. I printed out driving directions and we got in the car.

"People always think a farm is a green place with a tractor running through it," Owen remarked as we surveyed the mangy patch of land abutting some railroad tracks. "It's not always like that. This farm is not the classic." No, it was not. This farm was strewn with rusted car parts, overturned boxes of trash, empty 2-liter soda bottles, crushed cans, and downed trees, and through this *WALL-E* wasteland wandered dozens of chickens, cats, dogs, and three bloated, broad-breasted white turkeys—the standard factory breed. The bearded proprietor ambled through the debris and grabbed up a fat, hiccupping bird that he placed in a laundry bin in the back of our car. "You gonna—?" He made a throat-slashing motion and grinned. I gave him cash. The turkey may well have ingested STP, Mountain Dew, and crystal meth, but I remain confident that she was never polluted by an antibiotic.

We loved her instantly, perhaps because she was such a tragic figure. If a turkey could get a bad boob job, smoke a pack a day, and drink three martinis with every lunch, she would resemble this wheezing, sclerotic bird. From supporting the weight of an oversize breast, her scrawny, scaly legs were bowed and she staggered and lurched. Moreover, separated from her companions, she showed signs of depression. She barely ate, we couldn't get her to drink, and she passed her days in one corner of the yard, staring at a fence post. It seemed terribly wrong that she should spend her final weeks in such a funk.

A real farmer would have shrugged and sharpened his ax. But I'm a fake suburban farmer and announced my intention to find her a companion, in part to alleviate her woe, in part because having a turkey was so freaking cool that I wanted another. My mother called to say that she really hoped I'd stop with "this whole turkey thing." Apparently, backyard chickens were cute and trendy; turkeys were creepy and redneck.

There might be something to this. Owen and I went to collect our second turkey, a Narragansett turkey—after dark, when the proprietor got off her shift at McDonald's—from a farm that could have been the setting of a horror movie, complete with boarded-up house and a ramshackle barn crammed to the rafters with squawking poultry. This turkey was, however, truly stunning—slender and nimble, with a long, velvety neck and mottled dark feathers. I handed over forty dollars cash and we drove away as fast as we could.

This second turkey was far too attractive for his pudgy, clumsy bride, but they hit it off instantly. The heritage bird ran very fast around the yard first thing in the morning, flapping his wings and trilling musically while the factory-bred girl stood there, phlegmatic and blinking. How could I kill one or even both of them when they were just settling into their new home? I couldn't.

I had shelled out seventy-five dollars and driven all over Northern California, and I still didn't have a damned turkey.

I bought one at Whole Foods.

A few weeks later, though, it became clear that the turkeys had to go. The hen could not make the leap onto the roosting pole, and at night she huddled directly beneath the other birds so that in the morning she lurched out of the coop spattered, sometimes blanketed, in feces. Meanwhile, her dopey boyfriend loped around the yard, whooping and whistling loudly enough that I began to worry about our neighbors.

"The turkeys are gross," Mark said one morning.

"You're just realizing that?" said Isabel.

"They're funny," said Owen. "I like them."

"I know you do," I said. "But I think we have to get rid of them."

"Thank you," said Isabel.

"No!" Owen said. "I love the turkeys."

"They're not pets," I replied primly.

"Yes they are. Pretty much."

"Okay, here's the deal," I said. "If you go out and play with the turkeys for an hour this afternoon and every afternoon, we can keep them."

And so that day, after school, Owen dutifully went outside to play with the turkeys. Fifteen minutes later, he came back in. "You can do it," he said, "but I don't want to watch."

When my father came over a few days later, Owen turned on the TV very loudly and we killed the turkeys. It occurred to me standing there with those two unwieldy birds dead at my feet that I could just put them in the trash.

But no. I couldn't. My father went home and I set up an old propane burner in the driveway, boiled a ten-gallon pot of water, and dipped the turkeys, one at a time. Then, in the wintry dusk, I crouched in the gravel and plucked them bare. I cleared off the kitchen counter and lined it with newspaper. Cleaning those big birds took close to an hour and the mountain of gore was chilling to behold. Then I put the turkeys in black garbage bags, rubber-banded them shut, and stuffed them into the freezer. It felt more like cleaning up a crime scene than putting aside stores for the winter.

Months later, we finally hauled those turkeys out of the freezer. The hen was a fat beauty on the platter but, even brined, she was as dry as any turkey I've ever eaten. Perhaps drier. The six-pound heritage bird looked like a long-legged chicken. In my butchering, I had broken off the knob at the end of a drumstick, which now resembled something out of a horror comic. Contrary to everything I'd read about the succulence of heritage turkeys, he too tasted like every turkey I have ever eaten. Perhaps drier.

TURKEY

Make it or buy it? Buy it.

Hassle: Yes

Cost comparison: After killing, plucking, and cleaning, I paid close to $7.00 per pound for my heritage bird. I could have bought an organic heritage turkey for $7.00 per pound and avoided the mess. The other bird wasn't a heritage bird and for her I paid effectively just over $2.00 a pound. Going rate for ordinary turkeys at Safeway: $1.00 per pound. Of course, my turkeys had okay lives, however short. That's something. If not enough.

CHAPTER 16

THANKSGIVING

Even if you don't kill the turkey, you probably like to cook something from scratch on Thanksgiving. But do you have to cook everything?

STUFFING

I grew up on Pepperidge Farm stuffing and I like it more than I probably should. Those little cubes of sagey bread develop a custardy texture that is quite appealing. But commercial stuffing has none of the depth and character of homemade stuffing. I once did a side-by-side tasting of homemade stuffing and Pepperidge Farm. Mark said, "Yours is better." I said, "Can you elaborate?" He said, "Tastes better." And walked away.

I can do better than that. The bread has some chew to it and the pieces vary in size and crustiness, which makes eating it more interesting. The flavors are fresh and round, not cloying and monotonous.

Make it or buy it? Make it.
Hassle: It takes maybe 5 minutes longer to make scratch stuffing than to mix Pepperidge Farm.
Cost comparison: Homemade: $0.99 per cup. Pepperidge Farm: $0.89 per cup.

8 tablespoons (1 stick) unsalted butter, plus more for the casserole
8 cups bread cubes (any kind, or a mixture of sandwich bread, levain, croissants,
     whatever; crust adds texture)

1½ cups pecan halves or pieces

1 big onion, chopped

1½ teaspoons dried sage, or 1 tablespoon fresh, chopped

½ cup currants

Lots of freshly ground black pepper

Kosher salt to taste

2 cups chicken or turkey stock

1. Preheat the oven to 350 degrees F. Butter a 2-quart covered casserole.
2. Spread the bread cubes on a cookie sheet and toast in the oven until firm but not totally desiccated. Coarsely chop the pecans, spread on another cookie sheet, and slide this into the oven as well. Toast until golden.
3. Melt the butter in a skillet and add the onion. Cook until very soft. Stir in the sage, currants, pecans, and bread cubes. Add salt and pepper to taste.
4. Stir in about 2 cups stock.
5. Pour the mixture into the casserole and bake, covered, for 30 minutes. If you're serving people who love a crusty stuffing, uncover the casserole for the last 10 minutes or so.

Makes about 8 cups

CRANBERRY SAUCE

My brother-in-law makes a cranberry sauce that entails poking each individual cranberry with a needle, thereby allowing it to release its juices without bursting. When cooked, the berries resemble a bowl of jewel-like cherries. That is his family tradition and it is lovely. About fifteen years ago, I made Paul Prudhomme's fresh cranberry relish, which involves grinding cranberries with a lot of sugar, oranges, lemons, and a full tablespoon of vanilla. It's fruity and supersweet, and that's become our family tradition. It is also lovely. My friend Melanie likes cranberry jelly that slides from the can and keeps the cylindrical shape. That's her family tradition and it's as good as any other. Cranberry sauce is there to embellish a piece of poultry and pretty much any sauce—homemade or canned, spicy or sweet—that makes you remember happy Thanksgivings past is going to be the right one.

MASHED POTATOES

Though I'd never bought them before, I was dead certain of what I thought about Betty Crocker Potato Buds: disgraceful. Then one rainy fall evening, I opened a box. I boiled water with a chunk of butter and a big pinch of salt, and then poured in a little cold milk and a cup of the buds, which looked like goldfish food. I stirred the bizarre mixture with a fork. Man, was I slumming.

What happened next shocked and chastened me.

"Isabel!" I yelled. "Come look!"

"What is it?" she said.

"Mashed potatoes!"

She peered into the pot and said, "So?"

"It took five minutes."

She was underwhelmed. But then she has never peeled potatoes. She has never experienced the tedium, the damp knuckles, the grimy bits of brown skin stuck to every surface. In the pot was a cloud of beautiful, fluffy spuds. We tasted the buds. Good! Perhaps a bit stickier than home-mashed, but certainly acceptable. I could have sat down and eaten the whole pot.

As with biscuits (page 73), I had to reexamine my snobby prejudices. I can see that a convenience like this must have meant a lot to someone in my grandmothers' generation, when mashing potatoes was a more regular part of daily life, when you couldn't just say, nope, I don't feel like making mashed potatoes and pot roast, tonight, we're having quesadillas.

Were I expected to mash potatoes for my pin money, I would find potato buds very alluring. But I only mash potatoes when I want to—mashed potatoes are a choice and a treat. And real mashed potatoes are better.

Make it or buy it? Make it.

Hassle: Peeling potatoes

Cost comparison: Homemade: about $0.40 per cup. Betty Crocker Potato Buds: $0.50 per cup.

2 pounds russet potatoes
Salt
1 cup milk, heavy cream, buttermilk (page 53), or half-and-half
4 tablespoons (½ stick) unsalted butter

1. Peel the potatoes, cut them into chunks, and drop them into a pot of cold, salted water.
2. Put the pot on the stove over high heat and bring to a boil. Simmer for about 25 minutes, or until the potatoes are soft.
3. Meanwhile, in a small saucepan, gently heat the milk and the butter until the butter melts.
4. Drain the potatoes in a colander and return them to their dry cooking pot. With a masher, start pounding them.
5. Add the butter and milk, a little at a time, mashing and pouring until the liquid is absorbed and the potatoes are as smooth or lumpy, thin or thick, as you like them. Salt to taste.
6. Serve immediately.

Serves 4

SWEET POTATOES

Mashed potatoes from buds aren't all that bad; canned sweet potatoes, soggy and stubby, are a woeful substitute for fresh sweet potatoes.

Make it or buy it? Make it.
Hassle: Hardly any
Cost comparison: This recipe costs about $1.25 per cup to make. An equivalent amount of Princella canned yams costs $0.67 per cup.

4 tablespoons (½ stick) unsalted butter
1½ pounds sweet potatoes, peeled and cut into round slices about ½ inch thick
Pinch of kosher salt
⅓ cup maple syrup

1. Preheat the oven to 450 degrees F. Put the butter in a small casserole and slip it into the oven to melt.
2. When the butter is melted, pull out the casserole and turn the sweet potatoes in the butter until they are well coated on all sides. Add salt and turn again.
3. When the oven is hot, roast the potatoes for 15 minutes.
4. Pull out the casserole, pour the syrup over the sweet potatoes, return to the oven, and roast for 15 minutes more. The potatoes should be completely tender, the edges starting to carmelize.

Makes 4½ cups, to serve 6

PUMPKIN PIE

The very existence of Libby's canned pumpkin throws Barbara Kingsolver into a tizzy. "Come *on*, people," she laments in *Animal, Vegetable, Miracle*. "Doesn't anybody remember how to take a big old knife, whack open a pumpkin, scrape out the seeds, and bake it? We can carve a face onto it, but can't draw and quarter it? Are we not a nation known worldwide for our cultural zest for blowing up flesh, on movie and video screen and/or armed conflict? Are we in actual fact too squeamish to stab a large knife into a pumpkin?"

I had always used canned pumpkin for pie, because it was what my mother and grandmother used. In my family, canned pumpkin is traditional. But I liked the idea of starting with a whole food rather than a can, and what if canned pumpkin turned out to be just as inferior as canned sweet potatoes and I just didn't know better?

I baked two pies, identical except for the source of the pumpkin. Pie number one contained the flesh of a sugar pie pumpkin that I roasted for an hour, peeled, seeded, de-stringed, and forced through the food mill. Pie number two contained the flesh of a pumpkin that Libby's had processed in a plant and I scooped out of the can.

Results: The canned pumpkin was (obviously) more convenient, and I did not have to wait for it to roast. It was also slightly more expensive—about $0.50 more than the whole pumpkin. But those were fifty cents well spent, because it made a superior pie—the flavor was bigger, rounder, more pumpkin-y. I have no idea how you get more pumpkin-y than an actual pumpkin. According to the label, Libby's canned pumpkin contains nothing but pumpkin. Did I just have a dud pumpkin? Confusing.

My advice: When you're standing at the supermarket the day before Thanksgiving pondering your pumpkin options, grab the can and get in the checkout line before it grows any longer. You're not being squeamish, you're being sensible.

However, you should absolutely bake your own pie.

Make it or buy it? Make it.
Hassle: Once you have the crust, it's just stir, pour, bake.
Cost comparison: Homemade: $3.68. Sara Lee frozen: $5.99. Safeway in-house bakery: $8.79.

1¼ cups canned pumpkin puree
2 large eggs
⅓ cup granulated sugar
⅓ cup light brown sugar, packed
⅛ teaspoon ground cinnamon
⅛ teaspoon freshly grated nutmeg
⅛ teaspoon ground ginger
1 cup half-and-half
One 9-inch pie crust (page 153), partially baked

1. Preheat the oven to 375 degrees F.
2. In a large bowl combine the pumpkin, eggs, sugars, cinnamon, nutmeg, ginger, and half-and-half and beat until smooth. Pour into the crust.
3. Bake for 35 minutes. This is incredible served warm out of the oven, and almost as good cold.

Serves 8

WHIPPED CREAM

Although it's fun to spray and makes an exciting sound, most aerosolized cream tastes fake. Because it is. Reddi-wip, for instance, contains eight ingredients, including mono- and diglycerides and corn syrup. At least it contains a modicum of dairy. Cool Whip is essentially hydrogenated oil churned with corn syrup, and while I don't find it disgusting, it's nothing like freshly whipped cream. I always assumed synthetic whipped cream was cheap because only a French person or a snob would insist on the real thing. In fact, Reddi-wip and Cool Whip cost more than real cream.

Make it or buy it? Make it.
Hassle: Minuscule
Cost comparison: Home-whipped cream is half the price of a canister or plastic tub.

> *1 cup very cold heavy cream*
> *2 tablespoons sugar*
> *½ teaspoon vanilla extract (page 260), optional*

Pour the cream and sugar into a large bowl and beat until soft peaks form. If you want to use vanilla, add it after peaks have formed. Serve immediately.

Makes 1¾ cups

CHAPTER 17

DRINKS

I wanted to make wine. I tried to make beer. But for those ambitious beverage projects I think you might need a garage, or a basement. We stored our beer-in-progress in our pantry and every time people went in or out, they knocked the air lock off. We lost track of how long the beer had been sitting there and my husband eventually poured it into the ivy. But there are plenty of less ambitious drinks I have made at home, both alcoholic and not.

LEMONADE

Lemonade is mostly water, which flows freely and cleanly from First World taps. Is it the wisest use of dwindling fossil fuels to truck cartons of lemon-flavored water hundreds, even thousands, of miles? The Newman's Own lemonade at a supermarket in California, where lemons grow like kudzu, is manufactured in Washington State, where lemons don't grow easily, if at all. If you buy lemonade, the green choice is probably concentrate. Homemade lemonade tastes brisk and sharp and clean and can be as sweet or tart as you want it to be.

Make it or buy it? Make it.
Hassle: I enjoy squeezing lemons almost as little as I enjoy gutting turkeys.
Cost comparison: If you have a lemon tree, lemonade is effectively free, but if your lemons come from the supermarket, it costs between two and four times as much to make lemonade as to buy it.

1 cup sugar
10 lemons

1. In a saucepan over low heat, dissolve the sugar in 1 cup water. Cool completely.
2. Squeeze the lemons and collect the juice in a pitcher.
3. Stir in about half the syrup and taste. Add more until you get the sweetness you desire. Measure your liquid and add an equal amount of cold water to the pitcher. Chill. Serve. Drink.

Makes 1½ to 2 quarts

SIMPLE SYRUP

The sweetener used in the lemonade is called simple syrup, and it turns up in many cocktails, like the Lemon Drop and the Old-Fashioned. I was puzzled one day when I saw a bottle of simple syrup at the supermarket. Made by a company called Stirrings of Nantucket, it cost more per ounce than Bacardi Gold. You can buy a 12-ounce bottle of Stirrings simple syrup for $5.99 or you can put 1 cup sugar and 1 cup water in a saucepan and heat until the sugar dissolves, which costs $0.22. Store in a jar in the refrigerator.

GINGER ALE

Soda is surprisingly easy to make. For this ginger ale you need a funnel and a clean, empty 2-liter plastic bottle—a rinsed-out plastic soda bottle is perfect—with a screw-on lid. I don't like commercial ginger ale because my mother believed in its healing properties and gave it to my sister and me when we were home sick from school. This recipe makes an extra-spicy, slightly tart ginger ale that, unlike Canada Dry, brings back no memories of the stomach flu. This is more appropriate in a Dark & Stormy rum cocktail than the sickroom. Be warned: you'll have some sediment in your homemade ginger ale.

Make it or buy it? Make it.
Hassle: Amazingly simple
Cost comparison: $1.59 for a bottle of homemade. $1.79 for Canada Dry.

> *1 lemon*
> *2 tablespoons finely grated fresh ginger (from a 2-inch chunk)*
> *1 cup sugar*
> *¼ teaspoon instant yeast*
> *Cold tap water*

1. Place the funnel in the mouth of a 2-liter plastic bottle with a screw-on lid. Juice the lemon and strain the juice into the bottle through the funnel.
2. Add the ginger, the sugar, and the yeast. Don't worry if some of it gets stuck in the funnel—the water will flush it out. Now pour in enough water to fill the bottle. Cap tightly.
3. Gently shake to release the sediment and yeast from the bottom of the bottle. Press on the bottle; you'll notice there's some give.
4. Let the bottle sit at room temperature for about 24 hours. You'll know the soda is done when you press on the bottle again and it feels very taut and hard. Put the bottle in the refrigerator. As soon as it's cold, it's ready to drink. Open the bottle with care—it may be very bubbly. It will lose effervescence over the next few days, so enjoy it promptly.

Makes 2 liters

MARGARITAS

I started out drinking frozen strawberry margaritas when I was in college, and if a margarita wasn't sweet and rosy pink and so cold my head hurt when I swallowed, I wouldn't drink it. I have changed, probably for the worse. I now drink only margaritas made with fresh lime juice (in a pinch you can use lemon), decent tequila, and $45-per-bottle Grand Marnier, served straight up. No rocks, ever. Ice dilutes the alcohol. Which is what I mean by changing for the worse.

I think fresh lime juice is more important to a top-shelf margarita than top-shelf tequila. But squeezing limes for more than a few margaritas can make you tetchy, which presents a quandary when you serve margaritas at a biggish party. Good margaritas or crabby hostess? At my first-ever barbecue party, I wanted to serve margaritas, so I bought a bottle of pale green margarita mix. Before anyone else arrived, as my sister and I set the table, we made ourselves "good" margaritas with fresh lime juice, decent tequila, and $45-per-bottle Grand Marnier. I felt stingy, drinking good margaritas while mixing bulk margaritas in a pitcher for the guests. But I really do dislike squeezing limes.

My father arrived. The man who taught me to show a horse who's boss, appreciate crime fiction, and kill a chicken. Could I really give him a mediocre margarita? I could not. I made him a good margarita too. Then my inimitable and dear ninety-nine-year-old grandmother arrived, the woman who taught me to wear dangly earrings, and to pat corn tortillas by hand. Could I really give her a second-class margarita? Of course not. She got a good margarita. My friends Melanie and Stan arrived. I love Melanie and Stan—that's why we were having them over! I couldn't give them bad margaritas! In the end, everyone got good margaritas and I didn't even mind squeezing the limes because I was drinking a good margarita.

You can buy margarita mix, and it is very convenient and very cheap, and it tastes very cheap. I'm against it. As Christopher Hitchens says of choosing one's booze, "Pick a decent product and stick with it. Upgrade yourself, for chrissake. Do you think you are going to live forever?" Always buy more limes than you think you need; limes can be very stingy with their juice and it's hard to know what you're dealing with until you cut them.

Make it or buy the mix? Make it.
Hassle: Squeezing limes

Cost comparison: $0.78 for a margarita made from mix. $5.68 for a margarita using the following recipe.

¼ cup tequila, as good as you can afford
¼ cup Grand Marnier (or Cointreau)
¼ cup freshly squeezed lime juice (from 2 to 3 limes)
Kosher salt, optional

1. If you want salt on the glass, run a squeezed lime around the rim of a martini glass and dip in a saucer of salt to coat.
2. Pour the tequila, Grand Marnier, and lime juice into a cocktail shaker with a handful of ice. Shake vigorously. Strain into the glass.

Makes 1 generous margarita or 2 little ones

BITTERS

For $900 you can buy a copper still that looks like a cross between a samovar and Ali Baba's lamp. Although the Manhattan used to be my favorite drink, I was not up for making bourbon, which takes years to age. But when I was flipping through my mother's 1975 copy of *Liqueurs for All Seasons* one day, it occurred to me that bitters were completely within my grasp and time frame. Just a single drop of a potent aromatic bitters transforms a rude slug of whiskey and vermouth into a Manhattan. I went on to make a lot of bitters, including one with cherry and vanilla, another with orange peel, and an extremely complicated bitters recipe that required multiple steepings and strainings and decantings and the purchase of gentian. This was the finest of all bitters, tasted from a spoon, but once it went into a cocktail I couldn't tell the difference between this and other bitters—unless they contained orange, which I love.

This is a shortcut bitters I liked very much that you can make with ingredients you may already have in your cupboard. Don't bother with a premium bourbon. I used Jim Beam.

Make it or buy it? Make it.

Hassle: Easy. Fun.

Cost comparison: Homemade costs $0.64 per ounce. Angostura: $2.25 per ounce.

Peel from 1 orange
One 750-milliliter bottle 80-proof whiskey
6 vanilla beans, split in half lengthwise
1 teaspoon anise seeds
2 juniper berries
2 whole cloves
2 allspice berries
2 teaspoons cardamom seeds

1. Preheat the oven to 200 degrees F.
2. Put the orange peel in the oven—you can set it directly on the rack—and roast for 1½ hours, until very dry.
3. Combine the orange peel and all the remaining ingredients in a large jar. Cap the jar, give it a vigorous shake, and let it sit at room temperature for 2 weeks.
4. Strain into a clean jar or bottle. Store in a cupboard indefinitely.

Makes a little over 3 cups, more than enough bitterness to last a lifetime

MARASCHINO CHERRIES

Some people think a twist of orange peel makes a more elegant garnish for a cocktail than a lipstick red cherry, and they are right. But elegance is overrated. There's something festive and charming about a drink embellished with a crunchy cherry, round and red as the nose on an alcoholic. I mean, clown. I poured so much money into attempting to make my own maraschino cherries that I could put a small down payment on an orchard. The results:

Maraschino recipe number one came courtesy of Melissa Clark's *In the Kitchen with a Good Appetite* and involved soaking sour cherries in Luxardo, an expensive liqueur made from Croatian Marasca cherries and their crushed bitter pits. Clark:

"They were seductively crisp-textured and steeped with an exotic, piney, floral flavor that was just sweet enough but balanced by the tart tang of the cherry." Since I could find neither fresh nor bottled sour cherries, which is what Clark calls for, I rinsed the goop off the sour cherries in a can of pie filling and macerated them in the Luxardo for five days. At the end of that time, I tasted one. It was too alcoholic, and it had neither snap nor stem. It was like eating a small, booze-soaked prune. Fail.

I moved on to maraschino cherry recipe number two, which I found in the online archives of the *Seattle Weekly*. (The author refers to the store-bought maraschino cherry as a "humiliated, flavorless fruitard.") This recipe called for brining fresh bing cherries and covering them in Luxardo, which I now had on hand. This approach held promise. While pie cherries are limp to begin with, bings are naturally crunchy and it was just a matter of capturing and preserving that. I carefully pitted the cherries, keeping the stems attached, and dropped them into the brine. Yet even these firmest of cherries lost all their structure during their saline bath. They came out salty and, again, overly boozy for my tastes. I know "overly boozy" is a strange criticism from someone who loves booze, but it seems wrong to garnish alcohol with more alcohol. Aren't garnishes about complementary contrast?

I found the alcohol-free recipe I was looking for in Linda Ziedrich's brilliant *Joy of Jams, Jellies, and Other Sweet Preserves*. (Despite what I'm about to say about this particular recipe, if you buy one preserving book, Ziedrich's is the one.) In the headnote, Ziedrich explains that the gaudy American maraschino cherry we all know and joke about was invented in Oregon during Prohibition. Because the local trees produced yellow cherries, red dye came into the equation. Ziedrich offers a recipe developed by Oregon State University that entails brining with alum (aluminum hydroxide), an additive that makes pickles crispier, gingerbread harder, and maraschino cherries snappier. (Old cookbooks abound in recipes that call for alum.) I found it at Safeway in the spice rack; it looks just like cream of tartar and comes in the same little plastic jar.

I brined a two-pound bag of organic cherries with the alum, then drained, rinsed, and cooked them in a sugar syrup, and let them steep at room temperature for a day. I reheated them and let them sit another day. Then I added lemon juice and almond extract and I sterilized jars to can them. Everyone was going to get a jar of maraschino cherries for Christmas along with a small bottle of bitters. I was all set to can the cherries when I popped one into my mouth. This was the worst cherry yet—salty, sweet, soggy, absolutely revolting. I carried the pan of cherries out to the chickens, and even they weren't interested and the cherries lay there, soaking dye and alum into the dirt.

Make it or buy it? Buy it.

VERMOUTH

Vermouth is fortified wine infused with herbs, and making it at home is a delightful and ridiculous project. The results can be incredibly delicious. I found a recipe for vermouth on a blog called *Last Crumb* and this vermouth called for thirty-three ingredients, including dandelion root and pau d'arco, the medicinal bark from a South American tree. I trimmed the ingredient list down to a more manageable twenty-six components and ordered herbs from a botanicals supplier (see Appendix). A few days after that, the herbs arrived, packets of twigs and leaves and roots and barks and powders, enough to make cases of vermouth and clutter the pantry for the rest of my days.

I made my first vermouth that very evening, replacing the recommended brandy with Navan, a vanilla-infused cognac liqueur made by Grand Marnier.

Americans typically use vermouth only as a mixer in martinis and Manhattans, but Italians sip it straight up as an aperitif. Obviously, they are not sipping from $2.99 bottles of plonk; they are sipping Carpano Antica and Punt e Mes. I think this sweetish sipping vermouth belongs in that company.

Make it or buy it? Are you nuts? If so, make it.
Hassle: Sure
Cost comparison: Except the saffron, none of the herbs costs much—a pinch of angelica works out to less than a penny—but since I will never use them for anything else, and have made only three bottles of vermouth, I'm not sure I shouldn't allot the cost of the whole bag. But I won't. A bottle of homemade: $11.00. Lillet (the closest comparison): $17.00 per bottle.

INFUSION

5 pinches ground coriander

1 pinch dried sage

3 juniper berries

2 pinches pau d'arco

1 pinch dried oregano

2 pinches crushed dandelion root

1 cinnamon stick

1 star anise

1 pinch cardamom seeds

2 pinches freshly grated nutmeg

1 pinch dried rosemary

2 pinches dried chamomile

1 pinch crumbled angelica root

1 tiny pinch crumbled gentian root

1 pinch dried marjoram

2 pinches fennel seeds

2 pinches ground ginger

1 bay leaf

4 whole cloves

1 pinch saffron threads

3 black peppercorns

5 drops wormwood extract

1 whole vanilla bean

½ cup plus 2 teaspoons sugar

One 750-milliliter bottle dry, cheap, undistinguished white wine

⅔ cup Navan vanilla cognac liqueur, or brandy

1. Put all the infusion ingredients and 2 teaspoons sugar in a small saucepan. Cover with 1 cup of the wine.
2. Simmer gently for 10 minutes to infuse the wine with the flavorings. Cool completely.

3. Into a large, clean jar with a lid, pour the brandy or liqueur and the rest of the wine, leaving room at the top for the infusion. Rinse and reserve the wine bottle.

4. Line a sieve with a coffee filter or very fine-weave cheesecloth, doubled over, and filter the infusion, squeezing out all the precious bitter juice into a bowl.

5. Add half the infusion to the jar and shake. Taste. If you think it needs more flavor, add more infusion. (I used it all.) If you want a dry vermouth for your martinis, stop right now. Your vermouth is ready. If you want a sweet sipping vermouth, proceed to step 6.

6. Melt the ½ cup sugar in a small saucepan. Pour into the jar. It will crackle and harden the instant it touches the cool liquid, forming a crazy caramel spider, but in 20 minutes it will melt and disappear into the vermouth.

7. Decant into the empty wine bottle. Store in the refrigerator and serve well chilled. Invite friends over so you can show off.

Makes 1 bottle

COFFEE LIQUEUR

With very little effort, some sugar, vodka, and espresso powder, you can make coffee liqueur, though you will have to wait a few weeks to let it mellow before you mix that White Russian. The homemade liqueur tastes just like Kahlúa, which you can buy ready to pour from a thick brown bottle. They cost about the same.

Make it or buy it? Buy it.

CHAPTER 18

CANNING

And the canning season was on. How I dreaded it! Jelly, jam, preserves, canned raspberries, blackcaps, peas, spinach, beans, beets, carrots, blackberries, loganberries, wild blackberries, wild raspberries, applesauce, tomatoes, peaches, pears, plums, chickens, venison, beef, clams, salmon, rhubarb, cherries, corn, pickles and prunes. By fall the pantry shelves would groan and creak under nature's bounty and the bitter thing was that we wouldn't be able to eat one tenth of it. Canning is a mental quirk just like any form of hoarding. First you plant too much of everything in the garden; then you waste hours and hours in the boiling sun cultivating; then you buy a pressure cooker and can too much of everything so that it won't be wasted.

Frankly I don't like home-canned anything, and I spent all of my spare time reading up on botulism.

—Betty MacDonald, *The Egg and I*

I'm ambivalent about canning, despite the fact that—or more likely, because—I come from a long line of ace canners. My grandmother was a Mormon and if you're unfamiliar with the faith, one tenet is that every family keep a year's worth of food in the pantry in case of natural or financial catastrophe. In the back of the garage next to the washer and dryer was my grandmother's "pantry," its shelves sagging under the weight of mason jars filled with golden canned peaches and apricot halves bobbing in syrup, tomato sauce, bread and butter pickles, raspberry jam, currant jelly, spiced cherry syrup. There were also many boxes of Jell-O, bags of Lay's potato chips, and cases of Postum, the decaffeinated coffee stand-in. This was not a beautiful Martha Stewart pantry.

No, that would have been my mother's pantry, which occupied a corner of the basement under the stairs. Her reasons for canning were not religious but counterculture. She had to be one of the great commodity canners of the 1970s, making sure we would eat organic apricot halves in January rather than having to resort, God forbid, to Del Monte. Only children whose mothers weren't paying attention let them eat fruit cocktail with maraschino cherries.

I remember well and not fondly the black graniteware kettle rattling and steaming on the electric stove, every surface given over to widemouthed jars into which, sweating and impatient, my young mother—a math major, one of three women to graduate from her law school class in 1964—funneled apricots and cherries and plums and tomatoes so I could come home from school and pop open a jar of golden peaches for a snack. They were delicious, but when I think about it now, it seems almost tragic, a sacrifice of time and youth and spirit when we would have grown up just fine eating Del Monte. Everyone I knew who ate Del Monte and Wonder bread and Skippy and Pringles turned out okay. I see these people around town all the time.

When they were in their early forties, my parents divorced. I never saw my mother can anything ever again. There was no more family and there was really no point in canning 100 pounds of apricots anymore. Had there ever been? She got a job, she bought season tickets to the ballet, she bought new clothes, she started to travel. She made fun of her earnest, industrious young canning self, and she made it hard, if not impossible, for me to can.

I don't can fruit. But look at me now. Look at this book. How far does the apricot really fall from the tree? And I do like a homemade jam or relish.

Some jams are more worth making than others. Strawberry jam? Expensive and it tastes just like store-bought. On the other hand, there's my mother's orange-apricot conserve, the likes of which you will not find even in a gourmet supermarket.

ORANGE-APRICOT CONSERVE

This has the bite of orange, the sweet-tart tang of apricot, and the bitterness of apricot pits. About those pits: apricot pits contain trace amounts of cyanide and if that makes you nervous, leave them out. I grew up with this jam and am alive to write about it. I love their crunch.

This is not a canning manual. High-acid fruits and pickles are a very safe bet for the home canner, but for thorough instructions on canning and food safety, consult *The Ball Blue Book of Preserving*.

Make it or buy it? You can't buy this jam. Make it.

Hassle: In the dictionary under "hassle" there should be a line drawing of a woman standing at a sweltering canning kettle, lifting out jars.

Cost comparison: You can't really compare this with store-bought jam, as there is no product on the market like it. If you compare it with small-batch, artisanal jams, like those of June Taylor, the revered San Francisco Bay Area jam maker, per pint, this costs about half as much.

3 oranges
30 ripe apricots, about 3 pounds
Sugar
5 or 6 pint canning jars (you may well need fewer; it all depends on how much fruit you end up with, after measuring, which can vary)

1. Wash and slice the oranges thin, then chop. It is tempting, but don't use the food processor, which will turn the oranges to mush; you want discernible chunks of peel and fruit. Measure and note how many cups you have. Put the orange in a wide, deep saucepan, add 1 cup water, and cook, stirring often, for about 15 minutes, until the peel is tender.

2. Wash and chop the apricots, reserving the pits. Measure. Again, note how many cups you have. Add to the orange mixture on the stove. For every 4 cups fruit, both oranges and apricots, you need to add 3 cups sugar.

3. Simmer the jam, stirring regularly to avoid scorching. Meanwhile, put the apricot pits in a sealed plastic bag and smack with a hammer. You are trying to extract the

almonds in the middle of the apricot pits. When you've freed about 6 almonds, cut them into slivers.

4. While the jam is simmering, put some pint jars to boil in a large pot of water. Let them boil for 15 minutes to sterilize. You can use recycled canning jars, but must use brand-new lids and screw tops every time you can. Put the lids in a pan of hot water, but do not boil.

5. After about 1 hour, when the jam is thick and jammy—but still brightly colored—stir in the slivered "almonds." Ladle the jam into the jars. Put the caps on and gently screw on the lids. Sterilize in a boiling water bath for 10 minutes.

6. Remove from the water and set on a clean, dry dish towel on the counter. You should hear the lids click when they seal. Store sealed jars in a cupboard for a year or more. Refrigerate after opening.

Makes 4 to 6 pints

CHUTNEY

For people who only step into the kitchen to fool around once in a great while, chutney is the ticket: Practically foolproof, it is always good and hard to ruin. There is nothing like a homemade condiment, and, besides, you will never have to buy another bottle of wine to take to a dinner party.
—Laurie Colwin, *More Home Cooking*

A fine novelist and the most charming of food writers, the late Laurie Colwin was correct about almost everything, but when she got it wrong, she got it badly wrong. She got it wrong about chutney.

First of all, if you step into the kitchen only once in a great while, I can think of many more gratifying projects you might tackle before chutney. In no particular order: molasses cookies, fudge, duck à l'orange.

And while I agree it is hard to ruin chutney, that is because there is not all that much to ruin. One year I made plum-lavender chutney and it was okay. Another year I made cranberry chutney; another year, pear chutney; another year, apple. Also: banana. It was always pretty good, but nothing special. One year I had my father bring me all of his green tomatoes before he ripped out his summer garden and I made green tomato chutney. I was so proud of my thrift, turning green tomatoes into jars and jars of chutney. I made some crostini with goat cheese and fried green tomatoes and green tomato chutney. These crostini were stellar. That took care of half a jar of chutney. I had a dozen or so more. I brought my father a jar and made him taste it. He agreed that it was very superior chutney. "You can put it on sandwiches, eat it with meat," I said.

"Thanks!" he replied.

Yet he didn't seem as delighted as he'd been when I gave him the boxed set of *Sopranos* DVDs. When I looked in his refrigerator months later I saw the chutney where I had left it, untouched.

Don't kid yourself. If you ever want to be invited to another dinner party, you really need to bring a bottle of wine.

Make it or buy it? Neither

SWEET-HOT PICKLE RELISH

This is adapted from *The Book of New New England Cookery* by Judith and Evan Jones. It's sweet and hot and adds zest to every hot dog.

Make it or buy it? Make it.
Hassle: I don't love "finely" chopping anything, but this a relatively simple canning project with a big payoff.
Cost comparison: It costs a dollar a cup to make this relish. Vlasic: $2.40 per cup.

4 cups finely chopped pickling cucumbers, 8 to 10
2 cups finely chopped onion, about 2 large onions
2 cups finely chopped red bell pepper, about 2 large peppers
¼ cup kosher salt
2 cups cider vinegar
3½ cups sugar
1 tablespoon celery seeds
1 tablespoon mustard seeds
¾ teaspoon cayenne pepper

1. Mix the cucumbers, onion, and bell pepper with the salt in a large bowl and add enough cold water to cover. Let rest, covered, overnight at room temperature.
2. In the morning, drain the vegetables.
3. In a large pot, bring the vinegar, sugar, celery seeds, mustard seeds, and cayenne to a boil, stirring to dissolve the sugar. Add the vegetables and simmer for 10 minutes.
4. Pack immediately into sterilized canning jars, place the lids on the jars, loosely screw on the rings, and boil for 10 minutes in a boiling water bath. Remove from the water to a clean dish towel and wait for the pop of the lids sealing. Store sealed jars in the cupboard. Refrigerate after opening.

Makes 4 pints

BANANA KETCHUP

Until the mid-twentieth century, ketchup was any smooth semisolid condiment, concocted from ingredients ranging from green walnuts to oysters, mushrooms, and cranberries. But most of us will never know what green walnut ketchup tastes like because there is really only one kind of ketchup in the world today: tomato.

Just about every preserving manual and chef's cookbook touts a recipe for a wondrous tomato ketchup that will supposedly ruin you for Heinz forever. I've made the ketchup from *The River Cottage Cookbook* and Cindy Pawlcyn's *Mustards Grill Napa Valley Cookbook*, and while they were estimable dipping sauces, they were not ketchup. Heinz is ketchup and if you miss by an inch you miss by a mile. Buy the ketchup.

Tomato ketchup, that is. The banana ketchup from Helen Witty's *Fancy Pantry* misses by a mile and therein lies its charm. It's not trying to be anything but its own spicy, fruity, homely brown self. This freckled condiment improves pork or chicken sandwiches, and, of course, a burger.

1 cup golden raisins
¾ cup chopped onions, from one medium onion
4 garlic cloves, peeled

One 6-ounce can tomato paste

2⅔ cups cider vinegar

3 pounds overripe bananas

1 cup dark brown sugar, packed

1 tablespoon kosher salt, plus more to taste

1½ teaspoons cayenne pepper

½ cup light corn syrup

4 teaspoons ground allspice

1½ teaspoons ground cinnamon

1½ teaspoons freshly grated nutmeg

1 teaspoon freshly ground black pepper, plus more to taste

½ teaspoon ground cloves

⅓ cup dark rum

1. Combine the raisins, onions, garlic, and tomato paste in a blender or food processor and puree until smooth, adding some of the vinegar as necessary to help the job along. Scrape the puree into a large pot. (Don't wash the blender just yet.)
2. Peel the bananas and puree until smooth, again adding some vinegar if the mixture needs liquid. Add the bananas to the mixture in the pot, along with the balance of the vinegar, 4 cups water, the brown sugar, salt, and cayenne.
3. Bring the mixture to a boil, stirring frequently. Lower the heat to medium-low and cook, uncovered, for 1¼ hours, stirring often. If it feels as though it will stick, add additional water, up to 3 cups.
4. Add the corn syrup, allspice, cinnamon, nutmeg, pepper, and cloves. Cook, stirring frequently, for 15 minutes longer, or until thick enough to coat a spoon. To test its consistency, remove the pot from the heat, spoon a little ketchup onto a saucer, and let it cool. If very little or no liquid pools around the dollop, the ketchup is ready. If liquid does pool, resume cooking for as long as necessary. Cool to room temperature.
5. Puree the ketchup again in the blender or food processor until very smooth, working in batches if necessary. Rinse the pot. Return the ketchup to it. Taste for salt and pepper and adjust.
6. Bring the ketchup to a boil again over medium heat, stirring constantly. Add the rum.

7. Ladle the boiling-hot ketchup into sterilized half-pint canning jars. Tap on the sterilized lids, and lightly screw on the rings. Process in a boiling water bath for 15 minutes. Remove to a clean dish towel on the counter and wait for the lids to seal. Store in a cupboard for a year or more. After opening, refrigerate.

Makes 7 half-pint jars

CHAPTER 19

HAVING PEOPLE OVER

When I got married, my mother told me I needed to register for an ice bucket. She said, "You need pieces for entertaining." She said I should register for good china. That I needed table linens. I needed cocktail napkins. I needed trays.

I told her that I didn't see myself ever needing an ice bucket when I could just grab a handful of ice out of the freezer, and that people of my generation didn't call things "pieces." We didn't "entertain." We "had people over."

So I didn't register for an ice bucket. Nonetheless, I ended up with two ice buckets, both of them crystal, both of them beautiful. And for the next fifteen years, as I stubbornly "had people over," I floundered trying to figure out how to make every party look casual and effortless. I would have been embarrassed to pull out a crystal ice bucket.

I used to cry every time we "had people over." I became overwrought trying to deep-fry arancini while shaping the homemade spinach gnocchi and whipping up a soufflé for dessert and grabbing handfuls of ice out of the freezer for the gin and tonics. Every party was full of angst. I deserved it.

My mother was one of the most social people I know. In the decades after she and my father divorced I can't remember once seeing my mother chop a clove of garlic or peel a potato, let alone fry arancini. Opening bottles of wine and boxes of Bremner wafers? That, I remember. She threw parties all the time, and her invitations always came with a breezy disclaimer: "I think I'll just get a Costco lasagna. After all, it's not about the food, it's about the company." I hated it when she said that.

Of course, she was right. You never caught my mother in the kitchen reducing a sauce when there were friends laughing in the living room. She set a glamorous table with her own wedding china, put ice in the ice bucket (hers was green teak), transferred the Costco lasagna to some glitzy serving plate, and brought it out with fanfare. Everyone had fun at my mother's parties.

Only very recently did it dawn on me that "entertaining" is exactly the right word for "having people over." The dinner party is a work of theater, and the linens and candlesticks and ice bucket are props and they are every bit as important as the food. So is your own relatively calm presence. It ruins the show if you're in the kitchen in a pair of sweatpants and a jog bra, swearing over some misguided cioppino. Fifteen years into my marriage, I used the ice bucket for the first time. I put it on a tray (another wedding gift) with all the other cocktail fixings, lit candles, brought out the wedding china. My sister said, "Look at your little bar setup! Look at this *table*!" It put everyone in a festive mood, and I didn't know why I spent all those years resisting. And then I put out store-bought crackers with a tuna dip for an appetizer, and since I can't do Costco lasagna, I brought out one of my three time-tested alternatives. But more about them in a minute. First, about the crackers.

CRACKERS

My mother believed in crackers. Crackers were her little black dress. You could serve crackers with store-bought pâté, or peel off the foil on some Philadelphia cream cheese and pour over it a jar of chutney the color of lentil soup that some dear, dear friend gave you for Christmas in 1967. ("Oh, stop looking at me like that, Jennifer. Chutney gets better with age.") The perfect accompaniment: crackers, naturally. The leftover crackers you could spread with peanut butter for dinner—a week later, a month, a year!—with a glass of chardonnay while watching *Masterpiece Theatre*. After all, peanut butter is full of protein. You could make an easy but fabulous dessert with crackers—angel pie (page 258)—and there was nothing better than crackers when you fell sick. My mother collected crackers, and when my sister and I cleaned out her drawers after her death we found gluten-free rice crackers and RyKrisp and Ritz and table water crackers and Bremner wafers, crackers for every occasion, all neatly rubber-banded in the sleeves and arranged in the drawer. I think she chose the crackers to serve or eat on a given day based on the geometry of that drawer.

I've tried making crackers, and some of them have been great, like the Thomas Keller crackers you run through the pasta machine and which take several hours and two people to produce. But they never have quite the crunch or longevity of store-bought, and the whole point of crackers is that you don't have to hunch at a pasta machine for an hour. The point of crackers is to make your life easier. There are two crackers I actually like to make.

MELBA TOAST

I know. Why bother? Why eat melba toast at all? It's dry and bland, but good with a strong cheese—and it's inexpensive. It also has a certain 1950s glamour—I imagine melba toast and Champagne are what Bette Davis ate on a diet.

Make it or buy it? Make it.
Hassle: Zero
Cost comparison: You can buy a 5-ounce box for under $3.00. Making it from sandwich bread that's about to go stale: free.

Sandwich bread, store-bought or homemade

1. Preheat the oven to 375 degrees F.
2. Lightly toast the bread—it should be firm on the outside, still tender and bready in the middle.
3. Lay out the bread on a work surface. Cut off the crusts. Place the flat of your hand on a slice and cut the bread horizontally into two thinner slices. Now cut these thinner slices into thirds.
4. Put these in the oven on an ungreased cookie sheet and bake for 15 to 20 minutes until completely dry. Store in a cookie tin at room temperature.

CHEEZ-ITS

In her magnificent cookbook *Around My French Table*, Dorie Greenspan includes a recipe for "Cheez-It-Ish" crackers made with Gruyère and cut into circles. It gave me an idea to make actual Cheez-It clones. I took her recipe, substituted orange cheddar, and added some Worcestershire sauce. Then I cut the dough into postage-stamp squares, poked holes in the middle, and baked them. Owen came home from school and tasted them, and his face lit up. He said, "Will you make these for my snack all the time?" And I thought, *When there are twenty-five hours in a day!* But I lied, "Of course!" These crackers are a natural with tomato soup—use them as soup crackers. And if you put out a bowl of them with drinks when you have a party, the bowl will be empty within the hour.

Make it or buy it? Make it.
Hassle: Even cutting them isn't that bad.
Cost comparison: Homemade: $0.32 per ounce. Store-bought: $0.39 per ounce.

8 tablespoons (1 stick) cold unsalted butter, cut into small chunks
¼ pound extra-sharp orange cheddar, grated (about 1 cup)
½ teaspoon kosher salt
⅛ teaspoon freshly ground white pepper
Pinch of cayenne pepper
1 cup plus 2 tablespoons all-purpose flour
1 teaspoon Worcestershire sauce (page 166)

1. Put the butter, cheese, salt, white pepper, and cayenne in a food processor and pulse until the butter is broken up into bits and the mixture forms small curds, like cottage cheese. Add the flour and pulse until well combined. It will now look more like wet couscous. Add the Worcestershire sauce and pulse again. The dough should be moist and come together in your hands.
2. Turn the dough onto a work surface and knead it once or twice until it forms a ball. Pat it into a disk, wrap in plastic, and chill for at least an hour.
3. Preheat the oven to 350 degrees F.
4. Roll the dough out a scant ¼ inch thick. (If the dough seems sticky, flour the work surface, though you probably won't need to.) Using a fluted wheel cutter (if you have one; if not, a knife is fine) and a ruler, cut the dough into long 1-inch-wide strips, and then cut the strips into 1-inch squares. Gather and reroll the scraps and continue cutting.
5. Place on an ungreased cookie sheet. The crackers won't expand, so you can

fit them fairly tightly. Make a small hole in the center of each cracker with a skewer or the stem of an instant-read thermometer. A toothpick isn't quite big enough.

6. Bake for about 15 minutes, until the crackers darken just a bit. Cool completely on a rack and store in a cookie tin for up to a week.

Makes 70 to 80 crackers

WHITE PEPPERCORNS

Until I bought white peppercorns for the first time quite recently, I assumed the difference between white and black pepper was strictly cosmetic. After all, the white peppercorn is simply a pepper berry that has been allowed to ripen and had its husk removed. But something dramatic happens when you remove that husk. White pepper has less up-front bite and a long, more complex finish. While I've never been a big fan of black pepper, I love white pepper. Just one more reason to buy a spice grinder and find a good ethnic market: A 1-ounce jar of McCormick ground white pepper costs $6.15. I can buy an equivalent amount of white peppercorns from a Middle Eastern market and grind them fresh at home for $1.50.

ALTERNATIVES TO COSTCO

Even though it's delicious, I will never buy a Costco lasagna. I spent too many years rolling my eyes at my mother's dedication to the $12 casserole. But all of the following three dishes are good for parties, because you can make them ahead of time.

OLIVE PASTA

This recipe, and the following, is adapted from *We Called It Macaroni* by Nancy Verde Barr, a fabulous cookbook and one of the first I ever bought as an adult.

Make it or buy a Costco lasagna? Make it.
Hassle: Easy
Cost comparison: $2.50 per serving versus $1.00 per serving for a Costco lasagna.

½ cup olive oil
1 medium onion, minced
¼ teaspoon red pepper flakes
4 garlic cloves, minced
One 15-ounce can chopped tomatoes, drained
1 cup drained oil-cured or brine-cured olives, black or green, or a mixture, pitted
2 tablespoons capers
1 tablespoon red wine vinegar
2 teaspoons dried oregano
Pinch of sugar
Salt and freshly ground black pepper
1 pound fusilli
1 cup grated Parmesan or pecorino

1. Heat the oil, onion, red pepper flakes, and garlic in a large skillet or Dutch oven and cook until the onion is softened but not browned, about 8 minutes.
2. Stir in the tomatoes, olives, capers, vinegar, oregano, and sugar. Simmer for 15 minutes over low heat. At this point you can leave the sauce, covered, on the

stove until you are ready to eat. When that point comes, turn the heat on low to warm the sauce.

3. Cook the pasta in a pot of boiling salted water until al dente. Drain and pour into the hot sauce and stir for 1 minute. Add the cheese; salt and freshly ground pepper to taste.
4. Serve immediately.

Serves 6 to 8

LAYERED POLENTA

This also comes from Barr's cookbook, but I've made some changes over the years.

Make it or buy a Costco lasagna? Make it.
Hassle: Lots of work
Cost comparison: $2.08 per serving. Hard to beat the price on that $1.00 per serving Costco lasagna!

TOMATO SAUCE
5 tablespoons olive oil
1 big onion, finely chopped
Two 28-ounce cans whole peeled tomatoes, drained and chopped
Kosher salt and freshly ground black pepper to taste
1 teaspoon sugar
Finely chopped fresh basil (optional)

¼ pound pancetta, homemade (page 176) or store-bought
1 tablespoon kosher salt
¾ pound coarse polenta
1½ cups grated Parmesan
1 pound sweet Italian sausage
3 tablespoons unsalted butter, plus more for the baking pan
½ pound fresh mozzarella, store-bought (homemade would be wasted), cut into 1-inch pieces

1. In a large saucepan over medium heat, cook the onions in the oil until softened, about 8 minutes. Add the tomatoes, salt, pepper, and sugar and simmer, stirring occasionally, until the sauce is thick, about 30 minutes. Stir in the basil, if using, about 5 minutes before you're done.

2. In a medium skillet, fry the pancetta over low heat until it is brown and crisp. Set aside.

3. In another large saucepan, bring 2 quarts water to a boil, add the salt, and add the cornmeal in a slow stream, stirring constantly. Cook over medium heat, stirring occasionally, until the polenta masses together and begins to pull away from the sides of the pan, 20 to 30 minutes. Remove from the heat and stir in the pancetta plus its fat and ½ cup of the Parmesan. Pour onto a cookie sheet and smooth the surface with a wet spatula. Let cool until set. Cut into 2-inch squares.

4. Squeeze the sausage out of the casings into the skillet in which you fried the pancetta. Fry, breaking it into smallish clumps and cooking until all traces of pink are gone.

5. Generously butter a 9 by 13-inch pan. Spread a thin layer of tomato sauce over the bottom. Arrange one-third of the polenta on the tomato sauce in a single layer. Sprinkle half the mozzarella and half the sausage over the polenta. Spoon on one-third of the tomato sauce. Sprinkle one-third of the Parmesan over the sauce. Dot with 1 tablespoon butter. Repeat with half the remaining polenta, all the remaining mozzarella and sausage, half the remaining sauce, half the grated cheese, and 1 tablespoon butter. Top with the remaining polenta, tomato sauce, and grated cheese. Dot with the last tablespoon of butter. You can now put it in the refrigerator and bake it up to 5 days later.

6. Preheat the oven to 375 degrees F.

7. Bake the polenta, uncovered, for 30 minutes, or until the cheese is bubbling and the dish is piping hot throughout.

Serves 12

VADOUVAN MAC 'N' CHEESE

I found that as the working parent of small children at the turn of the most recent century, boxed mac 'n' cheese was as essential to my sanity as *Dragon Tales* and sauvignon blanc. It was easy, affordable, and much loved, and because it was served hot, I could pass it off as a wholesome dinner, which I knew it wasn't. I didn't do that very often. I would have needed less sauvignon blanc if I had.

My children are growing up now and their tastes have broadened impressively. The first time I met my editor, she pressed upon me a recipe for something called "Vadouvan Mac 'n' Cheese." Vadouvan is a muddy-yellow seasoning mix of curry leaves, onions, turmeric, and sundry other spices. I went straight from our lunch to an Indian grocery to buy vadouvan and when I got home I made the mac 'n' cheese.

"This isn't macaroni and cheese," said Owen. "It's green." Actually, it was a jaundiced yellow, but I didn't correct him. He was hungry, so he took a bite, and approximately one minute later he asked for seconds. The trouble with a lot of mac 'n' cheese is that it's monotonously rich, an exhausting song in the key of cheddar. But here, the spice cut the incomparable creaminess and richness of the cheese, and the cheese mellowed the spice. It was a huge hit. Six weeks later, Owen requested it for the dinner at his sleepover tenth birthday party.

"Are you sure?" I said. "Are you sure you don't want pizza?"

"I want people to think I know a lot about gourmet food," he said. "I like it when people think I'm an expert in things."

The guests—swilling root beer and telling fart jokes—seemed unimpressed with Owen's sophistication, but seven boys vacuumed up mac 'n' cheese for twelve in fifteen minutes. I couldn't decide whether to put this recipe in the "Dinner" chapter or "Having People Over" chapter, but I decided on the latter because I now make it only for parties. The recipe makes a lot and you can have it all done ahead of time.

This recipe originally comes from the website Jane Spice and I have changed it only slightly.

Make it or buy it? Buy boxed mac 'n' cheese as your sanity demands, but when you have time, budget, and stamina, try this recipe. It is not only better than Kraft Mac 'n' Cheese, it is better than a Costco lasagna.

Hassle: I don't love grating cheese. Plus, there's a lot of pot scrubbing.

Cost comparison: Homemade: $2.40 per cup. Stouffer's frozen: $1.50 per cup. Kraft: $0.69 per cup.

Kosher salt

12 tablespoons (1½ sticks) unsalted butter, plus more for the casserole dish

6 slices fresh bread (about 6 ounces), homemade (page 8) or store-bought, crumbled
*   into feathery bits in a food processor; rye (page 12) is especially tasty*

5½ cups whole milk

½ cup all-purpose flour

3 tablespoons vadouvan spice blend (see Appendix)

¼ teaspoon freshly ground black pepper

1 tablespoon chili powder

4½ cups grated sharp white cheddar (about 18 ounces)

2 cups grated Gruyère (about 8 ounces)

1 pound elbow macaroni

1. Preheat the oven to 375 degrees F. Bring a large pot of salted water to a rolling boil. Butter a large casserole.

2. In a skillet melt 6 tablespoons of the butter and toss with the bread crumbs.

3. In a medium saucepan, gently heat the milk.

4. In a large pot or Dutch oven melt the remaining butter. When it begins to bubble, add the flour. Cook, stirring, for 1 minute.

5. Slowly pour the hot milk into the flour-butter mixture and whisk well. Continue cooking, whisking constantly, until the mixture bubbles and thickens. Remove from the heat and stir in 2 teaspoons salt, the vadouvan, pepper, chili powder, 3 cups of the cheddar, and 1½ cups of the Gruyère. Set the cheese sauce aside.

6. When the water is boiling, add the macaroni. Cook until it is just tender; the inside should still be somewhat firm. Drain the macaroni in a colander, rinse under cold running water, and drain again well. Stir the macaroni into the cheese sauce.

7. Pour the mixture into the prepared casserole. Sprinkle over it the remaining

SHOULD YOU MAKE YOUR OWN VADOUVAN SPICE BLEND?

When I ran through my little packet of vadouvan, I found a recipe online. The process involves chopping several pounds of onions, shallots, and garlic, then cooking them to a brown slurry in a skillet and tossing in fresh curry leaves, fenugreek, and various other spices. After this, I spread the sludge on a cookie sheet and roasted it for an hour until it formed a leathery mat that I broke up and stuffed in a plastic bag. The mat was delicious— salty, oniony, chewy—and I snacked on it straight from the bag. A few days later, I made our beloved mac 'n' cheese. But even when I added an extra tablespoon of homemade vadouvan to the recipe, everyone noted a decline in savor. I priced it out and by making my own vadouvan I spent a few cents more per ounce than if I'd mail-ordered a new package. Buy your vadouvan. Even if you don't make the macaroni and cheese very often, it's good in soups and to flavor chicken and steak. Stir some into milk mayonnaise (page 40) to use as a dipping sauce for french fries. You can use this yummy spice blend anywhere you might use curry powder.

cheddar and Gruyère. Scatter the bread crumbs over the top. Bake until browned, about 30 minutes.

8. Transfer to a cooling rack for 5 minutes before serving.

Makes 14 cups, to serve 12 (or 7 ten-year-old boys)

CURRY LEAF TREE

Even if you never make your own vadouvan curry spice (which you shouldn't), if you cook much Indian food there will come a day when you want a steady supply of fresh curry leaves. Confusingly, the curry leaf has nothing to do with curry powder. Curry powder is a blend of spices, available at any grocery store, that typically includes turmeric, cumin, and coriander and only occasionally crushed dried curry leaf. Curry leaf comes from the curry tree and is typically used fresh and green. It is about the size of a small bay leaf and has an intense fragrance—slightly smoky, slightly metallic—for which there is no substitute. It is as essential to certain Indian dishes as sage is to Thanksgiving stuffing, but it's much more delicious than sage. I drove all over the greater San Francisco Bay Area one winter looking for curry leaves during what turned out to be a temporary import ban. A friend gave me a few leaves from her freezer stash, which disappeared in one recipe of masala chicken.

I decided I needed a curry tree. After I asked at the local nurseries and was met with blank looks, I tracked down an outfit in New Jersey that would sell me a four-inch *Murraya koenigii* for fifteen dollars. Even after the gentleman on the end of the line calculated interstate inspection and shipping and announced, somewhat sheepishly, that the tree would in fact cost seventy dollars, I took a deep breath and ordered it. I assumed the tree would be the size of a healthy potted geranium and soon it would grow to the size of a ficus, become a feature of our living room decor, and I would be in curry leaves forever.

A few weeks later, a diminutive package arrived that contained a specimen resembling one of the bean seedlings a first grader brings home in a Dixie cup. It was a few inches tall, each of its eleven leaves the size of a lentil. I put it in a sunny spot, watered it faithfully, and fertilized it periodically, and after a year it grew perhaps an inch. Two years later, the wispy curry tree still sits on the living room chest, its twenty leaves now the size of navy beans. Perhaps it will surprise me with a growth spurt, but I fully expect it to accompany me to assisted living a few decades hence looking approximately the same and I will breathe its exotic fragrance and rue all the pilaus I never made.

If you are in a nursery and see a flourishing curry leaf plant for twenty or thirty dollars, pull out your wallet. If you're in an Indian grocery and see fresh curry leaves, buy the place out and put them in your freezer. The import ban has been lifted, and last I checked, I could have bought 280 curry leaves for the price of my bonsai.

CHAPTER 20

DESSERTS

When my children were little, my husband worked the night shift at the *San Francisco Chronicle*, which left the three of us at home alone most nights. I didn't want to watch TV—not the shows they liked, anyway—and I didn't want to play endless games of Candy Land, or any games of Candy Land, ever, so we'd have dinner and then I'd pour a glass of wine and Isabel and I would bake cakes or cookies or scones, sometimes all three, while Owen played with his trains at our feet. I'd have another glass of wine, and though I thought I was very unlucky to be stuck at home alone with small children every night, it was actually very merry. A friend started calling me the Tipsy Baker and when I started a cooking blog, that's what I named it, though now I am embarrassed to explain its origin.

I don't remember being particularly contented in those years, but now I look back at those nights standing around the mixer as some of the happiest of my life.

ANGEL PIE

This was my mother's recipe, passed down from her own mother, who probably cut it off the back of a box of crackers. My grandmother says you can make this heavenly pie with saltines, but I've only made it with buttery golden Ritz crackers. Although they contain both partially hydrogenated oil and high-fructose corn syrup, Ritz are worth buying if for no other reason than to make angel pie.

Butter and flour, for the pan
3 large egg whites
1 cup granulated sugar
½ teaspoon vanilla extract (page 260)
¾ teaspoon baking powder
18 Ritz crackers, broken into fairly large pieces
⅔ cup coarsely chopped walnuts
1 pint very cold heavy cream
Sugar to taste, for the cream
Fruit (such as strawberries), sliced and sugared to taste, for serving

1. Preheat the oven to 325 degrees F. Butter and flour a 9-inch pie plate.
2. Beat the egg whites until stiff, gradually adding the granulated sugar and vanilla. Fold in the baking powder. Mix the crackers and nuts and fold into the egg whites.
3. Scrape the mixture into the prepared pan.
4. Bake for 35 minutes. The pie will be craggy and cracked and set. Cool to room temperature.
5. Whip the cream until it's soft and thick and whip in sugar to taste. Fill the pie with the cream and serve with sweetened sliced fruit.

Serves 8

POUND CAKE

I still don't know Mrs. Funsten's first name, but when I was growing up she regularly donated this brick-shaped pound cake to the elementary school bake sale. This unshowy cake was famous in our community and rightfully so. My mother, who didn't bake, always made a beeline for it and my sister and I liked to break off shards of the sweet, crackly crust and eventually, if no one stopped us, the whole cake would be stripped, as if it had been peeled. The crust is incredible, but so is the interior, flaxen from the butter and eggs and generously freckled and perfumed with nutmeg. Sara Lee makes a tidy, trim, very tasty cake, but she's no Mrs. Funsten.

Make it or buy it? Make it.

Hassle: Like any old-fashioned scratch cake, this requires about 10 minutes of creaming, egg-cracking, beating, and measuring.

Cost comparison: Ounce for ounce, homemade costs about a third of the price of a Sara Lee frozen pound cake.

½ pound (2 sticks) unsalted butter, softened, plus more for the pan

2 cups cake flour or all-purpose flour, plus more for the pan

2 cups sugar

5 large eggs

¼ teaspoon kosher salt

¼ teaspoon baking powder

1 teaspoon freshly grated nutmeg

1 teaspoon vanilla extract (page 260)

1 tablespoon brandy or rum (optional)

1. Preheat the oven to 325 degrees F. Butter and flour a 9 by 5-inch loaf pan and put a piece of parchment paper in the bottom.
2. Beat the 2 sticks butter and sugar for about 5 minutes, and then beat a little more. The mixture should be pale and lemon-colored. Add the eggs one at a time, beating thoroughly after each addition.
3. Sift together the 2 cups flour, salt, baking powder, and nutmeg. Stir anything that remains in the sifter back in with the sifted ingredients.

4. Fold the dry ingredients into the batter. Fold in the vanilla and the liquor, if using.
5. Scrape the batter into the prepared pan and bake for 1½ hours. A toothpick inserted in the center should come out clean.
6. Let the cake cool in the pan. Well wrapped, this will keep for about a week.

Makes one 9–inch loaf

VANILLA EXTRACT

You can save a formidable amount of money by making your own vanilla—but only if you get a bargain on beans. For years, amazon.com has sold eight-ounce packets of fat, moist Madagascar vanilla beans for about $0.41 a bean, shipping included. As I type, Safeway currently charges $11.49 for a single bean.

Granted, to get the good price on beans you must buy in bulk, and most people don't really want fifty-four vanilla beans at a go. You can use the vanilla beans to make ice cream and crème brûlée or you could also just sextuple the following recipe and never have to buy (or make) vanilla extract again, depending on how much you bake. Vanilla extract keeps indefinitely, tightly capped in a dark, cool place, like your cupboard.

The big question with home-brewed vanilla is: what kind of liquor to use? To try to answer this question definitively, I brewed three batches of vanilla, one with dark rum, one with golden rum, and one with vodka. Then I bought a bottle of supermarket vanilla for comparison. I made custard sauce and divided it into four portions, flavoring each with a different extract. The differences in flavor were striking when you sampled the vanillas side by side. If you're looking for a plain-vanilla vanilla, the vodka-based extract is the most subtle, almost indistinguishable from store-bought. Golden rum is assertive and slightly rummy; dark rum extremely rummy. I loved the dark rum vanilla, but others, specifically children, did not.

Make it or buy it? Make it.
Hassle: Minimal
Cost comparison: To make 12 ounces of vanilla costs about $7.00. To buy an equivalent amount of McCormick vanilla: $53.00.

9 plump vanilla beans
1½ cups vodka (cheap is fine) or rum, dark or light

Slit the vanilla beans lengthwise and scrape out the seeds. Put the seeds and the pods in a jar with a tight-fitting lid. Pour the alcohol over the beans. Cover and shake. Put the jar in the cupboard and let macerate for 3 months, agitating the jar occasionally.

Makes 1½ cups

LEMON EXTRACT

Make it or buy it? Make it.
Hassle: Tiny
Cost comparison: Homemade: $0.53 an ounce, less if you have a lemon tree. McCormick: $6.29 per ounce.

2 lemons
⅔ cup vodka

Scrape the zest off the lemons, trying to avoid removing any of the white pith. Put the zest in a small glass jar. Pour the vodka over the lemon zest, cover, and shake. Let sit in a dark place for 10 days or more.

Makes ⅔ cup

ISABEL'S CHOCOLATE CHIP COOKIES

"All these recipes for chocolate chip cookies," Isabel said, flipping through some cookbooks one weekend morning. "They all *say* they're the best, but how can you tell?"

"Why don't you do a test?" I asked.

"Maybe," she said listlessly, and yawned. But about an hour later I noticed a sheet of binder paper on which she'd listed in her immaculate hand all the chocolate-chip-cookie recipes she wanted to try. Over the next four months, she went on to calmly and efficiently try every one of them. She didn't rush; she didn't procrastinate. The kitchen was usually cleaner after she finished baking than when she began; the cookies were stowed in a metal tin. I would eat four or five cookies. She would eat one.

The top three cookies from Isabel's test were a husky chocolate chip cookie made with espresso powder, from the memoir *Cakewalk* by novelist Kate Moses; a whole-wheat chocolate chip cookie recipe out of Kim Boyce's *Good to the Grain*; and Dorie Greenspan's classic chocolate chip cookie from *Baking*.

Isabel folded the three together. Isabel would never say this is the best chocolate chip cookie in the world. She's far too sensible. But I'll say it: this is the best chocolate chip cookie in the world.

Make it or buy it? Make it.

Hassle: No more or less than any scratch cookie

Cost comparison: Homemade: $0.23 per ounce. Nestlé's unbaked chocolate chip cookie dough: $0.21 per ounce. Chips Ahoy: $0.20 per ounce. Pepperidge Farm Nantucket: $0.58 per ounce.

½ pound (2 sticks) unsalted butter, softened
⅔ cup light brown sugar, packed
1 cup granulated sugar
2 large eggs, room temperature
2 teaspoons vanilla extract (page 260)
1 cup whole-wheat flour
1 cup all-purpose flour
¾ teaspoon baking soda

2 teaspoons kosher salt

2 teaspoons instant espresso powder

1½ cups semisweet chocolate chunks or chips

1 cup coarsely chopped walnuts or pecans, toasted

1. Cream the butter until very fluffy, then cream it a little more. Add the sugars and beat well, scraping down the sides of the bowl.
2. Beat in the eggs, one at a time. Beat in the vanilla.
3. Whisk together the flours, baking soda, salt, and espresso powder. Add the flour mixture to the butter mixture in three installments, beating well each time. Stir in the chocolate and nuts. If you are patient and have the time, refrigerate overnight.
4. When you are ready to bake, preheat the oven to 350 degrees F. Line cookie sheets with parchment paper.
5. Scoop tablespoons of dough onto the cookie sheets, 2 inches apart. Bake for 11 to 13 minutes until the cookies are firm and lightly colored. Cool on a rack and store in a cookie tin for up to a week.

Makes about 3 dozen cookies

FIG BARS

Despite the fact that they contain high-fructose corn syrup and partially hydro-genated oil, I've always loved Nabisco Fig Newtons. But these are a cut above, a substantial and healthy cookie-pastry that you can eat for breakfast. I started with Maida Heatter's recipe for Big Newtons, and while I've made a lot of changes, these cookies are still *big*.

Make it or buy it? Make it.
Hassle: These require concentration and manual dexterity.
Cost comparison: Homemade: $0.20 per ounce. Nabisco: $0.24 per ounce.

2 cups all-purpose flour
1 cup whole-wheat flour
1 teaspoon baking powder
½ teaspoon baking soda
1 teaspoon kosher salt
8 tablespoons (1 stick) unsalted butter, softened
½ cup brown sugar (light or dark), firmly packed
½ cup sugar
1 large egg
¼ to ⅓ cup whole milk

FILLING
1 pound dried brown or black figs, about 3½ cups
¾ cup sugar
2 tablespoons lemon juice, about 1 lemon

1. To make the pastry: Sift together the flours, baking powder, baking soda, and salt. Add whatever is left in the sifter to the sifted ingredients and whisk gently to blend.
2. In a large bowl, beat the butter with the sugars until light and fluffy. Add the egg and continue to beat, pausing to scrape down the sides of the bowl. When you have a creamy mixture, slowly beat in the dry ingredients. Add the milk, starting

with the smaller amount, and blend to form a soft, workable dough. If the dough seems dry, add more milk, up to 2 tablespoons.

3. Turn the dough out onto the counter, knead a few times, and shape into a disk. Wrap tightly and refrigerate for at least 1 hour.

4. To make the filling: Cut the tough stems from the figs and put the figs in a saucepan with the sugar, ½ cup water, and lemon juice. Simmer over medium heat for 10 minutes, until the figs are slightly softened.

5. Pour the figs and their juices into a food processor and grind until you have a thick, jammy mixture. (If you don't have a food processor, let the figs cool a bit and then chop them on a big cutting board—damp and sticky work, but doable.) Cool to room temperature, but don't let the figs sit for more than 30 minutes, lest they become too stiff to handle.

6. To assemble: Preheat the oven to 375 degrees F and line a large baking sheet with parchment paper. Working with half the dough at a time, on a floured surface, roll out the dough into an oblong about 15 inches long, 6 inches wide, and a scant ¼ inch thick. Trim the edges evenly so you have a neat rectangle. (A rolling pizza cutter is good for this, though a knife will also work.) Reserve the scraps to roll out with the second portion or to use for patching any holes.

7. Mound half of the fig filling along the spine of the rectangle, stopping ½ inch from the top and bottom. You want a band of filling 1 inch deep and 2 inches wide. Using a bench scraper or a spatula, carefully lift one long end of the dough off the counter and fold it over the fig filling. Repeat with the other side of the dough rectangle, overlapping by ¼ inch or so. Gently press to seal. Using the bench scraper or spatula, ease the dough off the counter and onto the parchment paper. Roll it over so the seam side faces down. Seal the short edges by pinching together. If there are any holes, patch them with the scraps.

8. Repeat with the remaining scraps, dough, and fig filling.

9. Bake for 15 minutes, or until golden and firm on top. Cool on a rack. Slice while still warm, horizontally into 1-inch bars. Store at room temperature in a cookie tin for 5 days.

Makes about 30 brawny cookies

OREOS

This recipe is adapted from Boston pastry chef Joanne Chang's gorgeous cookbook, *Flour*.

Make it or buy it? Make it.
Hassle: Yes. Worth it.
Cost comparison: Homemade: $0.16 per ounce. Nabisco: $0.18 per ounce.

½ pound (2 sticks) unsalted butter, melted
¾ cup sugar
1 teaspoon vanilla extract (page 260)
1 cup semisweet chocolate chips, melted and cooled
1 large egg
1½ cups all-purpose flour
¾ cup cocoa powder
1 teaspoon kosher salt
½ teaspoon baking soda

FILLING
8 tablespoons (1 stick) unsalted butter, softened
1⅔ cups confectioners' sugar
1 teaspoon vanilla extract (page 260)
1 tablespoon milk
Pinch of kosher salt

1. In a mixing bowl, whisk together the butter and sugar. Add the vanilla and chocolate and beat well. Add the egg and beat some more.
2. Sift together the flour, cocoa powder, salt, and baking soda and pour anything that remains in the sifter into the bowl and whisk to combine. Stir this into the chocolate mixture. It will look like a mistake—a tacky, fudgy brown mess. Don't worry. Let it rest for 20 minutes at room temperature to firm up.
3. Transfer the dough to a piece of waxed paper. Now you're going to try to ease the dough into a long log—about 22 inches long and 1¾ inches in diameter. The

dough is sticky, but if you briskly and lightly roll it back and forth on the waxed paper, you will end up with a log. If the chocolatey dough starts to stick to the paper, transfer it to a new piece of waxed paper. Once you have a log of dough, try to make it as smooth and even as you can. After all, you are trying to replicate cookies made by a machine. Refrigerate the waxed paper–covered log of dough for a few hours, or overnight, until very firm.

4. Heat the oven to 325 degrees F. Butter a baking sheet or line it with parchment paper. Cut the dough into scant ¼-inch slices. Place them on the cookie sheet. They can be as close as ¼ inch apart, so pack them on there.

5. Bake for 20 to 25 minutes until they're cakey but firm when you press with the tip of your finger. Cool completely on a rack.

6. To make the filling: Beat all the ingredients together until perfectly smooth. Spread onto the cooled cookies, about 2 teaspoons per cookie. Store the cookies at room temperature in a cookie tin for up to 5 days.

Makes 2 to 3 dozen

RICE PUDDING

Rice pudding is so dowdy and old-fashioned it seems like something you should make at home. But I can't make a rice pudding better than Kozy Shack. I've tried Mexican rice puddings and French rice puddings, baked rice puddings, and stovetop rice puddings. Kozy Shack is, to my taste, always creamier, more ethereal, altogether superior. The ingredient list is more than acceptable: milk, rice, sugar, eggs, salt, natural flavors. I give up. They win.

Make it or buy it? Buy it.

BUTTERSCOTCH PUDDING

Traditional butterscotch contains no Scotch, but I tried adding a teaspoon to my pudding, inspired by a *Cook's Illustrated* recipe. It's a genius touch. That wee dram of smoky liquor cuts the sweetness and brings the flavor of this dessert into focus. The pudding is satiny and complex. Jell-O brand butterscotch pudding mix contains no Scotch, of course, but also no butter. It does find room for disodium phosphate and yellow dyes 5 and 6.

Make it or buy it? Make it.
Hassle: Moderate. Cooking eggs on the stovetop is always a gamble.
Cost comparison: Jell-O pudding prepared from the box: $1.22 per cup. Home-made: $0.66 per cup.

> *2¼ cups milk*
> *¾ cup heavy cream*
> *4 large egg yolks*
> *¾ cup dark brown sugar, packed*
> *¼ cup cornstarch*
> *½ teaspoon kosher salt*
> *2 tablespoons unsalted butter, cut into bits*
> *1 tablespoon vanilla extract (page 260)*
> *1 teaspoon Scotch or bourbon*

1. In a medium saucepan, bring the milk to a boil. Remove from the heat.
2. Meanwhile, in a large bowl, whisk together the cream, egg yolks, sugar, cornstarch, and salt until well blended.
3. Pour a splash of hot milk into the egg yolk mixture, whisking constantly. Gradually whisk in the remainder of the milk.
4. Pour the mixture back into the pot and cook over medium heat, whisking constantly, until it begins to thicken, 3 or 4 minutes. Do not let it boil.
5. Remove from the heat and whisk in the butter, vanilla, and Scotch.
6. Strain the pudding through a fine-mesh sieve into seven 4- to 6-ounce ramekins. Teacups are another option, and cute. Chill for at least 4 hours until firm and cold.

Makes 3½ cups, to serve 7

VANILLA PUDDING

Replace the brown sugar with granulated sugar and omit the Scotch or bourbon.

CHOCOLATE PUDDING

Serve this rich pudding as soon as it's cold. After a day or two, it starts to weep and loses appeal.

Make it or buy it? Make it.
Hassle: Foolproof
Cost comparison: Cheap! This costs about half what you'll pay for Hunt's Snack Pack or Kozy Shack from the tub.

½ cup light brown sugar, packed
¼ cup cocoa powder
3 tablespoons cornstarch
⅛ teaspoon kosher salt
2¼ cups milk (whole is best, as usual)
1 teaspoon vanilla extract (page 260)
Whipped cream (page 226), for serving

1. In a medium saucepan, whisk together the sugar, cocoa, cornstarch, and salt. Stir in the milk.
2. Cook over medium heat, whisking constantly. It will start out looking like scummy hot chocolate, after which it will look like thin hot chocolate, until suddenly it becomes hot, bubbling, glossy pudding. This is how you know it's done. Remove from the heat and whisk in the vanilla.
3. Pour into four serving dishes and cover with plastic wrap. Chill.
4. Serve within a day with whipped cream.

Makes 2½ cups, enough for 4

VANILLA ICE CREAM

The difference between even a premium brand of ice cream and homemade is the difference between the poly-blend sheets you inherited from your grandmother and Pratesi linens. Or how I imagine Pratesi. I know vanilla ice cream sounds boring, but homemade vanilla ice cream is nothing like Edy's. For a sublime variation, try substituting ½ cup honey for ½ cup of the sugar.

Make it or buy it? Make it.

Hassle: Yes

Cost comparison: If you make this with supermarket vanilla beans, you will be crying foolish tears into your very delicious $25.00-per-quart ice cream. If you make this with affordable vanilla beans, because you shopped online (see page 260), you'll be gloating over your $3.50-per-quart ice cream and its beautiful flecks of vanilla seed. If you use homemade vanilla extract, you'll like your $3.00-per-quart ice cream a lot better than Dreyer's. Dreyer's costs $4.32 per quart. Häagen-Dazs: $6.79 per quart. Ben & Jerry's: $10.50 per quart.

2 cups heavy cream
1 cup whole milk
¾ cup sugar
½ teaspoon kosher salt
3 vanilla beans, split lengthwise, or 1 tablespoon vanilla extract (page 260)
2 large eggs

1. Combine the cream, milk, sugar, and salt in a saucepan. Scrape the seeds from the beans into the cream mixture, then drop in the pods. Heat to just below a boil.
2. Whisk the eggs in a bowl, then add the hot cream mixture, whisking. Pour the mixture back into the saucepan, return it to the heat, and stir constantly until thickened. Do not let it boil.
3. Pour through a fine-mesh sieve into a bowl and chill. (If using vanilla extract, stir it in before you chill the ice cream.)
4. Freeze in an ice cream maker according to the manufacturer's instructions. I

think ice cream is best when scraped, still slightly soft, out of the machine. But it will keep for about a week in a tightly closed container in the freezer.

Makes 1½ quarts

SORBET

Sorbet is easy and cheap to make at home, but I've made mango sorbet and it tasted a lot like Häagen-Dazs—it just required time and effort. When you go to the trouble of making sorbet, you should make a flavor you can't find at the supermarket. Like pink grapefruit or grape.

PINK GRAPEFRUIT SORBET

You can't buy anything like this shell pink dessert.

2 cups freshly squeezed grapefruit juice (from about 3 large pink grapefruits)
1 tablespoon grated grapefruit zest
1 cup sugar

1. Mix everything and chill in the refrigerator until very cold.
2. Freeze in an ice cream maker, according to the manufacturer's instructions. Serve immediately, or scoop into a storage container and freeze, tightly covered. Keeps for several weeks.

Makes 1 pint

GRAPE AMBROSIA SORBET

My paternal grandmother used to love the grape ambrosia sherbet at an ice cream shop called Farr's in Ogden, Utah. It was a milky lavender color and studded with walnuts. My grandmother died, years passed, and one day I realized I hadn't eaten grape ambrosia sherbet in over a decade.

Because I live 773 miles from Farr's, I started experimenting with recipes. Some of these were outlandish, particularly an Internet recipe that involved a bottle of Welch's grape juice and sour cream. Then I made the Concord grape sorbet from *The Last Course* by Claudia Fleming, the former pastry chef at Gramercy Tavern in New York City. This sorbet was tart, refreshing, and a vibrant purple. It was close, very close, to how I remembered Farr's grape ambrosia, especially when I added walnuts.

A year later, we were passing through Ogden on a road trip and I made a detour to Farr's. I told my kids about their great-grandmother and her love for this incredible sherbet, her baked beans, the funny things she said, like "Bob, would you like another bean?" I ordered us grape ambrosia cones and took photographs of the children with their cones. I tasted my grape ambrosia. *Why, this is odd*, I thought. I took another bite. It tasted exactly as I remembered. But it tasted nothing like the sorbet I'd been making. It tasted like Fanta grape soda.

> 1 pound Concord grapes, stemmed (don't worry about removing every twig;
>   you'll strain them out later)
> 2 tablespoons sugar
> ¼ teaspoon ascorbic acid
> ½ cup simple syrup (page 228)
> ½ cup walnut pieces, toasted

1. Put the grapes, sugar, and ascorbic acid in a food processor and pulse until roughly chopped. Let the mixture rest for 30 minutes.
2. Process the grapes again, this time until very finely pureed. Strain through a fine-mesh sieve into a bowl, pressing down on the solids.
3. Stir in the simple syrup and ¼ cup water. Cover and chill overnight.

4. Freeze in an ice cream maker according to the manufacturer's instructions, adding the walnut pieces when the sorbet is almost firm. Serve immediately, or scoop into a container and freeze for up to 2 weeks.

Makes a little less than 1 quart

ICE CREAM MAKERS

The days of hand-cranking ice cream in the backyard with rock salt are more fun in recollection than they were in reality. There are dozens of efficient ice cream makers on the market today, from a Cuisinart model that costs less than $50, to the break-your-back-carrying-it-from-the-car $700 Lello machine, to the $4,800 Swiss Pacojet. The primary difference is that with cheaper models you have to freeze the bowl for twelve hours before using, which requires both freezer real estate and foresight. With machines like the Lello, you can make ice cream on the spur of the moment—push a button and the engine both churns and freezes your dessert in under an hour. The downside of these premium machines is that they are expensive and they are mammoth—about the size of a microwave. (The Pacojet comes in compact sizes suitable for the countertop, but I'd sooner fly my family to Hawaii for a week than spend $4,800 on an ice cream maker.) Machines like the Lello can also be noisy. I've used both, and I recommend a cheap machine. With $650 you can buy a lot of premium ingredients.

MARSHMALLOW CREME

You can use this to top ice cream, or in a peanut butter and fluff sandwich. Home-made marshmallow creme is almost indistinguishable from store-bought, though there's a foamy crackle to commercial fluff that homemade lacks. Whether that's a positive or negative is up to you.

Make it or buy it? Make it.
Hassle: A cinch
Cost comparison: Homemade: $0.36 per cup. Kraft Jet-Puffed marshmallow creme: $2.75 per cup.

One ¼-ounce envelope unflavored gelatin (about 1 tablespoon)
2 cups sugar
1 teaspoon vanilla extract (page 260)

1. In a small bowl, soak the gelatin in ½ cup cold water.
2. Heat the sugar and ½ cup water in a small saucepan, stirring occasionally, until the sugar dissolves. Add the gelatin mixture and bring to a boil. Remove from the heat.
3. Pour the hot syrup into the bowl of a stand mixer, add the vanilla, and whisk until snow-white and cool, about 15 minutes.
4. Scoop into a storage container, such as a glass jar or resealable gallon plastic bag. Store in the freezer, where it will remain soft and scoopable indefinitely. Don't try to keep it for more than 1 or 2 days at room temperature, as it will begin to weep and disintegrate.

Makes 2½ cups

CHOCOLATE SAUCE

This is my sister-in-law Laura's recipe and it could not be easier.

Make it or buy it? Make it.
Hassle: None
Cost comparison: Homemade: $0.12 per tablespoon. Hershey's: $0.13 per tablespoon.

> 2 ounces (2 squares) unsweetened chocolate, chopped
> ¾ cup sugar
> 4 tablespoons (½ stick) unsalted butter, softened
> ½ teaspoon vanilla extract (page 260)

1. Melt the chocolate with ⅓ cup water in a small saucepan over very low heat, stirring constantly. Add the sugar. Heat to boiling, stirring constantly, until the sugar is completely dissolved and the mixture thickened.
2. Remove from the heat and stir in the butter and vanilla. Cool slightly and serve warm over ice cream. This can be stored in a jar in the refrigerator, but it is best eaten all at once, warm.

Makes 1 cup

ICE CREAM CONES

A tuile is a superthin French cookie that you slide off the baking sheet the instant it comes out of the oven and manipulate into a cone shape (or any shape you like) before it has a chance to harden. A few minutes later, it is stuck forever in that shape, crispy and delicate. (*Tuiles* is French for "roof tiles," which in France are, apparently, often curved.) If you can make tuiles, you can make ice cream cones.

I can't make tuiles. Whenever I have made tuiles, I have ended up with one or two tuiles and a small mountain of crumbs.

Once, I made some delicious, buttery ice cream cone crumbs and a single functional ice cream cone using a recipe from David Lebovitz's *The Perfect Scoop*. My friend Susan reported success making cones with her pizzelle press, which is a machine used to shape decorative perforated Italian butter cookies. I made some pizzelle batter and tried to replicate her results with a waffle iron but the grooves were too deep and I ended up with a colossal mess. Occasionally I buy ice cream cones, but at home we usually eat ice cream in bowls. If nothing else, it makes a trip to the ice cream parlor more of an occasion.

Make it or buy it? Buy it.

CRYSTALLIZED GINGER

My mother treated crystallized ginger as a sweetmeat, something dainty and refined to be savored after dinner as a treat, like a Godiva cherry chocolate or a glass of port. I always assumed crystallized ginger must be a luxury item and was convinced I could save money by making it at home. One day, I bought some fresh ginger root and made the hottest candied ginger I'd ever tasted. It reminded me of a sticky Chinese ginger confection people insisted would cure morning sickness, but didn't. The home-candied ginger was fantastic, but a few days later it hardened into tooth-cracking nuggets. I tried another recipe that involved boiling and rinsing the ginger root repeatedly, then simmering it for hours in syrup. This was tedious and after all that the sugar formed warty clumps on the surface of each piece. One day at Safeway, after I put some fresh ginger in my cart to give it another go, I decided to check the price of candied ginger. The candied ginger cost exactly the same per pound as the fresh ginger. A few days later I checked at Whole Foods. There, candied ginger cost less than fresh ginger.

Make it or buy it? Buy it.

BIRTHDAY CAKE

I like to bake and I'm a show-off and for Isabel's second birthday many years ago I baked a banana cake from *The Cake Bible* by Rose Levy Beranbaum, which may be the most finicky and intimidating cookbook I own. Even before I served it, I knew that any cake baked from *The Cake Bible* was chosen to impress adults, not to please children. The cake was dense and damp and I frosted it with a dark chocolate ganache so severe that people scraped it off and later I scraped it off their plates straight into the garbage can.

In later years when Isabel and Owen began requesting Safeway sheet cakes decorated with Snow White and Crisco roses or Batman and Power Rangers, I remembered that *Cake Bible* cake and bought the desired cake, however tacky and artificial. If a tacky cake was what they wanted, a tacky cake they got. Isabel graduated from princess cakes around the age of eight, and when he was nine, Owen made his last request for a monstrosity of crushed Oreos and bubble gum ice cream featuring a representation of Optimus Prime. Or something like that. I miss the innocent pleasure they took in bad cakes.

A few years ago, I picked up a vintage copy of Peg Bracken's *The I Hate to Cook Book* at the elementary school white elephant sale. Isabel began flipping through it and fixated on the "Cockeyed Cake." It's an easy cake that you mix in the pan in which it is baked. This is the perfect starter cake for a kid and involves less washing up than even mix. All on her own, Isabel baked it and said, "I don't know why anyone makes any other cake, ever."

Really, I don't either. The cake is chocolatey but not too chocolatey. It is supremely moist and somehow remains so for days. Isabel photocopied the recipe and put it in a plastic page protector that went in the binder she'd started for recipes. She baked it for my father's birthday one year and served it brownie-style, from the pan, unfrosted. It was, as always, perfect.

Recently, because I've been feeling sentimental, I called my aunt, Stephanie, to ask for the recipe for the chocolate cake that she served at all maternal family birthday parties. She said, "Oh, it's that one-bowl cake from Peg Bracken's book. I doubled the recipe and baked it in layers. Mother and I were talking about it the other day, how I made that birthday cake five times a year, every year, for thirty years. That's a lot of cakes."

So, the cockeyed cake from *The I Hate to Cook Book* is a family cake, twice over. Stephanie adapted Bracken's recipe to make two layers, so you do have to use a bowl. If you want to make it in the pan, just cut the recipe in half and mix it in a greased 9-inch square baking pan. If speed and simplicity are the goals, this trounces mix.

Make it from scratch or buy mix? Make it.
Hassle: Easiest cake ever

Cost comparison: Homemade cake: $3.50. Betty Crocker mix chocolate cake, prepared: $3.80. I priced the homemade cake using homemade vanilla (page 260). If you use McCormick vanilla, the price for the whole cake catapults to almost $7.00. Make your vanilla!

Butter, for the pan
3 cups all-purpose flour, plus more for the pan
⅔ cup cocoa powder
2 teaspoons baking soda
2 cups sugar
1 teaspoon kosher salt
½ cup neutral vegetable oil
2 tablespoons distilled white vinegar
1 tablespoon vanilla extract (page 260)
2 cups water or 1 cup cold coffee plus 1 cup water
White Mountain Frosting (recipe follows)

1. Preheat the oven to 350 degrees F. Butter and flour two 9-inch round cake pans and line the bottoms with parchment paper.
2. In a large bowl, whisk together the 3 cups flour, cocoa, baking soda, sugar, and salt.
3. Poke three holes in the dry mixture. Into one, pour the oil; into another, the vinegar; and into the third, the vanilla. (It's not strictly necessary to poke the holes, but it is traditional.)
4. Pour the liquid over everything. As Bracken puts it: "You'll feel like you're making mud pies now, but beat it with a spoon until it's nearly smooth and you can't see the flour." This can take a while. As my five-year-old niece, Stella, put it when we baked the cake together: "It looks all pimply." Keep stirring and most of the pimples will burst. . . .
5. Pour the batter into the prepared pans. Bake for 30 minutes. The cake is done when a toothpick inserted in the center comes out clean.
6. When completely cool, turn the cakes out the pans onto a rack, and spread the layers with White Mountain Frosting.

Makes 1 spectacular birthday cake, enough for 10

WHITE MOUNTAIN FROSTING

This was the traditional frosting in my mother's family and if the baker was in a generous mood, she (always a she) made a double recipe of the icing for the birthday honoree and presented it both on the cake and in a bowl with a spoon. I don't usually like ice cream with cake, but vanilla ice cream is sensational with this frosting. If you let the frosted cake sit for a couple of hours, the frosting sometimes develops a crust like that of a very crispy-creamy meringue. A forkful of cake with some crunchy-sweet frosting and ice cream will make your birthday very happy indeed.

This isn't how my grandmother makes her White Mountain frosting, but I find this method much easier. You need a candy thermometer for this.

> *1½ cups sugar*
> *3 large egg whites*
> *¼ teaspoon cream of tartar*
> *Pinch of salt*
> *2 teaspoons vanilla extract (page 260)*

1. In a small saucepan, bring the sugar and ½ cup water to a boil. Put a candy thermometer in the pot.
2. Meanwhile, with an electric mixer, start beating the egg whites with the cream of tartar and salt until foamy. Turn off the mixer.
3. When the temperature of the syrup reaches 240 degrees F, turn on the mixer once again and, beating ferociously, add the syrup in a slow drizzle. Keep beating as you add the vanilla, and continue for a few minutes until the frosting is glossy and barely warm.

Makes 7 cups, enough for one 2-layer birthday cake

SIMPLEST BUTTERCREAM

I love White Mountain Frosting, but my husband thinks it's too sugary. He prefers buttercream. I like that, too. There is only one frosting I don't like: canned frosting. The ingredient list (trans fats, preservatives, artificial flavors) is almost as nauseating as the synthetic flavors.

Make it or buy it? Make it.

Hassle: Hardly any if you soften your butter and own a mixer

Cost comparison: Betty Crocker canned frosting: $0.12 per tablespoon. Home-made buttercream: $0.06.

¾ pound (3 sticks) unsalted butter, softened
9 cups confectioners' sugar
1 tablespoon vanilla extract (page 260)
Scant ⅔ cup milk

In a large bowl, beat the butter very hard until fluffy. Add four cups of the sugar, then the vanilla and milk. Add the rest of the sugar and beat well.

Makes 6 cups

AFTERWORD

It's empowering to know I can cure bacon, brew vanilla, age Camembert, extract honeyfrom a hive, and behead a chicken, even if I have no desire to do at least one of those things ever again. Even if, in the end, I spent more money than I saved. (A few costly projects like the chickens and the bees ate up all the savings of from scratch cooking). Big food companies flatter us by telling us how busy we are and they simultaneously convince us that we are helpless. I am moderately busy, but not all that helpless. Neither are you. Everything I did in the course of my scratch-cooking era—with the possible exceptions of eviscerating poultry and stuffing hot dogs—was very, very easy.

But the more helpless we feel, the lower those food companies move the bar of our expectations, and the bar is now very low at your local supermarket. Trust me. I have eaten my way through mine. It makes me quite furious when I think about the sicketating powdered hollandaise sauce, the extortionate price of the vanilla extracts, the pathetic bread, the soups sweetened with corn syrup, the abomination of Pillsbury "creamy vanilla" canned frosting that contains neither cream nor vanilla. It upsets me that we pay as much for these foods as we do.

Almost everything is better when it's homemade. While this may have started out as opinion (though I'm not sure it did), I would now state it confidently as fact. Almost everything. But not everything. Which makes me inordinately happy. Because I think it's reassuring that you can walk into a supermarket and buy a bag of potato chips and a tub of rice pudding that are better than anything you can make at home. I wish there were more foods like that. I really don't want to spend my life standing over a stove, muttering about the evils of ConAgra and trans fats. It seems a tragic waste to shape one's life around doctrinaire rejection of industrial food. Which means, I suppose, both insisting on high standards most of the time and then, sometimes, relaxing them.

Moreover, in the United States, at least, it can be hard to feel connected to your mother's cooking or your grandmothers' without making some concessions to packaged foods. I'm unwilling to give those connections up, at least not all of them.

My mother wasn't much of a baker. On the rare occasions when she did bake a cake, she always made the same cake, which we called Skippy's Apricot Cake. You can find variants of this recipe on the Internet—it clearly wasn't the brainchild of my great-aunt Skippy, though in our family she got all the credit. I'm quite sure it was an invention of a home economist at the Duncan Hines company, but I've never seen the recipe printed precisely as we made it.

I loved this cake as a child, but I grew up to become a high-minded, adventurous, and snobbish baker who disdained cake mix, and when I went to my mother's house and she would pull this cake out of the freezer and offer me a slice, I would say, no thanks. Didn't she care that there were other cakes, better cakes, cakes that didn't involve mix? I wanted her to know I didn't approve by never once, after the age of fifteen or so, accepting a slice of this cake.

Recently, I was going through my mother's recipe file and discovered six copies of the recipe, each written out in her own hand on an index card. Why six? Was it in case she lost one? Was it to give to admiring friends who requested it? Why didn't more people request it? Ingrates. Starting with me. The cake is a wonder, the recipe a treasure. It takes a couple of minutes to stir together, and I make it all the time now, as does my sister. Our children love it. I hope they always will. I would rather it didn't involve a mix, but it's an almost perfect cake, a cake that strikes the balance between mindlessly shopping and compulsively making. You must buy the mix to make this cake.

SKIPPY'S APRICOT CAKE

Butter, for the pan
1 box Duncan Hines Lemon Supreme cake mix
1 cup canned apricot nectar, such as Kern's
¾ cup neutral vegetable oil
½ cup granulated sugar
4 large eggs

GLAZE

1 cup sifted confectioners' sugar
2 tablespoons fresh lemon juice

1. Preheat the oven to 350 degrees F. Butter a 9-inch tube or Bundt pan.
2. Stir together the cake mix, nectar, oil, and sugar. Add the eggs, one at a time, beating well after each addition. Pour the batter into the pan.
3. Bake for 50 minutes. When it's done, a toothpick inserted in the cake should come out clean.
4. Just before the baking time is up, mix together the ingredients for the glaze.
5. When the cake comes out of the oven, immediately turn it out of the pan onto a cooling rack positioned over a cookie sheet or large piece of newspaper—anything that will spare you having to later wipe down the counter. Pour the glaze over the top of the cake while the cake is still very hot. The glaze will melt and flow down the sides of the cake and harden into an irresistible lemony crust.

As my mother wrote on each copy of the recipe:
"Makes 12 large slices, 24 lady slices."

APPENDIX

CHEESEMAKING SUPPLIES

The Cheesemaker
Molds, cultures, rennet
www.thecheesemaker.com
W62 N590 Washington Avenue
Cedarburg, WI 53012
414-745-5483

New England Cheesemaking Supply Co.
Molds, cultures, rennet
www.cheesemaking.com
54B Whately Road
South Deerfield, MA 01373
413-397-2012

MEAT CURING SUPPLIES

Butcher & Packer
Pink salt
www.butcher-packer.com
1780 E. 14 Mile Road
Madison Heights, MI 48071
248-583-1250

Butcher Supply Company
Pink salt
www.butchersupplycompany.com
1040 3rd Avenue South
Nashville, TN 37210
800-896-5945

BAKING SUPPLIES

King Arthur Flour
Bulk yeast, high-gluten flour
www.kingarthurflour.com
135 US Rte. 5 South
Norwich, VT 05055
800-827-6836

HERBS FOR VERMOUTH AND BITTERS

Mountain Rose Herbs
Dandelion root, angelica, pau d'arco
www.mountainroseherbs.com
PO Box 50220
Eugene, OR 97405
800-879-3337

SPICES

Kalustyan's
Vadouvan powder, Aleppo pepper
www.kalustyans.com
123 Lexington Ave.
New York, NY 10016
800-352-3451

Penzeys Spices
Aleppo pepper
www.penzeys.com
12001 W. Capitol Drive
Wauwatosa, WI 53222
800-741-7787

ACKNOWLEDGMENTS

For testing recipes, sharing recipes, walks, and friendship, thanks to Melanie Hamburger, Layne Huff, Kathy Kirkham, Chris Myers, Mary Ann Myers, Mary Pols, Tom Russell, Laura Smoyer, Lisa Swanson, Stephanie Trimble, and the DOT sisters—but especially Marleen Roggow and Debra Turner. Thanks to Thom Geier, who, whether he knows it or not, got the ball rolling, and to my agent, Steve Troha, who kept the ball rolling. My wonderful editors, Leslie Meredith and Donna Loffredo, gently pointed me in the right direction, and Suzanne Fass raised my game. Thanks to my father, John Reese, a better cook than I ever knew, who appreciates my vermouth. Thanks to Isabel, my favorite baking companion; Owen, a fellow chicken enthusiast; and Mark, who put up with the goats, the ducks, the hulking prosciutto, and me. I could not have gotten through the last eighteen months without my sister, Justine Reese. Writing a book wasn't the half of it. Justine, thank you.

INDEX

ABOUT THE AUTHOR

Jennifer Reese is the former book critic for *Entertainment Weekly*. She lives in Northern California with her husband, children, and a few too many animals. She writes about her 1,000-plus cookbook collection at www.tipsybaker.com.